INFORMAL WORKERS AND COLLECTIVE ACTION

INFORMAL WORKERS AND COLLECTIVE ACTION

A Global Perspective

**Edited by Adrienne E. Eaton,
Susan J. Schurman,
and Martha A. Chen**

ILR PRESS

AN IMPRINT OF

CORNELL UNIVERSITY PRESS

ITHACA AND LONDON

First published 2017 by Cornell University Press
First printing, Cornell Paperbacks, 2017
Printed in the United States of America

Library of Congress Cataloging-in-Publication Data
Names: Eaton, Adrienne E., editor. | Schurman, Susan J., editor. |
    Chen, Martha Alter, editor. | Container of (work): Hawkins, Daniel
    (Daniel James). Port workers in Colombia.
Title: Informal workers and collective action : a global perspective /
    edited by Adrienne E. Eaton, Susan J. Schurman, and Martha A. Chen.
Description: Ithaca : ILR Press, an imprint of Cornell University Press, 2017. |
    Includes bibliographical references and index.
Identifiers: LCCN 2016047013 (print) | LCCN 2016050096 (ebook) |
    ISBN 9781501705564 (cloth : alk. paper) | ISBN 9781501705571 (pbk. : alk. paper) |
    ISBN 9781501707957 (ret) | ISBN 9781501707964 (pdf)
Subjects: LCSH: Informal sector (Economics)—Employees. | Informal sector
    (Economics)—Employees—Labor unions—Organizing. | Employee rights. |
    Labor movement.
Classification: LCC HD2341 .I53425 2017 (print) | LCC HD2341 (ebook) |
    DDC 331—dc23
LC record available at https://lccn.loc.gov/2016047013

Cornell University Press strives to use environmentally responsible suppliers and materials to the fullest extent possible in the publishing of its books. Such materials include vegetable-based, low-VOC inks and acid-free papers that are recycled, totally chlorine-free, or partly composed of nonwood fibers. For further information, visit our website at www.cornellpress.cornell.edu.

Contents

Acknowledgments

The research presented in this volume was made possible by funding to Rutgers University and the Women in Informal Employment: Globalizing and Organizing (WIEGO) network as part of a grant from the United States Agency for International Development (USAID) to the American Center for International Labor Solidarity, commonly known as the Solidarity Center.[1] The opportunity to conduct a study over multiple years and across diverse employment and geographic contexts is rare. It was feasible because we were able to work with the global contacts and relationships that have been created over many years by the Solidarity Center's global program, the networks of informal worker organizations supported by the WIEGO network, and Rutgers' membership in the International Federation of Workers' Education Associations. These relationships enabled us to assemble a global research team and to gain access to the informal workers' campaigns that are included in the book. They also allowed us to employ a multiple case study design in which we could develop detailed descriptions of each campaign in context and then analyze whether there are common elements that apply across the various contexts.

The preliminary research design for the nine individual cases that are the core of this volume emerged from the first year of work funded by the Solidarity Center in which both the Rutgers and WIEGO teams conducted broad literature reviews of organizing and campaigns by informal workers. Based on the findings of these reviews, and in consultation with the Solidarity Center staff, the Rutgers and WIEGO teams identified two themes to pursue in more depth and cases that fit within those themes. One, the focus of the Rutgers work, involved successful campaigns by traditional unions to organize subcontracted workers. The other, the focus of the WIEGO work, involved successful collective bargaining by organizations of informal workers. Rutgers and WIEGO then identified researchers with the necessary country or sectoral expertise and language skills to conduct the case studies using common sets of research protocols. The cases chosen also reflect, to some extent, focal countries for the Solidarity Center as required by USAID.[2]

By focusing on successful campaigns, our goal was to inform both other campaigns by or for informal workers as well as policy and academic discussions about the role of collective action in improving the work conditions of informal workers. We think that the case studies presented here more than achieve this goal. Each of the stories is inspiring, and together they demonstrate that informal workers are indeed engaging in collective action around the world, both organizing and negotiating. In our view, the campaigns described here indicate that the global labor movement has begun to understand that informal workers are an integral part of the twenty-first-century working class and that finding ways to help them be recognized, represented, and heard is essential to labor's future.

We are deeply grateful to the Solidarity Center staff for enabling us to conduct this research. In addition to providing us with the financial support to engage a talented and diverse team of researchers, the opportunity to interact with the staff and think through together the study design, implementation, and findings was invaluable. In some cases, the staff facilitated the field research, assisting with identification of or outreach to research subjects. The opportunity for collaboration among such a diverse group of scholars and practitioners would not have been possible without the support of the Solidarity Center staff. By working together to supervise the development and analysis of these cases, we have learned much from each other and, hopefully, have been able to generate insights that will be useful to practitioners as well as contribute to ongoing theorizing about how informal workers can engage in collective action to improve their circumstances.

We also want to acknowledge and thank each of the contributing authors. They each did an amazing job in the field, often confronting situations that were far more complex or ambiguous than originally expected. In addition, we thank the anonymous reviewer who provided us with excellent advice that has greatly improved the content and presentation of the book. Camille DiLeo did a marvelous job editing all the notes in each chapter. And of course, we owe a deep debt of gratitude to all the leaders and activists in each of the campaigns for allowing us their valuable time and insights. They represent the future of social and economic justice for workers!

INFORMAL WORKERS AND COLLECTIVE ACTION

Introduction

BROADENING LABOR'S REPERTOIRE?

Adrienne E. Eaton, Martha A. Chen,
and Susan J. Schurman

Sometimes you think that it is normal that the boss and the supervisors ride roughshod over you because you're from the lower class; it's normal that they tramp down on you. But when you hear someone tell you that this is not normal, that it's not normal that you should have to ask for your rights; that you have rights and you need to make sure that these rights are respected, well, you begin to say, what? What was I thinking? Was I asleep? Well, after this, you begin to wake up and see things differently.

—Colombian Port Worker[1]

Around the world, in countries as far flung as Cambodia and Brazil and in industries as diverse as transportation and hospitality, workers in informal employment, who labor every day with no legal or social protection, are organizing and negotiating for better conditions. Some of them are self-employed; others work for wages in either formal or informal enterprises. Some used to have jobs in the formal sector with a union contract; others have always worked informally. To achieve their goals they are mounting collective action campaigns that draw on the repertoire of past generations of workers, but they often recombine them or innovate to fit their unique contexts. Informal workers, their organizations and their campaigns, represent the leading edge of the most significant change in the global labor movement in more than a century. This book tells the story of nine such campaigns.

- In Monrovia, the capital city of Liberia, street vendors, the majority of whom were youth who had lost their parents in the civil crisis and had no other means of support, organized the National Petty Traders Union of Liberia, a member-based organization (MBO). Over the course of five years, in the face of repeated attacks by police, their union succeeded in persuading the city of Monrovia to negotiate a memorandum of understanding that recognizes their positive role in the economy and protects their right to engage in their trade.

1

- In the Brazilian state of Minas Gerais, waste pickers organized producer cooperatives and, over a long period of sustained collective action, succeeded in obtaining recognition for their role in the waste management and negotiated the first recycling bonus law to increase their income.
- In Cambodia, young women who work on commission from Cambrew brewing company to promote the brand in bars and restaurants, in the process enduring sexual harassment and other indignities, have been joining a traditional but independent union and engaging in collective bargaining after a campaign led by nongovernment organizations (NGOs) and international labor organizations helped them to obtain recognition as formal workers.
- In the Colombian port of Buenaventura, workers, pushed into informal employment by a neoliberal regime and abandoned when their union morphed into a labor intermediary, organized a new union and succeeded in restoring formal status to crane operators.
- The South African Commercial, Catering, and Allied Workers Union (SACCAWU) persuaded its members to accept concessions in order to include the growing number of informal workers who were working side by side with them without the benefit of a contract.
- The Transport and Road Building Workers Trade Union of Georgia organized informal minibus drivers—some of whom are self-employed and others who are informal wage workers—to join the existing union in their sector and campaign to save their jobs in the face of vehicle upgrading and formalization of the enterprises operating in the transport sector. The union has negotiated collective agreements that provide basic wage, hour, and safety protections but don't necessarily override the self-employed status of many individual drivers.
- In Uruguay, with help from the Gender Department of the national trade union center, domestic workers organized the sole union of domestic workers in 2005 and, over the next decade, succeeded in obtaining both legislative and collective bargaining protections. In the process, they helped to develop an organization that can act in the interest of employers and as the bargaining partner for collective bargaining.
- In the aftermath of the Arab Spring, the Tunisian General Labor Union capitalized on regime change to restore formal status and collective bargaining rights for sixty thousand low-wage government workers whose jobs had been informalized through outsourcing to multiple labor intermediaries.
- In the Dominican Republic, Haitian migrants make up a large share of informal workers. Beginning in 2007 a major national trade union confederation

launched the country's first campaign to organize Haitian immigrants working informally in construction and domestic work. This campaign came in the context of intensified efforts by the Dominican government to undermine the status of Haitian migrants and Dominican-Haitians.

These stories represent only a small sample of the variety of responses by informal workers and by labor organizations to the challenges associated with the changing nature of employment in today's global economy. They are an integral part of a larger pattern of change in the labor market and in labor organizing taking place globally. We believe that the lessons contained within these examples add significantly to the growing literature about how workers' rights can be advanced in the context of a global economy. Above all, our examples suggest that there is no single "right way" for workers to organize but rather that varieties of employment arrangements require varieties of unionism and collective bargaining.

Informal employment has long been the predominant form of employment in the developing world. More recently, changes in trade and technology, neoliberal policies, and global competition have pushed a growing number of workers from formal to informal employment in both the developed and developing worlds. By definition, informal workers do not receive legal or social protection through their work; most earn below the minimum wage and are from poor households. For decades, many trade unionists considered informal workers to be outside the scope of their responsibility and unorganizable. But a growing body of research documents that informal workers are both organizable and organizing.[2] They are doing so in a variety of ways: forming member-based organizations (MBOs) of their own; using the assistance of existing trade unions or NGOs to organize; joining existing unions; creating new unions, sometimes in opposition to existing unions; or by combinations of all these methods. Like workers in more formal employment relationships, informal workers are demonstrating that collective action is possible and can result in improvements in their lives. At the same time, the goals they are struggling for, the targets of their struggle, their campaign and negotiating strategies, and the forms of organization they create are sometimes quite different from those of traditional trade unions.

While the focus of this book will be largely the Global South, the issue of informal work is gaining attention in the United States as well. The news has been full of reports on the "gig economy," which makes substantial use of independent contractors who are not eligible for the protections of labor and employment laws in the United States nor for collective bargaining.[3] At the same time, Uber drivers and others in the gig economy have begun organizing and fighting back.[4] David Weil's important book on the "fissured workplace" highlights various types of informal employment (without calling it that) and the forces driving their growth, though he has little to say about collective action by the workers affected. A recent collection of case studies edited by Ruth Milkman and Ed Ott describes several new approaches to the organizing of "precarious" (often informal) workers in New York City. Their overarching concern is to what extent these new organizing campaigns constitute a new labor movement and whether the "old" and "new" labor movements can create a new synthesis.[5]

This book joins a growing body of literature that documents and analyzes the organizing strategies of informal workers. Based on the findings from nine detailed and at least partly successful case studies of campaigns to improve the working conditions of informal workers, this book seeks first to shed light on the nature of collective action by informal workers. The focus is less on the organizing process and more on the types of organizations that are created and the types of negotiations that take place once workers achieve sufficient collective leverage to induce employers, contractors, and/or government to enter into negotiations. In our view the literature on informal workers' collective action has emphasized the process of organizing but has paid less attention to the forms of organization that are created or the types of negotiation that take place.[6] The examples presented here illustrate that workers and labor organizations around the world are rediscovering the lessons of previous generations of workers who learned how to aggregate individuals' sense of injustice into forms of collective action that achieve a level of power that can yield important changes in their work and lives.

Informal Workers Organizing

Since the International Labor Organization (ILO) first called attention to the "informal sector" thirty years ago,[7] a growing number of labor scholars and activists have argued that organizing informal workers, especially women, in order to overcome the systemic disadvantages they face, is the best means for these workers to be seen and heard by decision makers with the power to affect their lives. A brief overview of this literature demonstrates the growing support for and efficacy of this view.

One strain of this literature approaches the issue of informal workers primarily through the lens of traditional unions. Much of this strain has relied on interviews with trade unionists and has focused on the barriers to organizing informal workers.[8] Some of this same work, nevertheless, concludes that unions should move toward inclusion of informal workers. In 1999, the ILO's Bureau for Worker Activities (ACTRAV) published a set of nine cases covering all continents that outlined the need for the trade unions to organize informal workers, and they followed up with another report in 2002.[9] In 2011, Bonner and Spooner were able to provide a variety of examples of trade unions organizing informal workers.[10] Nonetheless, their subtitle, "challenges for trade unions," underscores the slow pace at which unions were reacting. Likewise, based on a scan across all regions of the world, Schurman and Eaton reported that "trade unions are beginning to respond . . . [but] the data reveal the real difficulties that existing unions face in adapting their approaches and structures to atypical and informal economy workers."[11]

Meanwhile, informal workers were not waiting for existing unions to initiate campaigns. In 2007 Chen, Jhabvala, Kanbur, and Richards edited an important collection of papers on member-based organizations of the poor (MBOPs), many of which are worker organizations, noting that some have been successful while others have failed and examining the factors that account for success.[12] In 2012, Mather surveyed the literature on informal workers self-organizing in a variety of occupations and countries, calling attention to significant differences in organizing approaches in different sectors.[13]

Most studies of informal worker self-organizing are rooted in either single countries or single industries. Agarwala, for instance, focuses on informal workers' organizing in three Indian states. She argues that informal workers have been most successful in improving their lives by essentially giving up on attempting to bargain for better pay and standards with their employers and instead demanding state-provided social benefits such as housing, education, and health care.[14] In his book based on ethnographic studies of informal workers in different sectors in Brazil, Coletto discusses attempts at collective action among waste pickers and street vendors.[15] In contrast, Tilly, Agarwala, Mosoetsa, Ngai, Salas, and Sheikah examine informal workers' organizations as a strategy for improving subcontracted work in a single industry (textile and apparel industries) in four countries (Brazil, China, India, and South Africa). They conclude that these organizations have the potential to contribute to shoring up labor standards with the largest impacts coming from serving as "force multipliers" for government regulation, bringing collective voice to political and economic dialogues, and acting as advocates for sectoral economic development.[16]

The research presented in this volume builds on and extends much of this previous research. It differs from most of the research conducted so far in that it does not focus on a particular sector nor a particular country, although, interestingly, all nine cases involve the service sector, not by any intent on the research team's part. Rather, as one of the largest multicase studies yet conducted, it looks across quite divergent experiences in different industries, occupations, and countries and attempts to tease out new insights that can only be drawn from such a broad scope. The relatively broad scope of these nine cases also provides an opportunity to contribute to the debate about "narrow union" versus "broader social movement" strategies and tactics. At least in these cases, the answer is "both–and" rather than "either–or." The book also distinguishes between two broad categories of informal workers: the self-employed and the wage-employed, a distinction that is often obfuscated in the previous literature.

Defining Informal Employment

In 1993, the International Conference of Labour Statisticians (ICLS) adopted an official definition of the "informal sector" that refers to *enterprises* that are unincorporated or unregistered.[17] Later, in 2003, thanks to the joint efforts of the International Labor Organization (ILO) and the Women in Informal Employment: Globalizing and Organizing (WIEGO) network, the ICLS adopted a definition of "informal employment" that refers to *jobs without employment-based social protection*. Individuals in these jobs may be working for formal firms, informal firms, or households.[18] In this volume we are concerned with informal employment, both self-employment in informal enterprises and informal wage employment for formal firms, informal firms, or households.[19]

Some observers refer to informal wage employment, especially in global value chains, as work that has been "informalized from above."[20] The term "from above" refers to the fact that the work was formerly performed by workers in formal employment relationships but has been transformed into informal employment by various means as part of employers' efforts to reduce risk, gain flexibility, and reduce labor costs. Several of our cases were selected because they fit this description: port workers in Colombia, hospitality workers in South Africa, and low-paid government workers in Tunisia.

The defining feature of formal employment is that compensation, hours of work, and safe working conditions are covered by national labor codes and standards often further raised by union collective bargaining agreements. In most countries, formal employment presumes full-time work. By externalizing jobs to subcontractors—often termed "labor intermediaries"—employers sever the employment relationship and thereby gain what has been termed "external numerical flexibility."[21] Likewise, by modifying work schedules of directly employed workers to reduce hours below full-time, employers acquire increased "internal numerical flexibility." By escaping collective bargaining rules that limit their ability to transfer employees to different tasks and locations, employers gain "functional flexibility." And by instituting individual rather than collective pay rates, employers gain "wage flexibility." Combinations of these forms of increased flexibility allow firms to maximize profits and minimize risks. In the case of external flexibility this can actually change the nature of their relationship with workers from an employment to a commercial contract. Internal flexibility can be used to create work schedules that are not regulated by wage and hour laws.

The key characteristic of this first category of informality is that these workers remain "dependent" on an employer even though the employment relationship may be disguised, ambiguous, or third-party, while those in the second category are "independent," selling their goods or services directly in a market.[22] The work arrangements of the dependent informal wage workers result from what David Weil has called "fissuring" in the context of the labor market in the United States.[23] Often, what could be or once was a formal employment relationship has been distanced or mediated by a subcontractor or labor intermediary. In other cases, employees have been redefined—sometimes illegally—as "independent" (self-employed) contractors. In still other cases, the employment relationship has been informalized through employer scheduling decisions where workers are employed for limited time periods, sometimes on a daily basis. Most of these arrangements have the effect of removing the workers from the protections of labor and employment laws and access to employment-based benefits like unemployment and health insurance or pensions. In the developing world, however, most wage employment was never formalized in the first place. Most wage workers in developing countries were and are still casual day laborers or so-called "nonstandard" employees without written contracts, workers benefits, or social protection.

The second category of informality includes those more generally understood as constituting the informal economy: the self-employed, including micro-entrepreneurs who hire others, and own-account operators who work on their own or with unpaid contributing family workers. In urban areas, the self-employed tend to be concentrated in manufacturing, trade, transport, and personal services; in rural areas, the self-employed are concentrated in smallholder farming plus artisan production, livestock rearing, and fishing.

In reality, like all sociological or statistical ideal types, there is no bright line separating the two broad categories of informal workers. Workers themselves often cross these work boundaries, sometimes on a daily basis, as they strive to piece together a livelihood. And formal enterprises may well contract work out to informal enterprises or to industrial outworkers in what Slavnic calls "the informal outsourcing chain."[24] In this volume, the transportation case study from Georgia may best illustrate the complications. Taxi, minibus, and truck drivers—at least in the developing world—may be either self-employed, informal employees, or dependent contractors. In some cases, drivers may purchase a vehicle and set themselves up as owner-operators selling their services on the street or to companies (in the case of truck drivers). Or they may have been employees of a larger enterprise that changed their status—legally or not—to independent (or actually dependent) contractor. Or they may rent their vehicles from an owner who sets their routes and earnings but expects them to pay for gas and maintenance. The Georgia case involves a union effort to organize drivers who fit into all three categories.[25]

Unions and Informal Workers

When the Solidarity Center commissioned the case studies in this volume, it asked Rutgers University to focus on organizing waged informal workers by traditional unions and the WIEGO network to focus on cases of collective negotiations by organizations of informal workers regardless of organization type. In the Rutgers cases, the working hypothesis behind the focus was that traditional trade unions might find it easier to organize informal waged employees because they more closely resemble the unions' current membership and existing strategies. The WIEGO cases were motivated by Solidarity Center's interest in understanding the circumstances in which informal workers, especially the self-employed or those in disguised employment relationships, were self-organizing or organizing with the help of organizations other than traditional trade unions.

Here too clarity about terminology is important, in particular the definition of a union. While many labor scholars and labor leaders have come to equate unions with workplace organizing and the practice of collective bargaining, we do not. We prefer, with an important modification, the expansive definition of the renowned scholars and activists Sidney and Beatrice Webb, writing about the British labor movement almost a hundred years ago. They defined a union as a "continuous association of wage-earners for the purpose of maintaining or improving the conditions of their working lives." Our modification of their definition, for reasons that should be obvious at this point in the discussion, is to substitute the word "worker" for "wage-earner." Still, we find it useful to acknowledge that most unions throughout the world have focused on organizing and representing wage earners and doing so through collective bargaining. We follow Cobble in calling these "traditional unions."[26]

As discussed in our brief review above, for scholars of and participants in traditional unions, a crucial question is: How can those organizations depart from their historic position of "just saying no" to informal work arrangements, and therefore to informal workers as constituents, and embrace new organizing and negotiating strategies and structures? We see a shift from what Yun calls "exclusion to integration" or Heery calls "resistance to inclusion" as crucial to the future of labor movements around the world.[27]

As discussed above, the literature is replete with interviews with trade union leaders producing long lists of the challenges to traditional unions that informal workers present. These challenges include unstable relationships to the labor market and to any particular employer; workplaces outside factories or firms in public or private spaces; very low earning levels leading to low dues; demographic differences (by gender, race, ethnicity, and immigration status) between the formal workers who are typically union members and informal workers; and informal workers' suspicions of the motives of union representatives. A central issue—present most clearly in our South Africa case—is the relationship between formal workers, who are typically the backbone of the traditional union, and informal workers in the same sector or enterprise. Formal workers must come to see the poor conditions typically faced by informal wage workers working in the same enterprises or sectors as having the potential to lower their own standards rather than as a buffer that makes their standards possible. Yun developed his typology of union approaches to organizing and representing informal workers (exclusion, inclusion, proxy, integration) through an examination of the complex dynamics between formal and informal workers and their organizations in multiple cases in the auto industry in South Korea. Elbert describes a successful campaign to improve the conditions of informal workers (both internal and externally hired temporary contract workers) in a food processing plant in Argentina.[28] The campaign's success hinged in large part on the support from formal workers and their union. Interestingly, as the chapter on Haitian immigrant workers in the Dominican Republic in this volume demonstrates, the dynamics of union inclusion of informal workers closely parallels the dynamics of union inclusion of immigrant workers. We seek to build on this emerging literature by carefully documenting several more or less successful campaigns by traditional unions to bring informal waged workers into their organizations and to advocate for them.

For observers of traditional unions, an even more basic question exists concerning the second category of workers: Are traditional unions the right vehicle for organizing and advocating for those who are self-employed? Based on the South African experience, Theron concludes that nonunion MBOs, such as cooperatives, are a more effective form for raising standards for self-employed or own-account workers. Indeed, few would contest that the organization of informal self-employed workers is a heavy lift for traditional unions. Throughout the world, traditional unions have typically defined their membership as employees working for a particular employer or set of employers within an industry, or what can be called a "wage culture." Many trade unionists have come to equate unionism with collective bargaining for wages and benefits; this option may not always be the best or even a possible strategy for representing the interests of the self-employed. Fischer quotes a Tanzanian union leader who equates the informal sector with the self-employed in this regard: "What they need—those people in the informal sector—they need to know something about business, they need to know how they can get loans, how they can administrate these kinds of things. And that is not what the union are experts in."[29]

Extent and Dimensions of Informal Employment

The ILO, the International Expert Group on Informal Sector Statistics, and the WIEGO network have collaborated for two decades to improve statistics on informal employment. More and more countries are collecting data on informal employment. Recent estimates indicate that it constitutes more than half of non-agricultural employment in most of the developing world. Recent estimates are 82 percent in South Asia, 66 percent in sub-Saharan Africa, 65 percent in East and Southeast Asia, and 51 percent in Latin America.[30]

Study Design and Methodology

As outlined above, the two streams of research that yielded these nine case examples were initially conducted independently by the Rutgers and WIEGO teams. When the decision was made, in consultation with the Solidarity Center staff, to combine the two different streams of research into an edited volume as part of the final two years of the grant, we expected to find that there would be both similarities as well as differences in the strategies and tactics of these two different types of campaigns. The nine cases included in this volume were selected in large part because they were identified by the Solidarity Center as having achieved at least some demonstrable success in improving some conditions for some workers. Further, the organizations involved have proved sustainable; they continue to exist as of the time of this writing. The Rutgers research team was directly supervised by Susan Schurman and Adrienne Eaton, and the WIEGO cases were supervised by Chris Bonner and Marty Chen of WIEGO and analyzed initially by Debbie Budlender, an independent consultant in South Africa. Though each team had conducted its fieldwork with a separate protocol, all authors were asked to follow the same basic outline in putting their chapters together.[31]

This study thus falls in the category of multicase exploratory case study design, the goal of which, in this instance, is to discover patterns and add theoretical insights about successful informal workers' organizing. In the conclusion, we seek to summarize the significance of our findings and suggest their relevance to theory building. "Theory" in this case does not refer merely to "cause-effect" relationships, though we will make some claims in this respect. The strength of the cases in this volume is the scope and depth of the descriptions of the campaigns in different contexts but following similar case protocols, which allows us to use "replication logic," the appropriate analytic method for multicase studies.[32]

Organization of the Book

Following this introduction, this volume is divided into two sections focusing on the two main types of informal workers: waged workers and the self-employed. The chapters include case studies on a wide range of occupations and industries, each with its own particular economic realities. They are based on field research which relied primarily on interviews and focus groups with workers themselves and with organizational leaders and other stakeholders. A final chapter presents our concluding thoughts.

Section 1: Formalizing or Reformalizing Informal Wage Workers

In chapter 1, Daniel Hawkins describes a campaign for both formalization and unionization among port workers in Buenaventura, Colombia. These workers had been subject to a complex web of subcontracting arrangements leading to widespread informalization following the privatization of that nation's ports in 1993. While Colombia is perhaps the most dangerous place in the world for workers and unions to organize, the port workers in Buenaventura, with support from transnational labor organizations, created a new union, Union Portuaria (UP), in 2009. A new union was necessary because the older unions that had represented port workers prior to privatization had either disappeared or converted themselves into fake cooperatives, which constituted a particular form of labor intermediation. With the help of the global trade union movement and the political opening emerging from regime change, UP has been engaged in an ongoing battle to restore some elements of decent work for a small number of externalized workers.

In her case study of union advocacy for casual and contract workers by the South African Commercial, Catering, and Allied Workers Union (SACCAWU) (chapter 2), Sahra Ryklief reviews the new work arrangements that retail and hospitality sector employers have used to remove workers from legal protections and social insurance funds. In responding, SACCAWU accepted a certain level of nonstandard employment while also attempting to bargain for equity in pay and benefits. SACCAWU is attempting to apply the leverage gained and lessons learned from its success in the retail sector to organize and advocate for workers in the hospitality sector.

In the Dominican Republic (DR), as in many countries of the world, there is substantial overlap between being an immigrant and working informally: virtually all Haitian workers in the DR work informally but not all informal workers are Haitian immigrants. In chapter 3, Janice Fine and Allison Petrozziello examine this overlap and look at how organizing is taking place in the construction and domestic worker sectors. Beginning in 2007, with the encouragement and support of the Solidarity Center, the Confederacion Nacional de Unidad Sindical (CNUS), one of the major labor federations in the DR, began to make migrant worker rights a major focus of its work, leading it to begin organizing informal workers for the first time.

In chapter 4 Mary R. Goldsmith describes the remarkable case of the domestic workers union in Uruguay, the Sindicato Unico de Trabajadoras Domésticas (SUTD), which has collectively bargained contracts with the housewives league (the Liga de Amas de Casa, Consumidores y Usuarios de la República Oriental del Uruguay). In November 2006, the Uruguayan legislature adopted a law (Law 18.065) that gives domestic workers the same basic labor rights as other workers. On November 10, 2008, the government, employer, and worker delegates in Uruguay signed the first collective agreement for domestic service in Latin America. The agreement applied to all domestic workers and their employers throughout the country and was renegotiated in 2010. These agreements set a minimum wage and provided for across-the-board wage increases and called for decent working conditions. The second agreement added a premium for night work.

In Cambodia, beer companies hire women on an informal basis, often on commission, to promote their brands in bars and restaurants not owned or managed by the companies. In chapter 5, Mary Evans describes the way exposure to HIV and sexual harassment and assault brought these workers to the attention of NGOs and labor organizations both within and outside Cambodia. They pressed for an industry code of conduct, which led to the formalization of some beer promoters under the protection of Cambodian labor law. More recently, the Cambodian Food Service Workers' Federations launched a campaign to formally represent beer promotion workers at Cambrew, a subsidiary of Carlsberg, a Danish global beer producer. The situation is complicated by the presence on the scene of government-dominated or government-affiliated unions.

The Tunisian revolution brought a new regime to power in 2011, promising, among other things, social and economic justice. In chapter 6, Stephen King describes the successful campaign by the Union Général Tunisienne du Travail (UGTT) and by workers themselves to restore formal employment to low-wage government workers whose jobs had been privatized and subcontracted during previous regimes. Under subcontracting arrangements, work had become informal and working conditions, pay rates, and benefits had been severely undermined.

Section 2: Securing Livelihoods for the Self-Employed

The minibus sector in Georgia originally began with self-employed individuals purchasing vehicles and operating in an informal manner alongside the more traditional metropolitan bus companies. As the new regime that came to power in the "Rose Revolution" began to clean up corrupt local politics and formalize the minibus sector, a system of mediation arose with route operators or route owners bidding to control newly identified bus routes. The minibus drivers now operate in a mix of economic relationships: some remain self-employed owner-operators while others are employees of different minibus owners. Chapter 7, by Elza Jgerenaia and Gocha Aleksandria, describes the evolution of this sector and the campaign by the Transport and Road Building Workers Trade Union of Georgia (TRBWTUG), an affiliate of the Georgia Trade Union Confederation (GTUC), to organize and collectively bargain for drivers regardless of their employment relationship. This case examines the process and outcome of collective bargaining in three Georgian cities: Batumi, Rustavi, and Tbilisi.

In 2011, bargaining among various stakeholders including government representatives, leaders of waste picker cooperatives, and NGOs in the Brazilian state of Minas Gerais resulted in the passing of the Recycling Bonus Law. In chapter 8, Sonia Dias and Vera Alice Cardoso Silva describe the background to the passage of the law, which established a monetary incentive to be paid by the state government to waste pickers who are members of a recycling cooperative, another form of informal workers' association. It is the first law in the country that authorizes the use of public money for ongoing payments for work done by waste pickers. Provision of a monetary incentive aims to reduce loss of reusable materials and to supplement the income of waste pickers, who primarily earn money from selling recyclables within specific product markets. Some waste picker advocates view the bonus law as an important gain in their ongoing campaign to become a recognized and formal part of the waste-management system, while others are afraid it will divert waste picker energy away from more important goals such as bidding for solid waste contracts. This case also reviews bargaining around the initial implementation of the law.

Soon after her election as president of Liberia, Ellen Johnson Sirleaf appointed a new mayor of the capital, Monrovia, and gave her an explicit mandate to "clean up" the city and the city administration. This included reining in the activities and locations for street vendors, who allegedly contribute to congestion and uncollected garbage in the streets. In chapter 9, Milton A. Weeks and Pewee Reed detail how street vendors organized to fight back attempts to constrain their activities. Street vendors marched in protest of the repeated harassment from police, pushing the mayor to agree to negotiate with them. There have been repeated negotiations between a street vendors union created out of a merger of two associations and various local authorities. In the fall of 2014, the negotiations with a new mayor of Monrovia finally resulted in a formal memorandum of understanding (MOU) between the city, the union, and the Liberian Ministry of Commerce and Industry. The MOU sets up a licensing system and protects union members from police raids and confiscation of their goods but commits traders to operate in designated areas to allow for free movement of pedestrian and vehicle traffic.

Broadening the Repertoire?

As mentioned above, traditional unions around the world are often viewed as almost synonymous with collective bargaining for wages and benefits; in the minds of many trade unionists and their observers, you cannot have a union without collective bargaining and you cannot have collective bargaining without a union. Our cases challenge this notion, as well they should. In the nineteenth century, the early labor *movement* had a broader repertoire. At least in Europe, the labor movement was understood to include trade unions but also labor parties and cooperatives. Unions themselves raised standards in a number of different ways and, at least in the United States, collective bargaining was not always one of them. The Webbs described three "methods" of trade unions: collective bargaining, legal enactment, and mutual insurance.[33]

Today, advocacy for legal reforms, or more broadly reforms in government regulation or public policy, is a common tool of unions around the world. As Eaton and Voos point out, mutual insurance may be the oldest method of trade unionism.[34] The Webbs had in mind funds organized by early unions that workers paid into collectively to protect members against sickness, accidents, death, and even unemployment. More recently, some labor scholars have revived the notion of "mutual aid unionism."[35] For most of the past century the traditional labor movement globally has focused on workplace organizing and representing workers through collective bargaining with an employer or group of employers, often at the sectoral level. Given the centrality of collective bargaining to the repertoire of most unions, the main emphasis of their advocacy and representation of informal workers has been to structure collective bargaining relationships for them when possible, often by including informal workers in the legal framework that structures the collective bargaining regime in a particular country and by organizing an employing entity with which to bargain.

It is clear that diverse strategies are needed to effectively improve the conditions of informal workers. Rina Agarwala argues that informal workers in three

Indian states have been most successful in improving their lives by essentially giving up on attempting to bargain for better pay and standards with their employers and instead demanding state-provided social benefits such as housing, education, and health care. Agarwala argues that in states where the success of at least one political party depends on addressing the concerns of the poor, but where that party also supports economic liberalization policies, informal wage workers have been able to succeed in their demands for benefits by specifically accepting their informal status.[36]

Our cases also demonstrate the need for new approaches to collective bargaining. For instance, one of the central puzzles for any union of domestic workers that wants to raise standards through collective bargaining is: Who will act as the employer?[37] Our domestic workers case, set in Uruguay, provides a novel answer to this question: a national organization of "housewives." Whether they are self-employed or wage-employed or semidependent, many informal workers work in public spaces or their own homes without secure tenure and basic infrastructure services. So most informal workers need to bargain with government for tenure and services, not just in the market with employers, buyers, and suppliers.[38] The Liberian street traders provide an example: they had to negotiate with the country's president, the municipality, and both the national and municipal police. Other innovations might relate to what is being bargained for. The informal retail and hospitality workers in our South African case were organized into a traditional union that then attempted to represent their interests by bargaining for equity in pay and benefits with employers while still allowing irregular hours and shifts.

The ILO Convention 154 defines "collective bargaining" as "all negotiations which take place between an employer, or one or more employers' organizations on one hand and one or more workers' organizations on the other for: (a) determining working conditions and terms of employment; (b) regulating relations between employers and workers; and/or (c) regulating relations between employers or their organizations and a worker's organization or workers' organizations." Although this definition, by referencing "workers" rather than "employees," can include informal workers' organizations, clearly the language is geared toward formal wage employment. Limiting the bargaining partner to "employers" excludes forms of collective negotiations between informal workers' organizations and the entities—usually a branch of government—that in fact have authority to determine the conditions of their members' work. Horn suggests that informal workers identify "the entity or authority most responsible for the issues over which they wish to negotiate."[39] Budlender suggests that the term "social dialogue," which the ILO defines as "all types of negotiation, consultation or information sharing among the bipartite parties in the workplace or industrial sector or by tripartite partners at the national level on issues of common interest," may better encompass the types of negotiations described in several of our cases.[40] For example, in the Georgian transport workers' case, the traditional labor movement views its effort as an attempt to strengthen social dialogue in the country. In our view, however, "social dialogue" implies a process that is firmly established in law and therefore does not apply to any of our cases.

Self-employed informal workers have to bargain with multiple counterparts: suppliers, customers, and often government authorities. Taxi drivers' organizations, for instance, may negotiate with the municipality that essentially regulates their conditions of work, rather than with an employer per se. Street vendors and waste pickers are other categories of workers who often engage in or attempt to engage in some form of collective negotiation with municipal authorities, as in our case involving street vendors in Monrovia, Liberia. Another of our cases concerns waste pickers (recyclers) who negotiated with state-level authorities in Brazil first over the passage and then the implementation of a law that created a state-funded bonus for registered recycler cooperatives funded at the state level.

Beyond the specific tactics employed or forms of organization developed, our cases highlight the crucial importance of the normative or moral claim that undergirds each of these campaigns. Each campaign draws on international norms of decent work and human and social rights to highlight the injustices faced by the group of workers involved.

The set of cases in this volume add to a growing body of literature suggesting that a significant change in global labor movement strategy long advocated by labor studies scholars and labor activists may finally be underway.[41] The new strategy is in fact not so new; rather, as our cases demonstrate, what is "new" are new categories of workers availing themselves of a broad array of "traditional" forms of unionism, including those that predate the post–World War II model, and traditional unions adopting the "new" tactics of direct action and member involvement associated with social movements. This change reflects a growing recognition that the changes taking place globally in work and employment are permanent and, hence, the role of labor movements as vehicles for representing workers' interests must adapt.[42]

Our cases also clearly show why, after nearly three decades of debate about how to respond to globalized capital and neoliberal economic policy, there has been so little evidence of change on the ground. Caught on the horns of a dilemma between their historic raison d'être—the moral claim to advance economic and social rights for all workers—and entrenched, often competing, interpretations and institutional arrangements for how to achieve this in practice, most traditional unions have found it difficult to include new categories of workers in their organizations or to embrace new types of workers' organization as part of the structure of "organized labor."[43] We believe our cases represent an encouraging sign that traditional unions are learning a crucial lesson: informal workers are organizing and engaging in collective action with or without support from the existing trade union movement. Some traditional unions are also learning and adopting useful lessons from their efforts to organize informal workers, and organizations of informal workers are adopting useful lessons from traditional trade unions. We predict others will follow. In our concluding chapter we summarize the common elements of successful campaigns that we think are contained in this research. Our argument, in brief, is that if the global labor movement is to successfully adapt to the reality of work in today's global economy, it will need to recover its historic moral claim to seek human and social rights for all workers and to incorporate many new forms of organization.

Part I

FORMALIZING OR REFORMALIZING DISTANCED EMPLOYMENT RELATIONSHIPS

PORT WORKERS IN COLOMBIA
Reinstatement as Formal Workers

Daniel Hawkins

The privatization of Colombia's port sector in 1993 inaugurated a process of pervasive employment flexibilization. The thousands of port workers, previously unionized on a mass scale and protected by collective bargaining agreements and indefinite employment contracts, witnessed a rapid transformation in their working conditions, highlighted by the explosion of nonstandard work contracts, informal hiring and firing, and the gradual asphyxiation or transformation of labor unions. In Buenaventura, home to the country's busiest seaport terminal, the flexibilization of labor relations took on a decidedly robust form. A multitude of large, medium, small, and even one-person firms sprang up within the port, many of which specialized in nothing more than creating and expanding lines of labor intermediation: hiring out low-paid, temporary workers to the formally constituted port operating firms.

In response to the changing conditions at the port, the embattled labor unions, bereft of space for collective bargaining and faced with a dwindling pool of formally contracted workers, began to mimic many of the labor intermediation practices of other firms. Before long, the conversion process was complete: for all practical purposes these unions had become intermediaries themselves, and their registered members merely workers supplied to other firms under service contracts. As this small Pacific coast town grew at a staggering rate, unemployment reached untenable proportions. Intermediary labor firms responded by intensifying the exploitation of workers, lowering wage rates, hiring workers on day-based or even tasked-based oral contracts, most of which were entirely informal and did not adhere to the laws regarding social security benefits.

Faced with such deplorable working conditions, a group of longtime port workers in Cartagena came together eight years ago to discuss the founding of a new and novel union, one that would represent workers by pressuring the principal port operating firms—in Cartagena, Santa Marta, Barranquilla, and Buenaventura—to end labor intermediation and directly hire workers via fixed-employment contracts with all the associated legal social security benefits. This union, Union Portuaria (UP), formed with the support of the US-based Solidarity Center, began with a double-pronged campaign to affiliate port workers and also pressure for the formalization of work at the port. The year 2012 saw the recommencement of worker protest and strike actions, leading to the direct hiring of approximately eighty previously subcontracted machinery operators and the promise of future employer-union negotiations. But the employer response has been both furtive and assertive. New types of companies replaced the now outlawed, fictitious cooperatives, while leading firms continued their anti-union practices, seeking to fire or blacklist any worker affiliated with the UP.

At the same time, the long-stalled free trade agreement (FTA) between Colombia and the United States provided the political impetus necessary to begin a major reshuffling of the manner in which the Colombian state regulated the labor market. Pressured to more assertively protect and guarantee union rights and worker protections, the Colombian president, Juan Manuel Santos, signed a Labor Action Plan with President Obama in April 2011. Along with various normative reforms, this plan focused on improving the situation for workers in five key economic sectors, one of which was the port industry.

This chapter describes the multiple forms of contracting and resultant labor relations present at the Buenaventura port, focusing on the still prevalent anti-union tactics adopted by many port-based firms and the ambivalent role adopted by the Colombian Labor Ministry. The chapter first provides a brief overview of the economic, social, and labor contexts in Colombia and then illustrates the manner in which labor intermediation takes place, both normatively and in practice. This is followed by a detailed analysis of the UP's worker protest campaign for the formalization of work contracts and the termination of anti-union practices at the port. The chapter concludes with reflections on the successes, failures, and limitations of the UP-led worker formalization campaign.

Colombia's Economy and Labor Market

In recent years, the economy of Colombia, Latin America's third most populous country, has displayed a worrying trend of sustained economic growth, measured by an increase in its gross domestic product (GDP), alongside a labor market plagued by high levels of unemployment and informality. Indeed, while the economy grew 4 percent and 4.7 percent in 2012 and 2013 respectively, the unemployment rate was 10.4 percent and 9.6 percent for the same period, rates that are way above the regional average.[1] Alongside such high and ingrained levels of unemployment, the massive amount of labor informality throughout the country has meant that unprotected employment[2] and "indecent work" have become the norm for many of Colombia's workers. According to the National Department for Statistics (DANE),[3] in Colombia's thirteen metropolitan areas in 2013, 49.4 percent of all economically active people worked in the informal economy. If DANE included rural areas and used a more inclusive definition of informal work, this level would increase substantially.[4]

The Colombian Labor Movement

Today, after decades of extreme repression and state-condoned harassment, Colombia's union movement finds itself in a period of relative respite and even sees a glimmering of newfound possibilities for renewed organizational strategies. Nevertheless, in order to more accurately locate this recent flicker of opportunity, a brief synopsis of the systematic exclusion of Colombia's union movement, both from the workplace and the formal spheres of politics, must be offered.

In Colombia the union movement has experienced historical constraints of a severity more pronounced than in any other country of the world. While many unionists across the globe face harassment, employer and even state repression, and the structural hostilities wrought by neoliberal labor market flexibilization processes, unionists in Colombia have had to confront these issues in a sociopolitical and cultural climate of extreme anti-union practices. The number of trade unionists killed in Colombia is more than double that for the rest of the world combined. Between 1979 and 2010, 2,944 Colombian unionists were murdered, 229 disappeared by force, and a further 280 had attempts made on their lives.[5] Workers must contend not only with fear of losing their jobs when they embark on union organizing, but also fear for their personal safety.

In the face of such victimization, the Colombian union density and collective bargaining coverage have declined precipitously in recent decades. In 2014 the unionization rate came to only 4 percent of the economically active population, one of the lowest union density rates in the hemisphere. Furthermore, the vast majority of Colombian unions are small and therefore face huge obstacles when it comes to collective bargaining. Eighty percent of all unions[6] have fewer than one hundred members, and only a little more than 627,000 workers are covered by some form of collective contract,[7] a figure that comes to only 3 percent of the total workforce.

The industrial relations framework in Colombia offers little space for effective union organization. To create a union, there must be a minimum of twenty-five workers in the firm, and unions are not permitted to negotiate collective bargaining agreements (CBAs) by industry or sector, a factor that significantly lowers the rate of CBA coverage across the economy and the unions' ability to take wages out of competition.

The union movement in Colombia is institutionally divided into three confederations: Unitary Confederation of Workers (CUT), General Confederation of Workers (CGT), and the Confederation of Colombian Workers (CTC). The CUT is the largest of the three and was founded in 1985–1986.[8] The CUT is the most politically leftist of the Colombian union confederations and groups together some of the largest union federations of Colombia. The CGT, created in 1971, is numerically the second largest confederation and groups together twenty relatively small union federations. Lastly, the CTC, the oldest confederation, was created during the initial period of welfare-like political openings during the first Alfonso Lopez Pumarejo government (1934–1938). The CTC has seventeen affiliated union federations, all of which are relatively small both numerically and in terms of their political influence.

Recent Developments

Following the trend to advance the global integration of economies, the first-term government (2002–2006) of President Alvaro Uribe launched an agenda that included the negotiation of various free trade agreements (FTAs), with emphasis on the world's largest and most prosperous economies, especially the United States, Europe, and Canada. Even though the Colombia-US FTA negotiations ended in February 2006 and the agreement was signed by both parties in November of that year, it took nearly six years before it received both US congressional approval and US presidential ratification.[9]

The principal reason for the slow passage of the FTA was the vociferous opposition to an FTA with Colombia, given the country's deplorable human and labor rights record. Indeed, the vehement opposition to the ratification of this and other FTAs by local and international unions and by social movements brought together, under a consolidated union front, a transnational advocacy network (TAN),[10] which simultaneously opposed the ratification of the FTA while also calling for concrete improvements to be made to both the Colombian legal framework and the state's effectiveness in enforcing its labor laws.

During Uribe's two presidential terms, there was little concrete improvement in the protection of labor rights. First, the Uribe government accorded the newly created Ministry of Social Protection the power to negate the registration of 253 unions between 2002 and 2007, in clear violation of the 1991 Colombian Constitution and the International Labor Organization (ILO) Convention 87. Second, the Uribe government implemented a state-funded criminal web of espionage, harassment, and murder of numerous unionists, other human rights defenders, and leading figures of the Colombian opposition. Numerous unions and their leaders were illegally spied upon by the State Department of Security (DAS), and a list of twenty-two unionists was handed to paramilitary leaders by high-level DAS officials.[11] Last, the regime propelled a prolific expansion of associated work cooperatives (CTAs), legal entities that made a mockery of the historical conception of the cooperative movement inspired by Robert Owen in Britain in the early nineteenth century.

CTAs in Colombia

CTAs in Colombia have a long legal history dating from 1931. It was not until the present millennium, however, that they really took hold, just as their "social objectives" became tainted. Initially, perhaps, CTAs were promoted as true cooperatives, offering workers the possibilities of forming collective associations of mutual benefit. Nonetheless, especially during the Uribe governments, this conception of workers' cooperatives was set aside by a double drive to cut business costs while simultaneously crippling union activity.

CTAs were not bound by the Substantive Work Code (CST) because the "associated workers" were simultaneously workers and, in theory, owners of the cooperative. "Workers" in a CTA were thus not paid a salary but rather received "compensation," which did not include any of the protections provided by the CST.[12] Firms took advantage of the legal status of CTAs by outsourcing work to them.

Under Uribe, the number of CTAs expanded from 710 (with 54,000 "associates") to 4,000 (610,000 associates).[13] The expansion of CTAs during the Uribe period, especially the hundreds that obtained contracts with public entities,[14] opened up a new sphere for political influence and enrichment. At the same time, congressional proposals to reform the CTAs were unceremoniously dropped.[15]

Alongside the opportunities for patronage and corruption, the CTA model allowed businesses to save substantial money on wage costs. There were no requirements to pay parafiscal costs,[16] weekend pay rates, night rates and, prior to the 2010 and 2011 reforms, social security contributions, which created savings of up to 50 percent in overall labor costs. The Colombian port sector was one of the industries most plagued by the expansion of CTAs, especially after the privatization process the sector underwent during the 1990s. In 2011, it became illegal for CTAs to use personnel for permanent core business activities.

The Transformation of Work in Colombia's Port Sector Firms

The firm at the top of the ladder at Buenaventura's main seaport, and the one under discussion in this chapter, is the regional port firm of Buenaventura S.A., Sociedad Portuaria Regional de Buenaventura S.A. (SPRBuen).[17] This firm was constituted in December 1993, after the privatization of the state-owned port firm Colpuertos (in 1991). The SPRBuen originally signed a contract for the concession of the Buenaventura port with the general superintendent of ports for a twenty-year period. In 2008, the Ministry for Transport of Colombia extended the concession until February 2034. The SPRBuen is constituted in the following manner: 83 percent private funds (importers, exporters, port operating companies, naval line operators, export workers, and other "natural" people); 15 percent belonging to the Mayor's Office of Buenaventura; and the remaining 2 percent belonging to the Ministry of Transport. According to a study undertaken by the Superintendence for Industry and Commerce, it transports 60 percent of Colombia's foreign commerce.[18] The SPRBuen also has controlling shares of a number of port operating firms including TECSA (Terminal Especializado de Contenedores de Buenaventura S.A.), ZELSA Ltda (Zona de Expansion Logistica), Sociedad Portuaria de Caldera S.A., and Sociedad Portuaria Granela de Caldera S.A.

Trade Unions

Currently, there are a number of unions present at the SPRBuen terminal, but only four[19] are officially registered and have some degree of union history and practice, and only one is currently functioning as an actual trade union.[20] Three of these unions are described below. Sintramaritimo (National Union for Cargo Handlers at Colombian Seaports) has roughly a twenty-year history and is present at the Buenaventura port. Although this union makes a pretense of having a national reach, it only has a union office in Buenaventura. Since privatization, Sintramaritimo has opted to utilize the models of CTAs and, more recently, *contrato sindical*[21] as a means of survival. Sintramaritimo is affiliated with the CUT. It claims to have 1,212 affiliates nationwide, although numerous Buenaventura port workers, as well as members of Union Portuaria, state that these "affiliates" are actually workers who have signed up as casual laborers as a means of getting rudimentary work through past and present Sintramaritimo union leaders.[22]

Simbrasemar (Union of Laborers, Stevedores, and Auxiliary Services of Maritime Firms) has also long been associated with the model of labor intermediation, with the president and director's board having close ties with many of the firms involved in "hiring out" workers for the principal operating firms. Neither

Simbrasemar nor Sintramaritimo have attempted to negotiate collective agreements recently. Sintrabrasemar currently counts 510 members, although, as with Sintramaritimo, these affiliates are passive.

Union Portuario (UP), initially consolidated in Cartagena in 2009 after a six-year process of planning, discussion, and worker consultation, had approximately three hundred members at the time of its Caribbean inauguration. The elected president, Javier Marrugo, ex-unionist of Sintramaritimo and current pensioner, was the linchpin in the efforts to create a new national level union from 2002 onwards. Marrugo, with the support of the US-based Solidarity Center, began a series of nationwide visits to the main Colombian ports in an effort to drum up port worker backing for the formation of port-based UP sectional offices. In Buenaventura, after much on-the-ground union canvassing, port workers came together to attend numerous assemblies (in 2006, 2007, and 2008) organized to discuss the formal creation of a union office of the UP in Buenaventura. Three to four hundred people participated in these assemblies, which focused on the need to promote union unity in the port sector nationally via the creation of a truly national port workers' union that would have offices in the main Colombian ports. Further discussion revolved around the need to reinvent what unionism meant to port workers after many local union leaders had veered into the role of middlemen in the complex web of labor intermediation.

Labor Degradation at Buenaventura

In 1993 the Colombian state formally relinquished its control of the country's ports. This process was pushed forth as part of the hegemonic regional policy discourse and the "Washington Consensus" as a means of lightening the state's economic load and providing much-needed resources to pay for the burgeoning foreign debt.

Colombia's ports had been under state control since 1959, run and administered by the firm Colpuertos. This firm was set for liquidation with the passing of Law 1 in 1991. The new Statute for Maritime Ports outlined that regional port societies (RPS) (*sociedades portuarias regionales*) would administer the country's ports, and initially nine such concessions were obtained by businesses and public entities. These partnerships were promoted to expand the activities and efficiencies of the country's ports: introducing new technologies, protecting the environment, using beaches efficiently, and reducing port costs.[23] Part of the process of reducing port costs involved downsizing the workforce and increasing flexibility in the labor regime.

The dismantling of Colpuertos led to the termination of more than ten thousand employee contracts.[24] Many of these workers were rehired by the newly founded RPSs or by the numerous operating firms that began to appear from

1993 onwards. Employment conditions, however, were markedly different from those the majority union, Sintrapuertos, had upheld during the period of Colpuerto's monopoly of the port sector. First and foremost was the new legal framework governing the period of employee hiring. With the passing of Law 50 of 1990, firms could now hire workers for set periods, rather than the "indefinite" contractual period set out in the CST. Secondly, the reconstitution of port operations and management opened the way for the expansion of outsourcing and labor intermediation. CTAs became one of the most lucrative forms of intermediation. The Buenaventura port, perhaps more than any other of the country's principal ports, was the most affected by the privatization of Colpuertos and the subsequent revamping of labor relations.

Buenaventura is a city plagued by informality and mass structural unemployment. Outside of the port sector there is little formal industry, and the very existence of the port ensures that tourism is nonexistent in the city. This mid-size city is thus highly dependent on the port industry. Nonetheless, the main port and the other minor ports fail to employ a sufficient portion of the economically active labor force. According to the Labor Market Observatory of the local Chamber of Commerce for 2010, there were 284,069 residents of working age in the city. In 2013, after years of modernization and downsizing, there were roughly four thousand people working at the main port terminal, a drop of nearly 60 percent from the preprivatization period.

Nonstandard and Precarious Work at the Buenaventura Port

Buenaventura appears to have been the laboratory for labor intermediation in the Colombian port industry. According to a survey of 195 workers of various occupations at the SPRBuen-controlled port terminal, conducted between April and September 2011 by the National Union School of Colombia (ENS),[25] 66 percent of all workers were subcontracted by either a temporary employment agency (EST) or a CTA. Only 27 percent of the workers (or 52 workers surveyed) had a direct labor contract with either the SPRBuen or one of the main port operating firms (see Figure 1.1).

The great majority of the surveyed port workers have spent the main part of their adult life working at the port. Only 3.9 percent had worked at the port less than one year. Due to the great instability and lack of employee contracts, however, only 20.2 percent of all people surveyed work at the port on a permanent basis.

The ENS survey of working conditions in the Buenaventura SPRBuen-run port terminal highlighted the precarious employment status of the workforce. Only 57 percent of respondents reported that they possessed a work contract.

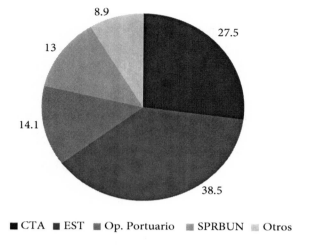

CTA ■ EST ■ Op. Portuario ■ SPRBUN ■ Otros

FIGURE 1.1. Percentage of surveyed workers by firm-type "Condiciones de Trabajo Decente de los Trabajadores de los Puertos de Colombia" (unpublished ENS document accessed by author, Santa Marta, Barranquilla, Cartagena y Buenaventura), 28.

The remaining workers labored under a different modality: 62.5 percent under a service contract (*orden de prestación de servicios*), which is of a commercial nature and does not include any employee benefits; 27.5 percent under a covenant of association with a CTA; 1.3 percent with a civil contract; and 8.8 percent under some other modality.[26] Of the workers who possessed an actual employee contract, only 46 (or 23.6 percent of all surveyed workers) had a full-time permanent contract. The remaining workers laboring under an employee contract did so for fixed time periods; the majority of these contracts last for three and four months. In addition, 44.5 percent of the 195 workers' surveyed stated that they worked for a firm different than the one that contracted them.

In terms of wages or income derived from working at the port terminal, a whopping 70.9 percent of surveyed workers received, as of mid-2011, a sum equal to or below the legal minimum wage (COP $535,600) per month.[27] The majority of surveyed workers obtained a monthly income between COP $50 and $400, a precariously low amount.

New Forms of Sidestepping Government Regulations

As noted by numerous labor scholars, extensive labor laws are necessary but not sufficient; they must be supported by effective mechanisms to ensure compliance and enforcement. This holds particularly true for the case of the port industry in Buenaventura. The early and pervasive use of labor outsourcing in the newly privatized port sector exemplified the major discord between the written labor law and the labor law in practice in Colombia. Indeed, a popular Colombia saying states, "hecha la ley, hecha la trampa" (when the law has been made, so has the means of evading it).

According to Colombian legislation, the only types of firms that can legally undertake labor intermediation are ESTs (temp service agencies).[28] These firms can send employees to client firms where they will undertake core business activities. These employees, however, can only work at the client firm for six months, which can be extended for a maximum of a further six months. Furthermore, the EST must ensure that its employees are covered by the legal social security protections and the legal benefits associated with a labor contract. After the introduction of Law 1429 of 2010, CTAs, once the prime culprits in institutionalizing labor intermediation and promoting nonstandard work at the port, were no longer legally permitted to undertake labor intermediation that involved sending associated members to work in core business activities.

The pervasiveness of labor intermediation, carried out in a manner outside legal norms, was still starkly evident more than one year after the ENS's survey was conducted. In interviews with five tallymen and women,[29] it became clear that TECSA S.A. continued to hire workers "through" outsourcing firms, even though these workers were undertaking core business activities and even though they had been working in this occupation for longer than the one-year maximum period. The means by which TECSA overcame legal impediments to such continual intermediation was by terminating the contract of one temp service firm and then hiring a new one. The tallymen and women would then be told to hand in their CVs to the new firm, and they would immediately restart work. It is important to note that the actual working conditions and managerial hierarchy in the port did not change; TECSA, through its supervisory personnel, ensured that tasks were completed as required. Effectively, the outsourcing firms did nothing but permit TECSA to evade the payment of costs associated with directly hiring workers and paying their legal employee benefits. Even when an outsourcing firm's contract lasted longer than one year, the firm in question (Accion S.A.) would only hire its employees for a maximum period of ten months. After this period expired, the workers would receive their severance pay and the other legal minimum benefits and then be told that the contract had ended. Generally, they had to wait either one or two weeks before the firm would tell them to come back to work as "new" employees. A port machine operator with eleven years' experience confirmed that this practice was widespread among the labor outsourcing firms in the port.[30] Ocupar Grupo Empresarial also used the ten-month contract followed by a small nonworking period as a means of evading the legal regulations inscribed in Law 50 and Decree 4369 of 2006.

One curious piece of information that illustrated the fictitious nature of such outsourcing firms was a TECSA S.A. company brochure that used a photo of two tallymen (one female) as the "image" of its firm. Both of these supposed TECSA employees were interviewed by the researcher and, surprisingly, neither of them had a contract with the firm. Rather, they had been passed from one outsourcing firm to another, always undertaking the same task and always under the direct supervision of TECSA management.

Such worker rotation "between" intermediary firms has been one of the persistent realities of working life at the Buenaventura SPRBuen terminal ever since the liquidation of Colpuertos. These practices have made workers' lives much more precarious and have impeded opportunities for collective organization. Nevertheless, blame for the initiation and expansion of labor intermediation also rests with many of the previous union leaders at the time of port privatization. Indeed, some old-time unionists were the first to create labor-intermediary CTAs in the port industry, especially in Buenaventura. These unionists, with their extensive understanding of the industry and their wide array of contacts with workers, were often very well placed to take advantage of the many business possibilities available by promoting fictitious cooperativism at the port.[31]

With the explicit prohibition of CTAs from undertaking labor intermediation practices in core business activities in 2011, new business models have emerged and expanded that have, in many instances, continued labor intermediation. Particularly, two new business models—SASs (*sociedad por acciones simplificada*, or firm for simplified actions) and *el contrato sindical* with firms—have grown in number in Colombia in recent years.

SASs came into existence with the promulgation of Law 1258 of 2008, which defines this form of business as a society constituted by one or various natural or juridical persons. Under this model, the firm's owners are not held responsible for any labor-related obligations, thereby opening up further terrain for new practices of nonstandard labor contracts. Alongside SAS, the rise of *contrato sindical* between a union and a firm is perhaps one of the unhealthiest developments in the timid process undertaken to decrease labor intermediation in Colombia. When a contract of this kind is signed between a union and a firm, the union is held directly responsible for all the labor obligations. Furthermore, the second Uribe government (2006–2010) specifically stated that *contratos sindical* fell outside the labor laws on intermediation. Although contracts of this nature have existed in Colombian legislation since 1950 (article 482 of the CST), it was only with the outlawing of CTA labor intermediation and a subsequent legal amendment to the model of *contratos sindical* that this modality of outsourcing workers' labor became attractive to the business world and to certain sectors within Colombia's union movement.

Signing a *contrato sindical* creates ambiguity in the role of the union as it theoretically acts simultaneously as both employer and worker representative. One of the key reforms of the original CST disposition, set out in the Decree 1429, was that a *contrato sindical* need no longer be approved by a union assembly. Now the signature of the union's legal representative is sufficient for the union contract to be approved. Such a practice directly undermines the very structure of democratic unionism, opening the door to union leader corruption.

The Campaign to Formalize Work
Union Revitalization and Worker Protest in Buenaventura

Worker organizations were decimated by the privatization of Colpuertos. Many senior workers and unionists were offered retirement packages, and Sintracolpuertos (the main port sector union) was disbanded. Since privatization, there has not been one CBA negotiated in the port sector.

The UP was founded as a means of representing and organizing workers to improve their concrete working conditions, especially pressuring for the formalization of their jobs and obtaining wage increases. With the assistance of the CUT-National, numerous union pensioners from Cali, and the Solidarity Center, the UP opened a chapter in Buenaventura in 2009. At the moment of its formal creation, the Buenaventura office counted 120 members, most of whom were stevedores and winch operators as well as a few tallymen/women.

Initially, the UP-Buenaventura focused on fostering grassroots port worker support for the initiative and sought to unionize workers who were energetic about the struggle to improve conditions at the port. In the words of the elected regional president, Jhon Jairo Castro, the local union strategy "concentrated not on unionizing vast numbers of port workers just for numerical importance. Rather, importance was placed on unionizing people who were committed to the cause."[32] As noted by a fifty-four-year-old stevedore and member of the UP, the difference between this and other unions was that "it was the only one that has looked to represent workers rather than firms."[33]

In order to survive and undertake union activities, the UP began a port-wide campaign to raise worker consciousness, concentrating on informing workers of their rights at work and then on pressuring the SPRBuen and TECSA to formalize labor relations at the port. The following section will summarize and offer commentary on this campaign, highlighting both its successes and failures.

The FTA and the Labor Action Plan

The long, drawn-out, and hotly contested ratification process of the US-Colombia FTA created a window of opportunity for a consolidated transnational action network (TAN) between Colombian unions and labor activists and their US counterparts. Applying lessons from their experience in various FTA negotiations throughout the hemisphere, the Colombian and US union movement vehemently opposed the FTA given the country's systematic violation of worker rights.[34] Indeed, the Uribe government's staunch anti-union stance effectively ensured that the agreement would linger for five years in the US Congress, as broad sectors of the US union movement and NGOs such as WOLA (Washington Office on Latin America)[35] undertook major political lobbying campaigns in support of their Colombian counterparts. The goal of these campaigns was to convince political representatives that Colombia's horrid record on human and worker rights meant that without change, the FTA could not be sanctioned.

More than being an economic debate, it was a moral one, rooted in what Eddie Webster terms "humanitarian solidarity," a defensive strategy in which human rights violations activate moral outrage.[36] Feeding off the rights-based discourse, Colombia's workers were framed as victims in need of state protection and international union support.

After many years of intense lobbying against the FTA during the Uribe reign, the inauguration of the Santos government in mid-2010 brought about new opportunities for the TAN to move from denouncing labor violations to proposing new ways of protecting labor rights. Santos attained the Colombian presidency in the second round of elections on June 20, 2010, and he was inaugurated on August 7 of that year. While the Uribe governmental platform was based on division, Santos looked to promote conciliation and dialogue. This was confirmed by his proposal to form a cross-party coalition as a means of overcoming congressional stalemate and obstructionism. Part of Santos's strategy was to nominate Angelino Garzón, one of the founders of CUT Colombia and long-time unionist turned centrist-conservative politician, as vice president. Garzón was charged with monitoring human rights with a particular focus on labor rights as a means of displaying the Santos government's intention to improve union-government relations.

Moving the US-Colombia FTA past its congressional stumbling point attained pre-eminent importance. The TAN took advantage of the moment and brought forward diverse policy proposals to broaden the protections for workers and unionists in Colombia. These proposals were discussed and reworked by certain US congressional representatives as well as by Colombian congressmen and women, staff members at the then Ministry for Social Protection, and staff members at the vice president's dispatch. After much back and forth, the Obama and Santos governments formally agreed upon and signed the Labor Action Plan Obama-Santos, a side agreement to the FTA, in April 2011.[37]

The plan contained numerous legal modifications that addressed ten major themes.[38] Furthermore, the plan focused on improving the protection of labor rights and union activity and ending "illegal" labor intermediation, especially in five key economic sectors:[39] mining, African palm, sugar cane, cut-flowers, and the port sector. Perhaps the most positive aspect of the Labor Action Plan, beyond the specific institutional and legal reconfigurations it required, was its focus on increasing the presence and capacity of the state to intervene in labor relations to uphold labor rights. The creation of the Ministry of Labor was perhaps the first and most emphatic step in that direction. But in terms of harmonizing the often ambiguous terrain between norms and implementation, it was the plan to strengthen labor inspection that was most important. Under the plan, the Ministry of Labor was to hire 480 new inspectors,[40] 200 of whom would be assigned to the five key sectors. According to the then vice minister for labor relations, David Luna, the newly created ministry would widen its department of inspectors and improve their salary base, increasing the number of inspectors to 904 by 2013, after sitting at only 289 inspectors in 2010.[41]

The plan also targeted illegal intermediation, especially in the five key sectors. Law 1450 of 2011 directly prohibits the misuse of cooperatives or other forms of labor intermediation that negatively affect labor rights. Furthermore, Decree 1228 of 2011 authorized the transfer of 100 labor inspectors to a special branch focusing solely on cases involving cooperatives, especially in the five key sectors. And finally, Decree 2025 of 2011 set out to clarify and harmonize previous laws regulating cooperatives. This decree set out a clearer distinction between what could be termed "permanent core business" and "intermediation" as a means of more coherently addressing violations and abuses of workers' rights. Additionally, this decree clearly sets out the instances in which a cooperative would be found in violation of laws concerning intermediation.

Together with the many other normative and institutional reforms included in the Labor Action Plan, the stage was set for a new era in workers' protections in Colombia. How did the Labor Action Plan affect the conditions on the ground in Buenaventura? First, we must ask the question: To what extent did the moral-based international campaign of union solidarity link to local actions of protest and workers' organization that demanded respect for the rights of port workers? Second, we must then determine the degree to which the institutional and legal changes made as part of the Labor Action Plan were understood by workers and used as leverage in their demands. Finally, we must evaluate the extent to which these normative-institutional changes were actually enforced and upheld at the port.

Activating Worker Consciousness;
Protesting Labor Precarity

The discourse of rights does not only affect those in the formal and upper echelons of the political sphere. Indeed, many grassroots movements have appropriated the discourse of rights and used it to leverage the state and to demand concrete changes.[42] In the Colombian case, grassroots worker protest has been quite prolific in recent years: for 2013, for example, there were a total of 364 worker mobilizations (including strikes, work stoppages, marches, sit-ins, and so forth), the highest number in more than twenty years.[43]

Worker activism was also on the rise in the ports of Buenaventura. With the consistent political and logistical support offered by the Bogota-based Solidarity Center office, the newly founded UP Buenaventura office began to perceive a major disjuncture between the importance of human rights in international political discourse and government policy and the consistent violation of workers' rights at the port. Participating in a number of workshops financed by the Solidarity Center and undertaken by ENS's staff[44] and unionists from the CUT, the port workers began to awaken to the fact that as workers they had rights and that irrespective of the precarious socioeconomic situation of the city, their rights were inalienable and should therefore be guaranteed by the Colombian state.

Many of the UP members in Buenaventura mentioned the union workshops as being the trigger that activated their motivation to participate in the later protests and mobilizations at the port. In the words of interviewee 6, a forty-eight-year-old woman who had worked for a total of twenty-one years in different capacities at the port:

> Sometimes you think that it is normal that the boss and the supervisors ride roughshod over you because you're from the lower class; it's normal that they tramp down on you. But when you hear someone tell you that this is not normal, that it's not normal that you should have to ask for your rights; that you have rights and you need to make sure that these rights are respected, well, you begin to say, what? What was I thinking? Was I asleep? Well, after this, you begin to wake up and see things differently.[45]

Interviewee 4 also succinctly summarized the benefits that the workshops offered the UP unionists:

> It's a big plus when you can count on an organization that can provide knowledge to workers about their labor rights. This knowledge helps us to defend our personal patrimony. Just as the boss needs to find out the things that help him to be successful, us workers also need to find

out our rights at work. Before joining the UP and participating in the workshops, I didn't know that I had a right to health coverage, or that I had a right to a pension and to occupational risk insurance.[46]

Workshops alone, however, will never be sufficient to foment a change in consciousness and ignite a sense of worker or class solidarity aimed at challenging the powers that be or the status quo at work. Many workers who were interviewed during the fieldwork spoke of the initial work stoppage in January 2012 as being perhaps the key instigator of a collective sense of "enough is enough." The mere process of observing fellow workers publicly protesting the appalling working conditions and the perverse chains of worker subcontracting at the port allowed many workers to comprehend that their individual struggle to "get by" was really a broad collective one. Once this small protest and work stoppage began, it quickly drew in many spontaneous supporters and, at a later date, helped to ensure that more workers would begin to voice their demands in a collective and even contentious manner.

Pressing for Negotiations

Despite the rising consciousness of workers at the port, the elected leaders of UP's Buenaventura office faced an almost insurmountable task in pressuring for union freedom and the formalization of working conditions at the port. In the first two years of the UP's existence in Buenaventura, the elected leaders were not able to get SPRBuen and TECSA management to talk with them.[47]

In this climate, the UP was forced to adopt a different tactic to press for change. In 2010, Javier Marrugo, on invitation from the Solidarity Center, traveled to Washington as part of an exchange program to help Colombian union leaders network and acquire new skills. The following year, the president of UP-Buenaventura, Jhon Jairo Castro, together with a small delegation of union leaders from the sugar cane sector, education sector, and private security industry, was invited by the AFL-CIO to travel to Washington to denounce the continued violation of labor rights and the anti-union behavior of employers in the SPRBuen port terminal. Upon his return to the city, Jhon Jairo was threatened and, along with the UP's general secretary, was issued a bulletproof vest in the event of an attempt on their lives. Meanwhile, WOLA sent staff members to Buenaventura to assist the UP in publicizing the labor rights violations at the port.

With the promulgation of the Labor Action Plan, the UP and its Colombian and US supporters began to pressure the Colombian government to oblige the SPRBuen and the principal operating firms to restructure their hiring practices in accordance with the new laws and decrees. Unfortunately, such efforts went nowhere. Although management personnel from the SPRBuen did eventually meet and discuss the UP's proposals, they clearly stated that their hands were tied, and they could not get involved in regulating the labor relations at the port; SPRBuen was nothing more than an administrative firm, not a port operator. Attention then turned to TECSA, the most important primary operating firm at the terminal, which also refused to meet. UP members then decided to adopt the only tactic that remained, which was worker mobilization and protest designed to hurt the employers where they most felt it: in their profits. They would rattle the local political sphere in the hope that, with international support, their plight would reach the ears and eyes of the Colombian government and influential members of the US Congress.

UP members had begun canvassing for support among diverse work sections of the port terminal. Winchers and stevedores were by far the most numerous occupations in the UP-Buenaventura, alongside the *braceros* (casual laborers). In order to adequately pressure the TECSA management, the UP's local leaders realized they would have to attract support from a wider occupational base, particularly as the stevedores and winchers were the easiest workers to replace if a protest, worker slow-down, or stoppage were to be organized. A small group of machinery operators who had discreetly affiliated with the UP began the difficult task of convincing their coworkers of the need to join the UP and demand that TECSA contract them directly.

Conjuring up worker support outside the UP base was an arduous task. Organizers found workers bitter and dismayed at the precarious working conditions at the port.[48] "Trade union" was a distasteful term for more than just the port terminal's employers. The perilously thin line between unions and sham cooperative firms in Buenaventura was a daily reminder of prior betrayals by union leaders. Furthermore, the last terminal-wide work stoppage in 1997, which had been advanced and organized by diverse union leaders, had been a major failure. The SPRBuen and the main operating firms wriggled their way out of negotiating and signing a CBA with the unions, leaving the small and diverse contracting firms responsible for an agreed-upon salary increase. Many workers today complain that the failure of this stoppage and negotiation process was due to union corruption; many still believe that certain union leaders of the time were paid off to ensure that no enforceable CBA came into existence.[49] Whatever the truth may be, the UP unionists faced an uphill battle in assuring their fellow workers that without worker collective action and a combined show of strength, all the labor law changes in the world would come to nothing in the Buenaventura port.

In the case of the machine operators, although there were only a few UP members as of 2011, worker discontent was rife. These male workers were qualified machine operators with certificates from SENA,[50] but they were paid less than the minimum wage. The principal complaint they had against TECSA, which was their boss but not formally their employer, was that their jobs were both underpaid and unstable, with no fixed or permanent shifts. Instead, workers would turn up daily and hope that the management would put them to work. If hired, they would work twelve-hour shifts without the required contributions to health, pension, and occupational risk insurance.[51] By the end of 2011 their patience had run out. After repeated discussions with UP members, these workers decided that to effectuate change they needed to move from debate and complaints to action and protest. The stage was set for the first work stoppage at the port terminal in nearly fifteen years.

Work Stoppages in Buenaventura

After many fruitless attempts at negotiating better working conditions for TECSA's principal and key workforce, the UP, bolstered by the new unionization of 110 TECSA machine operators, decided to undertake a work stoppage at the SPRBuen terminal. On the 17th of January 2012, 160 TECSA workers stopped work and began a UP-organized worker meeting directly outside the entrance to the port. These workers, under precarious, paid-by-the-hour work contracts with the TECSA contracting firm, Accion S.A., demanded that TECSA directly contract them and increase their salary base and improve their overall working conditions. The UP argued that these operators undertook "permanent core business" at the port and that TECSA could not therefore continue to utilize illegal labor intermediation—through Accion S.A.—as a means of avoiding the costs associated with formal employment contracts.

As word traveled around the port installations, more workers joined in the work stoppage. Particularly notable was that approximately eighty crane operators who had direct work contracts with the SPRBuen united in the stoppage to demand that their salaries be increased to the level of their colleagues in the Cartagena port. Such a decision demonstrated a sense of unity between the mass workforce of casual and nonstandard workers and the small population of directly contracted workers. Indeed, in Buenaventura, even the few workers who had formal work contracts still received menial wages while being forced to labor in strenuous, inhospitable conditions.

The TECSA-focused work stoppage took place at a key moment in the FTA-related discussions. International and particularly US union pressure was still high and, as the port sector was one of the targeted focal points of the Labor Action Plan, the Santos government was under pressure to show that change was taking place outside the formal realms of Bogota's political sphere.

The work stoppage continued for eight days, hurting TECSA's bottom line and hurling port workers and the UP into the spotlight locally and nationally.

A bilateral negotiating commission including TECSA management, a commission of port workers, UP union leaders, and representatives of the CUT-National, came together on January 24 as a means of bringing the stoppage to an end. This commission finally signed an agreement that had as its basis the direct hiring under indefinite contracts of eighty of the machine operators that were previously paid by Accion S.A. The remaining operators would not be immediately hired directly by TECSA, but they would receive the same wages as their eighty counterparts, what amounted to an increase of approximately 20 percent.[52]

The relative success of this work stoppage and the UP-led process of fomenting worker consciousness had a ripple effect throughout the port. Shortly after the machine operators had achieved the previously unthinkable goal of attaining direct contracts with TECSA, a group of roughly thirty maintenance workers presented a petition to TECSA demanding direct contracts and the corresponding benefits.[53] And perhaps more striking than direct petitions, workers across the terminal now understood that a new type of union was on the horizon and, even more importantly, that workers did have rights and that they could fight for them.

Many tallywomen had taken note of the January work stoppage even while they had not participated directly in it. The situation for female port workers was even more onerous than for men. For instance, many of the female workers were excluded from any job mobility. Supervisors were almost always men and mid-level and senior managers were only men. In the words of one tallywoman, "There has always been lots of discrimination in terms of ascents. Women can never be more than supervisors, and it's doubtful that you can even reach this role. Meanwhile, men scale the ladder."[54] Few tallywomen were members of the UP-Buenaventura at the beginning of 2012. This was due to the explicit anti-union sentiment that prevailed throughout the port. Even to voice support for collective action or unionization was sufficient reason to lose favor with bosses and risk losing one's job. This preference to "aguantar todo lo malo calladamente"[55] (silently put up with one's plight) would change as worker militancy grew across the terminal.

The initial relief for unions and workers following the success with TECSA turned into despair as the months wore on. UP members and CUT representatives realized that despite all the Ministry of Labor's rhetoric, it did not appear to be taking real interest in the plight of port workers. On the one hand, the ministry, in accordance with the Labor Action Plan, had set out to improve its system of prevention, inspection, and control. According to the subdirector of territorial management of the Ministry of Labor, Stella Salazar, the revamped ministry began a new program of inspection and control that had two phases. The first was prevention-oriented, focusing on giving administrative assistance to firms so they could comply with labor norms, especially regarding intermediation. The second phase focused on visits to the many EST, the CTAs, and other contracting firms, as a means of regulating their activities.[56] As part of this plan, the ministry had undertaken twelve investigations and countless visits to the offices of port-based businesses, which culminated in the imposition of ten sanctions as of October 2012, for a total of US $7 million in fines.[57]

On the other hand, while such heavy fines had never before been heard of in the sector, there remained serious questions as to the willingness of the ministry to pressure for union freedom and labor-management dialogue at the port. Leaders of the UP stated that the local labor inspectors had never consulted the workers about labor relations and intermediation practices at the terminal. The inspections and fines focused on establishing the degree of "financial independence" of the contracting firm in question and whether or not CTAs functioned in line with Decree 2025 of 2011.[58] The ministry was not, however, really pushing for social dialogue.[59]

The lack of commitment from the ministry to actually examine how the fundamental labor rights of port workers were being violated day in and day out created renewed cynicism from UP members and leaders. It seemed that while the Labor Action Plan was being hailed as a new beginning in labor relations in Colombia,[60] workers were still facing an uphill battle to organize and effectuate positive change. For many of the tallywomen and men who were shuffled between contracting firms, according to the whims of TECSA management, their patience was fast running out.

Backlash from Employers

After the January work stoppage, TECSA made a bid to separate and disperse workers as a means of reducing the chances of any future collective unrest. A group of roughly seventy tallymen and women had worked for Accion S.A., which had been awarded the tally contract by TECSA for approximately two years. When the work stoppage finished, TECSA unilaterally terminated this contract and its supervisors told half of the workers that they had to take their CVs to a different firm, Empresa Colombiana, to be considered for hiring. The remaining workers stayed with Accion S.A. The new tally contracting firm rehired the same workers, but they were coerced into working three days without pay (as a supposed means of evaluating performance) and were then given a two-month trial period. After this period came to an end, a number of these workers were told they had failed the trial and were fired. In response, the tally workers organized, without UP assistance, a work stoppage, which lasted from June 3 to 6, 2012. This pressure forced the firms' hand; the fired workers were reinstated and the two-month trial period was eliminated. But once again jubilation turned to despair as they were pressured into working twelve- to sixteen-hour shifts.

After many informal and formal discussions and meetings with UP leaders, the seventy tallymen and women joined the UP. From here the union decided to undertake another work stoppage, this time one that would incorporate various occupational work groups. The new work stoppage and worker protest took place at the end of August and lasted four days, with mass worker support and participation. But while the first stoppage had led to a relative union victory, the second major stoppage ended in major defeat for the workers. During the work stoppage, TECSA unilaterally terminated its contract with the Empresa Colombiana due to its failure to keep the workers in line and out of protest activity.[61] The workers who had participated in the stoppage were fired because they had not presented themselves for work during three consecutive days. During the work stoppage, the UP had petitioned the Ministry of Labor to undertake an inspection of port-located machinery, ensuring that it was all safe and not in danger of vandalism and to ensure that the labor conflict was officially authorized. But the officials never arrived. In their place, the state sent its repressive arm, authorizing the entry of police into the terminal to assist "scab workers" to replace those workers who had joined the stoppage. Furthermore, the ESMAD, the special antiriot police unit, arrived to break up the peaceful worker protest. In the process, numerous workers, both men and women, were injured, including a pregnant tallywomen who was beaten to the ground.

In the wake of this violently repressed work stoppage, TECSA and many of its intermediary firms began firing workers who had taken part in the protest. Indeed, according to Jhon Jairo Castro, while the January work stoppage had led to the direct hiring of eighty machine operators, the August stoppage left in its wake approximately eighty workers from diverse occupations "vetoed" from entering the port. No new contracts were negotiated, and while the UP-Buenaventura had the same number of members, many of them now were either banned from working at the port[62] or precluded from obtaining work because of their association with the union.

Indeed, while the work stoppages and initial growth and visibility of the UP at the port terminal appeared to offer hope of a new dawn for labor relations in Buenaventura, the structural power of SPRBuen and the port operators, and the tame response of the Ministry of Labor, vanquished such enthusiasm. According to the president of UP-Buenaventura, Jhon Jairo Castro, in mid-2013 there were only forty-five dues-paying members of the UP in Buenaventura and another fifty members who were at the time unemployed.[63] Jhon Jairo and members of the National Office of the UP blame the dramatic fall in the fortunes of the local UP office on continued union persecution throughout the port. They argue that firms share a "black list" of supposed union agitators to ensure that the workers identified are not hired.[64]

How to Improve the Enforcement of Labor Standards and Labor Law

It is important to look further into the failure of the Colombian state to protect worker rights at the port. This failure is central to understanding the still significant constraints facing workers and the UP in the SPRBuen port in attempting to uphold their formal labor rights. Is the answer simply to bolster the Ministry of Labor, providing it with more resources and more labor inspectors who are better trained and better compensated? Looking at the Chilean, Dominican Republic,[65] and more recently the Colombian case, this has been the preferred response. While one should be hesitant to offer evaluations so early on in the process of institutional transformation, the results of this case study do not provide much support to such arguments.

Rather, this case has shown that the problem of regulating firms in Buenaventura and Colombia in general and ensuring that they respect the labor law and guarantee the labor rights of the Colombian workforce has structural and cultural-political roots. In particular, some experts have argued that states expend less effort on the protection of enabling rights, such as freedom of association (FoA), than on upholding minimum labor standards.[66] In the case of countries with long and pervasive anti-unionist violence, such as Colombia, FoA rights are even more tenuous.

According to Oscar Gutierrez from the vice president's office, overall change in the manner in which labor relations are managed and governed has been too slow. The vice president's office, understaffed and underequipped, has assumed the complicated role of "putting out fires" in various parts of the country rather than working on designing, effectuating, and monitoring changes in how labor rights are upheld. While the Ministry of Labor has begun the task of internal restructuring in line with the new normative and administrative dictates, it has yet to adequately enforce compliance with the laws concerning the prohibition of illegal labor intermediation. The ministry is in the process of reactivating its department for inspection, which was for too long understaffed, underfunded, and undertrained.

More and better-paid labor inspectors may ameliorate the problem, but it will not overcome it, especially when these labor inspectors, however knowledgeable about the specificity and breadth of labor law, remain removed from what actually happens at the workplace. An alternative approach to ensuring compliance with labor laws is one in which the onus is on state officials but is shared by recognized worker representatives to "enforce and monitor." Such an approach would involve a vision of enforcing labor standards that is rooted in tripartism, not a new form of nonstate governance of the labor market. Indeed it really only broadens what exists in traditional collective bargaining relationships, in which union representatives monitor the employer's compliance with the CBA. In this case, unionists would monitor not a CBA, but rather compliance with fundamental labor rights as set out in national legislation.

Neither would this tripartite proposal be directly linked to the bilateral initiative promoted by global union federations: international framework agreements (IFAs). While such mechanisms do bring trade unions to the negotiating table, they remain plagued by problems with their geographical reach.[67] As a side point here, the case study suggests that the UP lacks international industry-based worker support. Due to unhelpful personal disputes between union officials, the UP has yet to negotiate its affiliation with the International Transport Federation (ITF), one of the strongest and most collaborative global union federations. This seems like a missed opportunity as the ITF, based on the transport industry's logistical power in an ever-more integrated global economy, has done much to improve working conditions in seaports and in sea vessels the world over. The UP could benefit from its support and experience of negotiating with and pressuring port-based firms.[68]

The five key sectors marked for special monitoring and attention by the Labor Ministry of Colombia as part of the Labor Action Plan could be used as a pilot program for the design and implementation of such a collaborative government-union partnership that would count on employer representation, at least in its initial period of design, setup, and implementation. It would require time, additional resources, and strong support from all levels of the Colombian state. If given a political and financial mandate, it could be a novel and deep instance of true dialogue, one that helps to strengthen the binding force of legal rules and improve everyday business practice. Furthermore, it could help give workers and their unions the chance to actually push forth and consolidate the minute space they have been given via the Labor Action Plan.

Reflecting on the campaign to formalize the precarious state of workers at the Buenaventura port, a conclusive evaluation remains elusive, as the struggle is far from over. Few workers have seen positive changes in their working conditions. The initial success of the January work stoppage was reversed by the subsequent anti-union actions by port employers. As argued by Luciano Sanin, however, with such categorical employer anti-unionism combined with labor supply that far outstrips demand, one cannot expect triumphant union success on a short-term basis. The success of the Buenaventura and indeed nationwide organizing and formalizing campaign in the port sector is based on the fact that after two decades of union demise, workers have rediscovered their consciousness and unionization is now a theme that is discussed throughout the ports, both by workers and firms.[69] According to Fabio Arias of the CUT, the success of the initiative lies in its ability to mobilize workers around the theme of worker formalization and decent work. Furthermore, the manner in which the UP and its leaders have stuck with their goals of pressuring for work formalization at the port has ensured that the union has gained notable appreciation and support from the port workers. This in itself is a marked turnaround from recent decades.[70]

Perhaps in the case of the UP-based campaign some degree of blame for the failure to protect members from being fired can be placed on the union's national strategy. As a means of ensuring its national reach and tapping into the opportunities created by the development of the Labor Action Plan, the UP attempted to move quickly. Its leaders looked to organize workers as quickly as possible as a prelude to handing in a list of demands to the principal operating firms and pressuring for negotiations. The power of mobilization was used as a direct threat, as it still remains the biggest form of union power. The UP failed, however, to develop a strategic plan of action that could ensure both a strong mid- to long-term organization plan as well as protecting members from the heavy-handed reprisals of the business sector. Before thinking about presenting lists of demands to firms, a union should have in place a definitive structure. This is built by following the steps of unionizing workers and notifying the respective authorities of their affiliation; determining the makeup of union leaders protected by union law (*el fuero sindical*); and unleashing a political campaign that highlights the precariousness of working conditions in the sector as well as the prevalence of anti-union practices. Finally, when enough workers are unionized and organized, one can present a list of demands.

Such a critique, however, should not be stretched too far. This case has clearly illustrated that despite the many positive reconfigurations set in place as part of the ratification of the long-frozen US-Colombia FTA, especially the Labor Action Plan, concrete, large-scale, labor-related changes on the ground have yet to be made at Buenaventura's SPRBuen-run port. Here, union freedom remains an entirely foreign concept to the business sector, and workers continue to be fired and mistreated simply because they ask for workers' rights to be respected.

RESEARCH METHODS

In order to get inside the Buenaventura case study, this research combined numerous formal interviews with key actors involved either directly or indirectly in this labor dispute, as well as more informal conversations, particularly with workers—both union members and nonmembers—at the port, including:

With Local Unionists (interviews)

- The president of Union Portuaria-Buenaventura
- The general secretary of the Union Portuaria-Buenaventura
- Six women unionists who work as tallywomen
- Five male stevedores
- One wincher
- One female "oficinista" (person charged with registering merchandise)
- One male cleaner
- The secretary of the Union Portuaria-Buenaventura

Focus Group Session

- With thirty-two members of the Union Portuaria-Buenaventura

With National Union Leaders

- Fabio Arias (fiscal, CUT-National)

Non Unionist Workers (inside the port)

- Male stevedore in the coffee section
- Male cleaner in the grain section
- Female cleaner in the grain section
- Female "distributor" in the grain section
- Male security supervisor

Colombian Government Officials

- David Luna (vice minister for labor relations)
- Stella Salazar (subdirector of territorial management of the Ministry of Labor)
- Giovanni Saavedra (director of the department for inspection, vigilance, and control, Ministry of Labor, Valle de Cauca)
- Oscar Gutierrez Guateca (head of labor issues, vice presidency of Colombia)

US Government Colombia

- Andrea Aquila (US Embassy in Bogota; economic and social issues)

Others

- Luciano Sanin (general director of the National Union School of Colombia)
- Carlos Guarnizo (Solidarity Center of the AFL-CIO in Bogota)

In addition to the many interviews conducted during an almost three-week period in Colombia, the research benefited from the author having worked at the National Trade Union School of Colombia (Escuela Nacional Sindical: ENS), in a period during which researchers conducted a diagnostic study of working conditions in the port sector of Colombia. This study, financed by the AFL-CIO Solidarity Center in Bogota, formed the basis of the author's understanding of the working conditions and the prevalence of indecent work in the port sector, particularly in Buenaventura. Complementing this in-depth study, the researcher made a detailed literature review of the Colombian port sector, focusing especially on newspaper articles from the main national newspapers: *El Tiempo*, *El Espectador*, *Semana*, as well as the principal business magazines of the country: *Portafolio* and *Dinero*.

RETAIL AND HOSPITALITY WORKERS IN SOUTH AFRICA

Organized by Trade Union of Formal Workers to Demand Equal Pay and Benefits

Sahra Ryklief

Although the percentage of the workforce that works informally is much smaller in South Africa than in most of the continent, it is growing in size and significance. It poses a challenge to a labor movement that has played an important role in the country's political transformation but now struggles to keep pace with changes wrought from economic liberalization. This case study analyses the ongoing campaign of the South African Commercial, Catering and Allied Workers Union (SACCAWU) to organize and represent casual and contract workers in the retail and hospitality sectors in South Africa. It focuses on two national companies where SACCAWU has a clear majority of membership: Pick n Pay, a major retailing chain with holdings in several African countries, and Sun International of South Africa, a hotel chain with a similar expansionist program in the region.

The study points to some of the characteristics of flexibility in the South African labor market, labor law, and in the companies. It reveals that under certain conditions, permanent or core workers have sufficient commonalities with flexible workers to not only act together within the union but also to lead resistance to extremes of inequality, which they themselves, having legal protection, are only witness to on a workplace level. SACCAWU has made a commitment to organizing casual workers and has created enough leverage through traditional labor tactics such as strikes to force employers to convert many casual workers to permanent status and to provide guaranteed minimum hours and benefits equity for others. The employers have not given up their fight for flexibility, however, and the union's wins have been a result of compromises that leave many workers in exploitative nonstandard work arrangements.

Background

When viewed primarily in terms of a democratic dispensation, postapartheid South Africa has been widely held as a flagship on the African continent.[1] The governing party, the African National Congress, has retained a majority vote fluctuating between 62 percent and 69.7 percent since 1994. South Africa is also one of the wealthiest countries on the continent, and national efforts to reintegrate the South African economy into the global economy and shift foreign relations toward the African continent in the past two decades have positioned the country effectively as a key regional economic and political power.

South Africa has a population of fifty-four million.[2] Eighty percent of the total population classified themselves as African (formerly called Bantu or black); 8.4 percent as white; 8.8 percent as colored, and 2.5 percent as Indian/Asian. The average life expectancy is at fifty years; this is a low life expectancy, an empirical testament to the vast inequalities in South Africa. The country remains one of the most unequal societies in the world.[3] It is ranked 118th out of 187 on the Human Development Index and 85th (12,507) in the International Monetary Fund's (IMF) gross domestic product (GDP) per capita ranking for 2013.[4]

Large-scale unemployment, low wages, and poverty characterizes the socioeconomic landscape, both during and after apartheid, despite the country's experiencing a consistent growth curve for most of the past two decades. From 1993 until 2011, the average quarterly GDP growth was 3.32 percent.[5] The global recession in 2008 caused growth to slow sharply during the latter part of the year, leading to a decline of −1.5 percent in 2009. The economy recovered quickly, although the 2010–13 growth was less robust than the rates recorded in the mid-2000s, as reflected by 1.9 percent growth in 2013.[6] In the period from 1995 to 2001, full-time employment among the economically active population (EAP, meaning the labor force) declined by 20 percent, while informal occupations rose by 17–31 percent.[7] An adaption of Von Holdt and Webster's calculations in 2003–2004 performed by Pillay in 2008 puts the EAP at 20.3 million, with 8.4 million registered unemployed; 6.6 million in the formal economy with regulatory protections and secure employment; 3.1 million as "semiformal" workers in precarious forms of work, including outsourced, temporary, part-time, and domestic workers; and 2.2 million in informal economic activities, as categorized by Stats SA, which include unregistered small businesses, street vendors, and home-based work.[8] More recent estimates of informal employment put it at about 16 percent of total employment.[9] Unemployment figures are consistently high and stood at 24 percent in 2014.[10]

Industrial Regulatory Framework and the Coverage of Informalized Workers

South Africa's labor relations legislation was overhauled after the 1994 elections. The Basic Conditions of Employment Act (BCEA) of 1997 sets out minimum standards for most employers, excluding minimum wage requirements, while the Labour Relations Act (LRA) of 1995 facilitates collective bargaining agreements (CBAs), including the right to organize. CBAs are reached through majoritarian agreement and are then legislated to cover all employers and employees in the industrial sector.

If workers are not in an employment relationship, they are not protected by either act. The acts do, however, extend to casual and contract workers. In most cases, only workers working less than twenty-four hours per month are excluded from the legislation. A problem remains that although most workers are covered by legal protections, they are not effectively organized or represented and are often either ignorant of their rights or unable to access them due to deliberate strategies by employers to deny them access.

Company exemptions are allowed for small, medium, and micro enterprises, which may apply for exemption from coverage of CBAs by the Department of Labor. These applications are generally contested by the unions in the sector. The BCEA also provides for state legislated sectoral determinations that regulate wages, hours, and basic conditions for weakly organized, vulnerable, or special sectors.[11]

The determination of wage minima for sectors are generally pegged against existing levels of poverty and have as their main objective the protection of non- or underorganized workers from the extremes of poverty. These determinations are established outside the collective bargaining framework in those sectors where unions are too weak to attain the 50 percent representation of the unorganized workers required to set up bargaining councils with employers.[12] There is no doubt that these state minima lead to improved conditions for workers in unregulated sectors. As will be demonstrated in the case studies below, however, if the minimum wage is set at a lower rate than the actual wages won through collective bargaining processes,[13] the sectoral determination serves to drive down wages and conditions in organized workplaces in the sector by allowing employers to add to the ever-growing informalized underclass within the protected workforce.

Hours of Work Protected—or Not?

South African labor legislation is highly protective of working hours through the BCEA.[14] In the BCEA the maximum number of hours in a working week is forty-five. A working day (inclusive of overtime) cannot extend beyond twelve hours;

and a rest period (weekend) of thirty-six consecutive hours, which must include Sunday, is stipulated in the act. Overtime cannot be more than ten hours in any given week and has to average out to four hours per week over a period of four months. Employees can also agree, through a collective agreement, to "average out" their working hours over a period of up to four months. All work on Sundays and public holidays is voluntary. An employee who does ad hoc overtime work on a Sunday must be remunerated at a rate of double the usual wage or hourly fee. Even if an employee normally works on a Sunday (i.e., it is taken as part of the normal working week in the sector), she or he must still be paid one and a half times the normal daily rate.

Paradoxically, despite these explicit regulations, the legislation allows for employees to sign away these protective rights. In general, the law states that you cannot, through collective bargaining, agree to worse conditions than in the BCEA. Through CBAs, however, employees may agree to work a "compressed working week." If this agreement applies, employees can work up to twelve hours a day without getting overtime pay, although they may not work more than ten hours overtime nor more than five days in any given week.

Employees can also agree to Sunday work in the employment contract as a matter of course, as long as the week consists of forty-five hours and contains a thirty-six-hour rest period. If this applies, an employee no longer has the option of refusing to work on a Sunday (voluntary agreement is no longer necessary) and is remunerated at one and a half times the normal wage rate for each hour worked, not at double the rate of the act.

As the case studies of Pick n Pay and Sun International bear out, the options in labor legislation for employers to extend the working day and opt out of the protection of weekends and the legislation of sectoral wage minima in the wholesale and retail and hospitality sectors has set the scene for a long-range process of driving down overall wages while reducing protections against increased hours.

Unions and Informal Workers

In 2013, there were 191 registered trade unions in South Africa and three national trade union centers or federations.[15] The national trade union federations all belong to the Southern African Trade Union Co-ordinating Council (SATUCC) and the International Trade Union Congress (ITUC). Most of their affiliates, as well as some independent unions, belong to sectoral Global Union Federations as well.

Union density in South Africa stood at 34 percent of all employed workers in 2008 within the "organizable formal sector."[16] Trade union density varies enormously by sector, with high levels of organization in most industrial sectors and low levels in most service sectors and other marginalized sectors of the economy.

Trade unions still remain the largest and strongest social formations in South Africa and consistently deliver better wages and conditions of service to semi-skilled and unskilled, low-paid workers than those that prevail in nonorganized sectors or workplaces. Most South African unions collaborate relatively effectively in statutory social dialogue arrangements. While union advocacy for workers in vulnerable occupations does occur, most trade unions in South Africa are not articulating coherent and effective organizing strategies to deal with the trends of informalization and casualization. A 2012 survey by the largest trade union federation, the Congress of South African Trade Unions (COSATU), covering 3,030 workers in thirty-seven urban districts across the country, found that workers who were in temporary, casual, or seasonal positions or who work for smaller employers were less likely to be in a union, although this varied substantially between affiliates.[17] With the exception of a few small-scale sectoral initiatives, the only concerted strategy, spearheaded by COSATU, has been to lobby the government to ban labor brokers.[18]

The Hospitality and Retail Sectors

According to Stats SA, both the hospitality and the retail industries form part of the major trade division which includes wholesale and retail trade, repair of motor vehicles, motorcycles, personal and household goods, and hotels and restaurants.

The hospitality sector is one of the fastest growing sectors in the South African economy and in 2009 represented 7.6 percent of total formal employment.[19] The retail sector has grown an average of 4 percent annually over the past ten years (2004–2014), a rate above that of the total GDP growth in the country. Between 2009 and 2011, the wholesale and retail trade subsector (also referred to as the trade subsector) contributed approximately 13.7 percent to the economy. Formal employment in retail stood at 745,000 in 2010 or roughly 7 percent of the national total.[20]

Both sectors are characterized by a few huge chains, which are well-organized by the predominant trade union in the sectors (SACCAWU). In the hospitality sector, the vast majority of enterprises are very small, micro, and medium-sized enterprises (SMMEs) making up 90 percent of the sector and employing fewer than ten employees.[21] The retail industry is similar. Because of the preponderance of SMMEs, both the wholesale and retail sector (sectoral determination 9), and the hospitality sector (sectoral determination 14), are covered by state-legislated minimum wage and workplace protections.

The reduction of labor costs through the downward variation of hours, wages, and benefits among employees undermines those protections and frees up financial restrictions to trading hours in the wholesale, retail, and hospitality sectors. This trend is at the core of a protracted engagement between South African unions and employers in these sectors. The case study of SACCAWU at these two national companies is a tale of a valiant battle on the part of the union to resist this trend for employment inequality in the workplace.

The Union

SACCAWU is a registered trade union with 147,000 members. SACCAWU organizes in the private services sectors, which are made up of commercial (wholesale, distributive, and retail), catering, tourism, hospitality, and finance (banks and insurance). The majority of SACCAWU membership is in the wholesale and retail trades, and SACCAWU is the most representative trade union in the sector.[22] SACCAWU is also the most representative union in the hospitality sector. It has a nationwide membership in the hospitality sector of forty thousand workers.[23]

Due to the structure of the sectors and despite organizing the largest supermarket chains in the sectors,[24] SACCAWU cannot claim majority representation of all workplaces in the two sectors and has not been able to set up national bargaining councils, which require 50 percent union and employer representation. SACCAWU first resolved to set up national bargaining councils in 1990, but because any bargaining council requires 50 percent union and 50 percent employer voluntary representation, employers have resolutely ignored union attempts in this regard. Godfrey, Theron, and Visser confirm that there is strong consensus amongst major retailers not to agree to centralized bargaining in the sector.[25]

SACCAWU has determinedly organized the larger wholesale and retail chains since the rapid restructuring of the labor force in this sector, which began in the 1990s.[26] The union has, therefore, gained some experience in fighting back corporate attempts to "informalize" formerly protected jobs.

Having successfully thwarted corporate attempts at undermining long-standing workplace rights won through national bargaining with the larger supermarket chains, the union instituted a concerted campaign to take what they have learned in wholesale and retail organizing into national companies in the much more weakly organized catering and hospitality sector. These campaigns form part of the broader SACCAWU strategy to ban labor brokers.[27] SACCAWU is a COSATU affiliate and supports the COSATU campaign against labor brokers.[28]

Challenges to Union Organization in the Two Sectors

Employment flexibility gives companies freedom to pay low wages, change the number of workers during operational peaks and troughs, and decide unilaterally how and when work is conducted. Flexible trading hours bring increased profits if prohibitive legal protections intended to protect workers' family and social time are circumvented and labor costs are contained. Legal protections are supposed to provide a counterbalance to this, specifically for vulnerable workers, but the LRA of 1995, a product of social dialogue and compromise, opened the door to various forms of employment flexibility by allowing unions to opt out of the most crucial protections against flexibility.

Restructuring in South Africa's food retailing labor market has significantly contributed to the decline of union strength in the sector over the past fifteen years. The retail workforce has gone from one characterized by permanent and full-time employment in the mid-1980s, with minor use of part-time and casual employment, to an extensively restructured workforce in the 1990s. As collective bargaining secured a standard shift for permanent workers, retailers made greater use of casual labor and flexible shifts, leading to the next great challenge for union organizing. Employee scheduling was introduced, which utilized permanent workers in the "valleys" and casual labor, working flexible hours, in the "peaks."[29]

Similarly, employer-driven forms of flexibility in the hospitality sector have presented a significant obstacle to unionization.[30] The hospitality industry employs a significant number of casual workers and part-time workers, many of whom are students. The number of permanent workers has declined over the past two decades due to widespread restructuring and outsourcing.[31] Increasingly, workers are employed on a fixed-time basis for a specific event, such as a conference or festival. These irregular forms of employment hinder union membership, which requires regular payment of union dues.

Shift work is also widespread in the hospitality industry, with many workers employed at night. Indeed in the casino industry workers operate on a twenty-four-hours, seven-days-a-week system. Apart from the negative impact these hours have on family life, they make it difficult for the union to recruit or gather workers together at a single time.

Focus groups with workers confirm that shift work undermines unity, as there is never a time when all workers are at the workplace together.[32] Shop stewards tend to be permanent, full-time workers at the workplace, with working hours that conform to the traditional working day. Casual and contract workers only work the busy periods: early or late shifts. Access to early and late shifts brings problems of transport for shop stewards, as public transport is not reliable outside of normal peak hours.

Union members are victimized through being given fewer shifts and flexitime; unorganized workers are given more shifts so as to make it appear that being a union member is harmful to one's opportunities at the company. In one company, management promoted a company union to rival SACCAWU, giving it more space and opportunity to organize while limiting SACCAWU until SACCAWU was no longer representative. But the failure to make gains at the bargaining table resulted in an illegal strike, dismissals, and the collapse of that union.[33] There were also incidences reported of management using the allocation of work to play off permanent workers against casual workers by promising permanent status in return for working the less popular shifts.[34] Contract workers employed by labor brokers are known to tell SACCAWU organizers that their boss has told them not to join the union. It is often difficult to convince them that it is safe to join the union and keep their job.

While racism—often covert—remains prevalent throughout South Africa, according to focus group sessions and interviews workers do not regard the traditional South African racial divisions of African, white, colored, and Indian as obstacles to union organizing. The nonmanagement workforce in the retail and hospitality sector is predominantly black (inclusive of African, colored, and Indian categories). Increasing numbers of migrant workers from other African countries in the workplaces, however, were identified as presenting a challenge. Workers report that immigrant workers were an easy target for management abuse, as they are either ignorant of their labor rights or are docile and willing to give them up in order to keep their jobs. For instance, they do not question when they are given shifts on public holidays and are also known to work in a private capacity for managers without additional wages.

SACCAWU has tried to organize undocumented foreign workers in companies. Management states that because the workers are undocumented, they cannot be recruited to a union. SACCAWU counters that if management does not allow SACCAWU to recruit the workers, they will report them for breaking the law and hiring undocumented workers.[35]

This, however, brings its own issues between workers, as some participants noted that South African workers are not always willing to join the union if they see that foreigners at the workplace have joined it. This attitude is seen as nurtured by management, who are perceived to encourage South Africans to see themselves as different from or better than foreign workers. The opposite is also true. Foreign workers are encouraged to see South African workers as lazy and having too many rights and that the unions encourage this, even as they themselves are abused. While these divisions are encouraged by management, participants acknowledged that these perspectives have their origin within the labor force.

Gender can also present specific challenges in the hospitality sector. Union members, and especially shop stewards, tend to be predominantly male, and sometimes unorganized women—who may be the majority in the workforce—do not feel comfortable approaching them.[36] Further, many of the issues women are concerned about, such as sexual harassment, remain hidden and difficult to mobilize around publicly.

Union members, particularly in the hospitality sector, feel that the union is not visible enough at their workplaces, while there is a general acknowledgment that the elected shop stewards are the union and, therefore, the union is visible through them. There was a perception that increased official visibility of SAC-CAWU in the form of organizer's visits and written material would assist unorganized workers in seeing the union as a stakeholder at the workplace.

Overcoming the Obstacles: Case Studies

Methodology

The case study draws on a variety of sources, both primary and secondary. A literature review was performed to review the sectors and profile the companies, the demographics of the workforce, occupational distribution, extent of formal and informal work, and trends and reasons for informalization. In addition, the research drew on preliminary findings of a survey conducted by the Labor Research Service to establish union activity at workplaces with significant numbers of informalized workers.[37]

Semistructured interviews and focus group discussions were conducted. The focus groups reviewed the perspectives of union members of the extent of informalization in their sector, differences in conditions of work and wages between formal and informalized workers, perceived challenges and obstacles, and their views of union strategies for organizing the informalized in their workplaces.

Pick n Pay

The Pick n Pay Group is one of Africa's largest and South Africa's second largest retailer of food, general merchandise, and clothing. According to the 2014 company report,[38] it has a total of 1,076 stores, made up of hypermarkets, supermarkets, and family stores (which are franchise stores). In 2014, the group generated an annual turnover of ZAR 63.1 billion and employed more than fifty thousand people. It is estimated that in South Africa, 60 percent of these employees are women and that the ratio of women to men is constant among formal and informalized workers in the company.[39]

Pick n Pay ownership was known to have a markedly liberal approach to trade unionism in comparison with other South African retail chains. The company has been unionized since 1984, and in 1997 it introduced an optional employee share ownership scheme.[40] Even so, the union believes that the company is drifting toward a hard-line industrial relations stance, due to stiff competition and the entry of Walmart into South Africa. In recent years the company management strategy has been marked by intransigence and reduced consultation with the trade union.[41] Clarke, as cited in Mathekga,[42] confirms this and says that the Pick n Pay managers state that market competition among South African retail companies and the reduction of costs for pension funds, health care, and other benefits make casual workers preferable to permanent workers.

SACCAWU at Pick n Pay

SACCAWU has majority representation at the company and has had an agency shop[43] agreement in place for more than seven years.[44] SACCAWU organizes its members at Pick n Pay, like many of the other large retail outlets, into company councils. These union company structures are semiautonomous structures on a store, local, regional, and national level, functioning parallel to the actual SACCAWU structures. Shop stewards are elected at every store/workplace, form a workplace shop steward's committee, and elect their coordinating shop stewards, who then participate in electing local, regional, and national company council officeholders.[45]

Company Councils' Relationship to Union Structures

All members of the workplace shop steward's committee are entitled to attend monthly union local meetings organized on a geographical basis. At these meetings they raise their company issues and articulate their needs to the union. The SACCAWU local elects officeholders (chairperson, deputy chair, secretary, and treasurer), who run the affairs of the local and oversee the election of delegates to the regional general council, which meets annually, and the regional congress, which meets every three years.

Aside from the intersection at a local level, the hierarchical union representative structures and company councils run parallel to one another. Up until 2008, the company council structures functioned completely outside of the constitutional structures of the union. They have now been incorporated into the SACCAWU constitution as amended at their 2008 national congress, although the actual functionality of structures is not affected and continues as before. Company councils try to get their best people elected into the union through contesting for local and regional leadership, as this is their only way of influencing overall union decision making.[46]

A Confusion of Categories[47]

Pick n Pay has employed both permanent and casual workers for more than two decades. Initially, casuals earned the same hourly rate as permanent workers, supplementing the workforce over weekends. The main difference was that they had no access to company employment benefits, such as health care coverage, a provident fund,[48] and supplements to the state maternity benefits won through collective bargaining. They were also not included in the union's recognition agreement, and only full-time (permanent) workers could be recognized as shop stewards.[49] Over the years, as store hours increased, the company approach has been to gradually increase its casual workforce by appointing all new employees as casuals. Casual workers work the same jobs as the permanent workforce during peak periods of the week, month, and year. They are called in when needed by store managers and are given the hours and days they are to work on a weekly (scheduled) basis. During these peak periods, there are often more casuals than permanent workers working in any given store.[50]

In 2003 the government introduced sectoral determination 9, specifying minimum wages, hours, and conditions of service for the wholesale and retail sector, replacing the old wage determination 478 for the commercial distributive trade. The wage minimum in the new sectoral determination was lower than the existing hourly wage rate earned by both casuals and permanent workers at Pick n Pay. In the years that followed, the company's response was to appoint all new employees at the lower rate, conforming to the sectoral determination minima, thus creating a third differentiated layer among the workers.[51]

As early as 1991, SACCAWU launched a campaign "No to Flexibility—No to Casualization!" winning limited rights in some stores but no employer recognition to represent casuals. At the union's 1999 national congress, the union resolved to recruit casuals and encourage unity between casuals and full-timers. The first breakthrough came after a two-week national strike at Shoprite in 2003 by thirty thousand mainly casual workers. They won the rights to a guaranteed minimum of sixty hours of work per month, provident fund membership, and recognition as elected shop stewards.[52]

In 2005 the union declared a deadlock with Pick n Pay. The union put forward a wage demand as well as a demand for permanent employment for all casual workers. Pick n Pay company management offering varied hours, wages, and the same percentage increases for the minimum-pay new employees, older casuals, and full-time permanents. The deadlock resulted in a strike.

Permanent, casual, and even nonmembers of the union joined the eleven-day strike. They settled on a wage increase much closer to the company's proposal than to the union's demand.[53] SACCAWU regards its main victory as the agreement struck with the company to begin phasing in all casuals to permanent employ-ment, with a fixed number of hours per week, including the same benefits as the permanent workers, though proportional to the amount of hours worked.

After the settlement, casuals working an agreed number of years at Pick n Pay became "variable time employees," commonly known as VTEs. They earn the same and often still work peak times according to schedules, but are guaranteed 186 fixed hours averaged out over the month (forty hours per week). Employees formerly termed permanent became known as "full, or fixed-time employees" (FTEs). They worked 196 hours averaged out across one month (forty-five hours per week).[54]

The War of Hours

The guarantee of a minimum number of fixed hours and proportional benefits was viewed as a great victory by the workers at Pick n Pay. But their respite was short. The first big blow dealt to the union in 2009 was management's with-drawal of their joint "flexibility and mobility agreement." This agreement facili-tated joint union and management decision making in scheduling hours of work during peak and slow periods on a workplace level. Shop stewards and managers had to agree on the weekly staff time schedules for each department.

The union had negotiated this agreement to ensure fairness in hours allocated among fixed and variable staff and to protect the special needs of those workers with families and long distances to travel between work and home. The company withdrew the agreement unilaterally, arguing that the consultation was onerous and an infringement on the exclusive right of management to make operational decisions. The withdrawal caused widespread unhappiness as it affected both full-time and variable-time employees. SACCAWU challenged this withdrawal through private arbitration and lost the case on the basis that the agreement was no longer financially viable for the company. The union also lost its appeal to the Labor Court.

Further reduction of legislated protections was negotiated in 2011, when Pick n Pay management informed the union that they planned to retrench more than three thousand workers. The union entered into negotiations to prevent or alle-viate the retrenchments. They were presented with an option to retain all staff members if they agreed to treat Sunday as part of a normal working week. In return for halting the retrenchment of the workers, the union agreed to extend the working week from Sunday to Sunday, forgoing double pay for full-time employees working on a Sunday as under the BCEA.

This effectively means that there is no need to employ only casual or variable-time employees on Sundays, as all workers including the full-time employees with full protections are now eligible to work without the prohibitive double-pay clause. This united stand to stave off retrenchment was once again achieved at considerable cost to some of the workers. Although union members at the company agreed to this concession, it was not a popular one.

In 2012, the company proposed another change to working arrangements. After negotiation, the union agreed to abandon the fixed-hour/variable-time employment categories. There are now two categories of full-time workers, working either forty or forty-five hours per week. All workers are now eligible to work shifts. The union also agreed to institute a "compressed working week," in which the employee's total week's hours could be worked in a shorter period than five and a half days. The extended prevalence of shift work has placed the union's voice in determining the work schedules back on the agenda as a necessity. In 2014 SACCAWU declared a dispute with the company through the Statutory Center for Conciliation Mediation and Arbitration (CCMA). After the parties failed to reach agreement, a vote on whether or not to strike on this issue was to be taken in April 2015.[55]

A similar victory was won by SACCAWU at another huge retail chain, Shoprite/Checkers. Here, too, the union also engaged in a protracted battle and bitter strikes to increase the hours of casual workers.

The Case of Sun International of South Africa

Sun International of South Africa Limited (SISA) was formerly known as Kersaf Investments Limited. The group has generated a 25 percent increase in annual revenue over the past six years.[56] Its principal activities are the operation of leisure resorts, hotels, and casinos. Sun International owns hotels, leisure, and gaming operations in Botswana, Chile, Lesotho, Namibia, Nigeria, Swaziland, and Zambia.

In South Africa it has sixteen workplaces, including the head office of the group.[57] It employs 10,147 workers, excluding those contracted to provide services. Of these employees, 8,808 are permanent staff and 1,609 are casual or "scheduled," as casuals are known in the company. Fifty percent of the company's workforce is female and 50 percent is male.[58]

The Union at Sun International

SACCAWU began organizing union members at Sun International using the company council model it had initiated in the retail sector in the 1990s. The union has majority representation at the company and has had an agency shop[59] agreement in place since 2010.

The company council at Sun International operates slightly differently from the one at Pick n Pay. The CBA allows for one shop steward for every sixty members (not ten members as with Pick n Play). The union is entitled to one full-time shop steward for every three hundred members at the workplace.[60]

The levy is also much less than at Pick n Pay. Each Sun International union member pays a R50 per year levy into a fund to facilitate two national meetings of the national Sun International company council a year. The fund, as with Pick n Pay, is managed by the independently elected officeholders of the national company council. The fund pays for transport to the national meetings. Sun International provides accommodation for these meetings.

As with the Pick n Pay company council, the national and regional company council structures are semiautonomous, with only the intersection of the union hierarchy at a local level.

In December 2009 SACCAWU members embarked on a seven-week strike at Sun International workplace sites nationally, involving more than 70 percent of its members. The demands of the union were for an across-the-board increment for all workers, rather than a variable percentage increase that would lead to differentiated amounts between employees, and the conversion of "scheduled" employees, so called due to their hours of work being formulated on a weekly basis, into "core " employees with fixed hours and benefits.[61]

At the time of the strike, all new Sun International employees were employed as scheduled staff members. After working for the company for a number of years, they could apply to become core staff members. In many instances, their applications were denied. Core and scheduled staff members worked at the same jobs for the same hours and wage. But only core staff members were eligible for benefits, which were considerable, including a provident fund, health care coverage, housing subsidy, education subsidy for their children's education, and profit sharing through the Sun International Employee Share Trust (SIEST). At the time of going on strike, the majority of workers at SISA were scheduled employees.

The strike was a bitter one. The company instituted a lockout at three properties in December 2009 and obtained an interim order at the Labour Court enforcing a limited picketing distance. Contravention of the picketing distance by striking workers at Grand West Hotel and Casino in Cape Town resulted in assaults by police and arrests of workers.

The final agreement was far-reaching. The union settled on 8 percent, less than its asking amount of 13 percent. Despite accepting a lower wage increase, union shop stewards cite their biggest victory in the company's agreement to convert 90 percent of its scheduled staff members to core through a phased process, starting with those who had been with the company the longest, making them eligible for benefits. After the strike the company began reporting on the process (permanent scheduled to permanent full-time) in its annual report. It increased its number of core employees from 5,826 to 9,053 from 2008 to 2011 and reduced its number of scheduled staff members from 2,852 to 1,844 during the same period.[62]

The company also agreed to expand its education loan scheme to finance the primary, secondary, and tertiary education of the children of all employees with at least one year of service and to extend the housing subsidy to all employees with more than two years of service from 2010 onwards, whether scheduled or not. Nonscheduled employees are also eligible for shares payout from the Sun International Employee Share Trust.

This was regarded by the Sun International SACCAWU members as a major victory. In the light of this, they deferred their other urgent demands to further negotiations with the company. These included scrapping a 1998 agreement by the union that treated Sunday as a normal part of the working week at certain SISA workplaces, settling a dispute on the payment of tips for gaming staff, ending the procurement of casual and contract workers through labor brokering, and employing a permanent workforce.[63]

Sun International employs cleaners, gardeners, waiters, and kitchen staff through labor brokers. These workers earn much lower wages than those employed directly by Sun International, work nonstandard hours or peak periods, and have no access to a provident fund, health care coverage, the SIEST profit-sharing scheme, housing subsidy and education loan scheme. In 2011, the Sun International Shop Steward's Coordinating Committee decided to step up the campaign to bring all workers employed by contract service providers into Sun International's staff, in line with the SACCAWU and COSATU campaign to do away with labor brokers.

The union opened protracted negotiations with the company in 2012. In 2013, the group restructured its senior management team and shortly thereafter restructured its operations, specifically in the gaming and hotel divisions. In 2014 Sun International declared the need to reduce the workforce and offered a voluntary retirement/retrenchment package. Seven hundred workers took voluntary retirement packages, and an additional one thousand workers were retrenched.[64] In return, the company announced that all formerly contracted food and beverage operations on their premises will be "in-sourced" into Sun International.[65] The union reports that the company still remains committed to doing away with the category of "scheduled" workers in favor of full-time status.[66] This will put the company in active compliance with the new labor legislation.

As the management strategies in both Pick n Pay and Sun International demonstrate, the ability to opt out of the provisions of the BCEA regarding weekend work has enabled employers to restructure their entire workforce, either through imposing different conditions in the contracts of new staff members or through collective bargaining, such as when the union agreed to a change to the workweek at some Sun International workplaces in 1998 or was faced with the choice of retrenchment or a change of conditions at Pick n Pay in 2011.

The case studies also demonstrate how employers can use state-legislated minima, an agreed amount set by technical experts and adopted through a tripartite structure,[67] to weaken actual earnings negotiated through years of collective bargaining. This is corroborated by the LRS survey of informal work, in which organizers identified sectoral determinations as an obstacle to organizing and as limiting unions in negotiating better increases. Employers use it as a weapon against the unions, saying, "This is the wage instituted by your government" and thus refusing to negotiate any higher wages.[68] It is essential that trade unions defend existing wage minima attained through CBAs and put these forward as acceptable minima in tripartite negotiations for sectoral minima. Otherwise, the state-legislated minima aids those employers seeking to undercut actual earnings.

Analysis of the Union's Strategy of Resistance to Informalization

JOB SECURITY AS THE FIRST FRONTIER TO BE WON BACK

At Pick n Pay the union succeeded in improving the hours, wages, and benefit provision of casual and contract workers. The union did not, however, succeed in winning absolute equality. Rather, it has traded permanency for some for fixed hours for all, and all employees are now subject to shift work.

The union took what it learned in retail and applied it through the Sun International company council, which has succeeded in increasing permanent positions and improving hours, benefits, and wages for scheduled workers.

Reregulation is neither easy nor neat. In all workplaces, contract workers still earn much less than permanent workers. Often, the part-time workers cannot exercise their rights to the proportional benefits won through collective bargaining, as they cannot afford the employee portion of the costs.[69] Neither can they exercise their rights as members of the union, as employers refuse to grant them rights negotiated by the union for shop stewards who previously were all full-time, specifically time off arrangements to do union business.[70] To change this requires a reopening of negotiations with the companies on all aspects of the existing recognition agreement, which the union is reluctant to agree to for fear that it may lose more than it will gain.[71] It will also have to cope with new sets of employment groupings arising out of the new amendments to the LRA.

Yet it is undeniable that SACCAWU has provided an alternate scenario to the indiscriminate and unchallenged informalization so prevalent in the retail and hospitality industry in other countries and that, along with other South African unions, it won the battle against workers remaining casuals for years. In the companies reviewed, permanent workers were prepared to make personal sacrifices in the interest of improving workplace equality for all. In both Pick n Pay and Sun International, shop stewards who are permanent workers are doing all the negotiations for casual and contract workers and are even entering into mediated discussions on their behalf.[72] They take their mandate from these workers through the union.

Equally noteworthy, flexi-time workers are prepared to accept variable conditions in one workplace as long as they are given job security and permanency. When interrogating what this job security entails, the most common and important elements are a fixed number of hours per week (as close to a forty-five-hour week as is possible), a provident fund, and health care coverage. They are also prepared to accept, and elect, full-timers to represent their interests.

SOURCES OF LEVERAGE

Retail and hospitality workers in large chains like Pick n Pay and Sun International have some leverage. Sources of leverage include customer service and solidarity between permanent and contract workers; both sectors thrive on customer service and on creating an ambience of a competent workforce that builds a loyal customer base and attracts them back. The union at Pick n Pay and at Sun International have astutely used their companies' images to their advantage through collective bargaining. In Pick n Pay's case, the union used the company's emphasis on family values in their marketing to obtain parental leave. At Sun International, which includes high-end hotels, resorts, and casinos in their stable, the union and company have together taken the aspirations of contract and scheduled workers for permanency and company identity and styled them as a feather in the company's cap, something the company can report on in their annual report to their shareholders.

In the large retail chains characterized by peaks and troughs in trading days and hours, workers with varied hours, wages, and benefits share the same workplace and often do the same work. This leads to a strong impetus to recognize the commonality between them. It is in the interest of the permanent worker to reduce the number of casuals and contract workers or risk losing their increasingly precarious permanent status altogether. It is also in the interest of the organized workers earning actual wages and benefits much higher than the sectoral minima to bring other workers up to their levels of wages, or their income and jobs become unsustainable.

Unorganized workers, employed at lower rates and antisocial shifts, are witness to the superior conditions of the permanent, unionized staff at the same workplace and thus are eager to join the union.[73] Once the members of the union overcome viewing these workers as "other," the task of recruitment is easy. It appears that the union is relying on these embedded sources of solidarity among workers with different statuses rather than attempting to build that solidarity. When asked what the union does to build solidarity between these workers, the responses received failed to indicate a concerted plan.[74]

Union representatives are of the opinion that the union identity, coupled with a clearly articulated union vision that refuses to accept anything less than permanency for all as the common vision, was sufficient to build solidarity in fighting unfair differentiation between workers doing the same jobs or working at the same company.

PLATFORMS OF SELF-ORGANIZATION

Unique among trade unions in South Africa, the SACCAWU company councils are semiautonomous, expediting decision making and reporting directly to the members at the workplace. They set the agenda for collective bargaining demands in consultation with the members, and they make all decisions related to the collective bargaining process among them. They raise and control their own funds to facilitate this. They decide on what they need from the union and relay this through the local structures.

Company councils may be another reason perceived "otherness," due to employment or immigration status, can be overcome. All workers have, or seek, a common company identity *through* the union. Hence the structural barrier of externalized contract workers being employed by a labor broker provides the greatest obstacle, not only to representing[75] but even to recruitment.[76]

Things are not always rosy, however, between the company councils and the union structures. Shop stewards feel they receive insufficient support or delayed responses from their local union offices.[77] Shop stewards accuse the local union offices of being slow to respond to new recruits, of not keeping pace with their requirements, and of not creating sufficient visibility of the union at the workplaces.[78]

The role of shop stewards, especially full-time shop stewards, in driving the company councils also bears some scrutiny. Much mention has been made since the massacre of mineworkers at Marikina of the higher education and resource levels of shop stewards, especially full-time shop stewards, in relation to their peers; this is seen as inevitably leading to estrangement between union leaders and rank and file at the workplace.[79]

These case studies confirm that shop stewards at Pick n Pay and Sun International do have privileged positions at their workplaces vis-à-vis the general worker. They have more resources, often a modest union office, individual access to e-mail, ability to travel using their independent company council funds, and financial and company literacy. Some of them have company cars at their disposal. There is undoubtedly considerable status and privileges attached to the position of shop steward. Yet shop stewards have to work hard to retain these. The additional levy for the company council places even more emphasis on accounting to their workplace.

Far from this alienating them from rank-and-file members, the relentless struggle against flexibility has made stewards more attuned to worker needs to achieve or maintain their positions. Shop stewards all described the pressure as being intense. Every weekly schedule has the potential of becoming a battle. This is particularly the case when permanent workers represent part-timers who, due to the recognition agreement, cannot become full-time shop stewards. They have to prove they are beneficial to these workers, who elect them. At the cutting edge of daily conflict, they take issue instead with union staff and describe the union responses as lacking energy and urgency.[80]

SACCAWU has demonstrated that it is prepared to confront and reverse informalization from above through recruiting, organizing, and strategic collective bargaining. The union slogan of Unity, Democracy, and Socialism; a clear national policy position of the union on organizing casuals and demanding equal working conditions and wages; the union and federation (CASTU's) refusal to accept labor brokers and the abuse of the category of casual employment have set the value base that inspire shop stewards and workplace struggles and have thereby succeeded in preventing docile acceptance of this concerted global trend. Yet at the end of the day, the question must be asked: Who is winning, the employers or the union?

The case studies seem to indicate that despite these valiant battles to reregulate flexibility, the union is incrementally losing the war. At Pick n Pay, the union traded Sunday protections to stave off retrenchments and has had two more strikes against unilateral restructuring since the 2005 strike. It is now contemplating a third over the same issue: unilateral work scheduling.[81] During the same period, from having a sizeable protected core of workers on full-time, fixed-time arrangements, all workers at Pick n Pay have now been reduced to variable work-time arrangements.[82]

Over the same period, the union has lost its majority at both Shoprite/Checkers and Woolworths, and weekend protections no longer apply. At Sun International the scheme to make all scheduled staff members permanent was a lengthy, incremental one. During its implementation, the company introduced large-scale retrenchments. The tail end of the process is likely to be hastened by the new legislation, which has a much shorter limitation on casual status than that negotiated by the union.

Still, by facing flexibility, SACCAWU has led the way. The case studies point to what is regarded as most important by the workers affected by informalization from above. It comes as no surprise that they are job security, a minimum number of guaranteed hours a month to ensure basic earnings, health care coverage, a provident or pension fund, and union membership to attain and improve the conditions related to these and other workplace issues.

But the case studies also reveal the perils of relying on collective bargaining alone to contain or reregulate informalization in the workplace. Even if unionized in high majorities in a workplace with a known liberal approach to trade unions such as Pick n Pay, the operational freedom employers are entitled to as their constitutional right to their private property tip the scales in their favor.

In South Africa, labor rights are incorporated in section 2 of the constitution. The state can provide and enforce real protection and prevent the "clawback" that the SACCAWU workers, along with millions of others, face in every annual bargaining round in these sectors. But in order to do this, as these case studies demonstrate, the current conceptual premise of regulated flexibility has to be jettisoned. The law must do what it is supposed to: protect and regulate. Any legal protection that can be signed away under duress is no protection at all. The threat of retrenchment is all the duress that is required, and retrenchment is an operational prerogative of employers against which trade unions are powerless.

Furthermore, the case studies confirm what the LRS has been saying for many years and proving empirically through its Actual Wage Rates Database (AWARD), which is that legislated minimum wages as currently determined are undermining actual wages and contributing to the expansion of the working poor. Regulating flexibility is an oxymoron. Without changing this premise to one that protects vulnerable workers from flexibility, the BCEA will be in danger of becoming as obsolete as these case studies demonstrate weekend protections are becoming in the retail and hotel sectors.

Appendix 2.1

INTERVIEW SUBJECTS

Face-to-face interviews and/or written responses to questions were conducted with:

- two leading shop stewards of the retail food chain Pick n Pay;
- one leading shop steward from Shoprite/Checkers in the Western Cape;
- eight shop stewards at Sun International workplaces;
- three union officials.

A final focus group (F/G2) to discuss the research findings and verify facts was conducted November 23, 2012, comprising:

- thirteen representatives of the Sun International shop steward's coordinating committee, including the national gender coordinator of the Sun International shop steward's coordinating committee;
- one representative from SACCAWU's collective bargaining unit;
- The head of SACCAWU's international desk;
- three representatives from the IUF, the global union organizing in the hospitality sector;
- The senior specialist for Southern Africa of the American Center for International Labor Solidarity (ACILS).

Names of interviewees are not revealed in the study; instead, interviewees are numbered according to codes defining their roles in the union. Citation codes are as follows:

- F/G: focus group.
- S/St: shop steward.
- TU/O: trade union official.
- GUF/O: global union official.

Sex breakdown is as follows:

- F/G: focus group 1: female 18, male 28.
- F/G: focus group 2: female 4, male 15.
- S/St: shop stewards: female 3, male 8.
- TU/O: trade union officials: female 0, male 3.
- GUF/O: global union officials: female 2, male 1.

Opinions of management were taken directly from company reports and opinions of government from government statements and documents.

SACCAWU STATEMENT ON LABOR BROKERS

Total Banning of Labour Brokers

For years now the wholesale, retail and hospitality sectors, the sectors in which SACCAWU organises, have been faced with growing casualisation of employment with increasing worsening of employment contracts, wages and benefits. This situation has become substantially worse since the mushrooming of labour broking companies, where more and more workers are less likely to get full time and secure employment.

Labour Brokers Do Not Create Jobs!

We have pointed out many times that labour brokers are not employers. They do not create jobs but make huge profits by creating a pool of job seekers and then secure a deal to provide their services companies seeking workers but unwilling to take responsibilities that come with employment. It is through this arrangement, which does not include workers, except when they are delivered to companies to work, the Labour Broking Companies are then paid an amount out of which they then pay workers. This obviously results in conditions that are worse than what workers would have secured if they were directly employed by companies where vacancies exist. We must demand the banning of labour brokers because it represents nothing more than modern-day slavery under the so-called guise of creating jobs.

If we allow labour brokering to continue, then it will result in secure, full-time, permanent employment being eroded until it becomes part of the past. Labour brokering is the most severe onslaught on workers rights hard fought for over decades and if it is not banned much of what workers have won, through bitter trade unions struggles, will disappear. This is not in the interest of workers, not in the interest of the unemployed, not in the interest of decent work and not in the interest of the country at large.

With labour brokering there is no opportunity that we will be able to meaningfully bring new job seekers into the job market and this will not only have a problem with secure employment but will also have untold social problems flowing from it.

Source: http://www.saccawu.org.za/campaigns/57-anti-walmart-coalition-campaign/111-saccawu-supports-strike-against-labour-brokers, accessed February 6, 2012.

HAITIAN MIGRANT WORKERS IN THE DOMINICAN REPUBLIC

Organizing at the Intersection of Informality and Illegality

Janice Fine and Allison J. Petrozziello

In 2007, Cathy Feingold, the newly arrived Solidarity Center (SC) director in the Dominican Republic (DR) observed a puzzling disjuncture: while informal employment had grown to just under 50 percent of the labor force, the organization and its union partners were still trying to build a labor movement exclusively within the shrinking formal economy and relating only to formal sector unions, who had few members.[1] Scholarly research on informal employment in the DR in the 1990s supported Feingold's concerns. A lack of good quality jobs had led to high rates of mobility between formal wage employment, informal wage employment, and informal self-employment, not only among vulnerable workers like women and migrants but also among skilled men.[2] With the support of Feingold, who had developed interest and expertise in informal economy workers while on the staff of Women in Informal Employment: Globalizing and Organizing (WIEGO), the Confederación Nacional de Unidad Sindical (CNUS), one of the major labor federations in the DR, made the decision to place informal employment at the center of its agenda.

As a consequence of their immigration status, migrant workers in many countries are disproportionately concentrated in informal employment; thus when the Dominican labor movement turned its attention to these sectors, Haitian workers and their migration-related issues leapt to the forefront.[3] Faced with political instability, poverty, lack of jobs, and natural disasters, Haitians have increasingly looked to their closest neighbor for an exit option. Willing to labor under unpleasant conditions at low wages with great instability and little chance for advancement, Haitian workers have long been recruited by Dominican employers for work in the agricultural sector. Haitians also work in construction, domestic work, export processing, street vending and market trading, and tourism. Despite many years of living and working in the DR, Haitian migrant workers and their children born in the DR have been denied citizenship and basic social rights. In 2009, the continuing abuse of Haitian migrant workers landed the DR on the US Department of State's tier 2 watch list in its annual Trafficking in Persons report, for "its continual inability to enforce anti-trafficking legislation and failure to provide sufficient legal and social services to victims."[4]

Beginning in 2007, with the encouragement and strategic and financial support of Solidarity Center staff, CNUS began to make informal employment and migration issues a major focus of its work. Within a few short years, CNUS amassed a tremendous amount of knowledge about migrant worker conditions, created worker rights trainings, supported vibrant informal economy organizing projects, and mounted effective public campaigns to remind employers of their obligations to these workers. It also dramatically shifted its position on the role and necessity of migrant workers in the economy, becoming the only labor confederation with a migrant worker department, a key source of expertise on human trafficking, and an important national player on migration policy.[5] Its affiliate, the National Federation of Workers in Construction, Wood and Construction Materials (FENTICOMMC), had conducted a first-of-its-kind study in the DR on the role of Haitian migrant workers in the construction industry[6] and was employing two organizers. The Solidarity Center and CNUS also began working with domestic workers, helping to transform the Asociación de Trabajadoras del Hogar (ATH) from a small grassroots domestic worker organization into a thriving and effective force for change.[7] Rather than blaming Haitian migrant workers for the labor force travails of Dominicans, CNUS has been championing their rights. This chapter explores how the shift in the CNUS's position came about, describes the informal worker organizing and migrant worker projects in detail, and considers some of the reasons CNUS and its affiliated unions came to embrace them so strongly.[8]

Weak Unions, Labor Market Deregulation, and the Growth of the Informal Economy in the Dominican Republic

The labor movement has always been weak in the DR. Unions have never represented more than 15 percent of the workforce.[9] Unlike other Latin American states that began their industrialization processes earlier and integrated portions

of the working class into the governing coalition, the DR's industrialization pro-
ceeded for the most part under authoritarian regimes that excluded the majority
of the working class from economic or political benefits.[10] While the DR has
ratified all eight of the International Labor Organization's (ILO) fundamental
conventions and the ILO considers the DR constitution and labor laws to be
largely in alignment with the fundamental ILO obligations, both the ILO and the
International Trade Union Confederation (ITUC) have found that prohibition
of anti-union discrimination is not adequately enforced and many workers are
fired for being union members.[11] The ILO has consistently argued that core elements of the DR Labor Code have actually dramatically impeded the formation
of unions and a strong labor movement.[12]

A stronger labor movement might have been capable of pushing back on the
country's economic development policies of the past several decades, which have
largely been based upon ensuring a cheap labor supply through keeping real
incomes low, avoiding subsidies for collective consumption goods, and preventing the broad distribution of welfare-state benefits. Under a widespread import
substitution strategy, labor absorption into the formal economy reached its peak
during the 1970s. By the mid-1980s, the DR had transformed into a service and
labor export economy where tourism and manufacturing based upon cheap
labor became the key growth sectors.

A process of informalization took place in the urban labor markets of the
DR between 1980 and 1991, during which there was a reduction in waged work
and a steady increase in self-employment and unpaid work. Strikingly, in Santo
Domingo under the export-oriented growth model, skilled men actually dropped
out of the formal economy, switching to casual, informal arrangements where
they could move between jobs, set their own schedules, and often earn more
money. While there were increasing numbers of women in the low-paying jobs
in the formal export manufacturing sectors,[13] others preferred employment in
the small microenterprises of the informal sector, where they felt they had more
control over the process and pace of work. In fact, they tended to associate sweat-
shop conditions with formal employment in the export processing zones rather
than with informal employment in small workshops.[14] Additionally, a job in the
formal sector did not necessarily equate to access to health care or state contributions to pensions. Although officially required by Dominican law to contribute
2.5 percent of social security for each person insured, or about 21 percent of the
revenues of the pension system, the state contributed much less.[15]

While in the mid-1990s the DR had a thriving garment industry, only ten
years later, as a result of the expiration of the Multi-Fiber Agreement, garment
factories across the Caribbean began shutting down as their owners shifted production to countries in Asia where labor was even cheaper. The garment sector

decline worsened the difficult labor market conditions workers were already facing. With an unemployment rate of 16 percent overall and three times that for women as a group, the loss of garment manufacturing represented a huge hit for formal sector employment, particularly for women. The informal economy continued to expand, as large numbers became informal workers and some became self-employed, mostly as own-account operators and a few as informal employers. Many formal sector jobs paid so little that workers preferred to work in the informal economy or to supplement their incomes in the informal economy.

According to ILO estimates, 48.5 percent of the nation's workforce was in informal employment in 2012, meaning that their jobs lacked basic social or legal protections or employment benefits, whether in the formal sector, informal sector, or individual households. Almost 30 percent of the workforce was employed in the informal sector, which means they were working in enterprises that had informal characteristics with respect to their legal status, registration, size, registration of employees, or bookkeeping practices. Just under 20 percent were in informal employment outside of the informal sector, meaning they could have been working in the formal sector or individual households. There was a strong gender skew: 10 percent more men than women were employed in the informal sector, while 14 percent more women were employed in informal employment outside of the informal sector. This was the painful labor market context in which the SC began to persuade its partners in the DR to focus on the informal economy, which was inextricably linked to migrant workers and issues of migration policy.

Indispensable but Unwelcome: The Catch-22 of Haitian Workers in the DR

According to the World Bank, 78 percent of Haiti's population lives in poverty, and unemployment is estimated at 70 percent. Fully 75 percent of the population still resides in the rural areas of the country. The underdevelopment of the Haitian state led to weak financial institutions and infrastructure, poorly administered international aid, and low levels of education. Haiti's almost complete political isolation at the time of independence cut the country off from participation in broader economic alliances, and the lengthy US occupation in the 1920s and 1930s did little for it economically. International sanctions and denial of aid between 1991 and 1994 and again between 2000 and 2003 also hurt Haiti's economic development and increased poverty. Haiti and the DR had a contentious history that was exploited by unscrupulous leaders to popularize a racist ideology.

In 1804, the first successful mass slave revolt in world history resulted in the establishment of the first independent and explicitly black republic of Haiti, while the Spanish held on to Santo Domingo on the eastern part of the island of Hispaniola.[16] The Haitian government helped Santo Domingo gain its independence from Spain, only to establish its own colonial rule there from 1822 to 1844. Subsequent armed conflicts between the Dominicans and the Haitians, the former struggling for independence from the latter, contributed to an enduring belief on the part of the Dominicans in Hispanic nationalism, and a powerful current of "anti-Haitianism and pro-Hispanism" gained force.[17]

The rise of Rafael Trujillo during the 1920s, and his protection by the United States for thirty-one years,[18] resulted in what some have referred to as possibly the most absolute one-man dictatorship in Latin American history.[19] One legacy of *trujillismo* was racism and xenophobia toward the Haitians and the cultivation of a deeply race-conscious society in the DR. Trujillo relied upon the racist formulations of Joaquin Balaguer (who would go on to serve seven terms as president) such as: "The Dominican people are a white Hispanic nation whose population is weakened by a mixture with the blood of non-white races. . . . Settlement of Haitians in the country degenerates the moral and spiritual strength of Dominicans."[20] In 1937, as part of a campaign to reduce the number of Haitians in the country, the government launched a campaign for "Dominicanization of the frontier." Thousands of Haitians, primarily in the provinces along the border, were murdered when the army was ordered to kill all who could not produce proof of Dominican status, although the order for the massacre explicitly excluded Haitian cane workers on the sugar estates. Legislation was passed limiting the employment of foreign nationals to 20 percent and barring the entry of Haitians except for the sugar harvests. As discussed below, despite the country's reliance on Haitian labor, Dominican policy has made it close to impossible for Haitians to gain citizenship rights.

Haitian men have been actively recruited to work in the DR for close to a century, much of that time as *braceros*, or temporary workers, who crossed the border each year to work as sugar cane cutters and then returned to Haiti. From 1952 until 1986, the Dominican and Haitian governments operated an exploitative temporary worker program under a bilateral agreement to import Haitian laborers for the sugar companies. Due to international pressure, there were some gradual improvements in the terms of the agreement intended to improve the living and working conditions for the *braceros*, but conditions remained bad and there was ample evidence of bonded labor and slavery-like practices.

Haitian women were not actively recruited to participate in labor migration for the sugar industry. Historical evidence, however, suggests that Dominican authorities and plantation owners "tolerated" the presence of some women, whose unpaid reproductive labor or poorly paid service work (food preparation for cane cutters, sex work) was seen as a boon to male laborers' production and thus represented an economic advantage for plantation owners.[21]

Over time and for various reasons, some Haitian sugar workers became permanent. These workers and their partners formed families and settled in the *bateyes* (worker camps adjacent to the sugar cane fields), which grew into larger communities. This, too, was largely tolerated by plantation owners, who saw economic advantages to migrants reproducing the agricultural labor force *in situ*. With the decline of the sugar industry in the late 1980s and early 1990s, some unemployed male and female workers on the *bateyes* began to migrate elsewhere in search of work. Some found other agricultural employment while others went to work in the construction, tourism, service, and export processing industries and in the informal economy in cities. Employers in the construction sector adopted many of the exploitative labor practices of the sugar industry, including paying workers with *vales*, or coupons to use at company-controlled stores, and more recently withholding or delaying payment and then offering workers loans at exorbitant rates, creating a cycle of indebtedness among Haitian workers. While their descendants now hold jobs similar to poor and lower-middle-class Dominicans, they have been unable to fully assimilate due to the systemic denial of citizenship rights.

Prior to January 2010, the Dominican Constitution recognized the right to citizenship of all those born on Dominican soil (*jus soli* or birthright citizenship), except for the children of diplomats or those "in transit" through the country.[22] Starting in the 1990s, and increasingly as of 2007, Dominican authorities have used the "in transit" clause as justification for stripping Dominican nationality from the descendants of migrants by arbitrarily suspending their identity documents, a practice that has come under much criticism from human rights activists in the DR and internationally.

Other measures taken by the Dominican state to limit access to Dominican nationality include the introduction of the 2004 General Law on Migration 285–04 (GL: 16–92). In compliance with article 28 of this law, the Ministry of Public Health has been implementing a different process of birth registration for children born to undocumented immigrants, especially Haitians. Mothers perceived to be foreign—including both bona fide Haitian migrants and undocumented Dominicans of Haitian descent—are given a "pink slip," which supposedly enables the parents to visit their consulate and obtain a birth certificate from their country of origin. In practice, though, this is quite complicated and impossible beyond the age of two years, leaving many parents unable to obtain birth certificates for their children, either in Haiti or in the DR. Without birth certificates, these children are unable to acquire Dominican identity cards called *cédulas*, which are required for completing high school, enrolling in university, voting in elections, opening a bank account, cashing a check, signing a contract, or participating in the country's social security system, which was introduced in 2004.[23]

In 2005, the Dominican secretary of labor announced a plan to comply with 285–04 by "*dehaitianizing*" the country. Mass expulsions followed, along with a rise in anti-Haitian violence. According to Kosinski, "Regardless of the fact that many of these individuals, their parents and grandparents have lived in the country for decades, this exception is being used extensively to deny documents to Dominican-born Haitians."[24] They are rendered stateless and subject to deportation.[25] In 2010 the DR changed its Constitution, and "birthright citizenship" was replaced by a right to Dominican citizenship only if a child has at least one parent who is a "legal resident" (*jus sanguinis*).

A further step toward the implementation of GL: 285–04 was taken in 2011 when the Dominican government defined the Reglamento (Rules of Procedure) 631–11, which set forth the rules for acquiring new temporary worker visas. The Migration Directorate provided a window of opportunity for employers to regularize the immigration status of their workers before they would be held legally liable for having undocumented workers in their employ. Essentially, the Reglamento establishes a traditional guest worker program. Employers must apply for visas on behalf of their workers and take responsibility for transporting them from Haiti to the DR upon entry and from the DR back to Haiti upon exit. While employers in some sectors such as agro-fishery have taken steps to regularize their workers' status, others have criticized the Reglamento as impracticable due to complex requirements, high costs, and the difficulty of bringing workers into compliance.[26] Employers in construction, for example, argue that the norm in their sector is informal: workers are not contracted collectively but individually and come to work for employers on an ad hoc basis and move between employers frequently. Most construction workers would have some difficulty proving residency in the DR because they do not possess written contracts and are highly mobile.

Prospects for regularization took an unexpected turn when, nine years after the passage of the Migration Law, Dominican president Danilo Medina announced that the country would be implementing a National Regularization Plan as called for in that law. This came as a political response to the international outcry against the DR's practices of stripping the nationality of descendants of Haitian migrants, which threatened to be implemented on a mass scale following the Constitutional Tribunal's September 2013 issuance of sentence 168–13. That sentence effectively ordered the retroactive application of the 2010 Constitution's criteria for access to nationality to all those born to migrants with irregular status in the DR as of 1929. When critics argued that the country was disregarding international obligations to avoid statelessness, the government moved to approve a regularization plan in the hopes it could turn nationality-stripped descendants into migrants in need of regularization. When that proved legally impossible (the first requirement being identity documents from one's country of origin), the government swiftly passed Naturalization Law 169–14, dividing the affected population into two groups: group A, whose identity documents were to be restored, and group B, whose birth had never been registered and would in effect be treated as migrants who could apply for naturalization after two years' time.

From mid-2014 to mid-2015, the Dominican government implemented these three processes in parallel: regularization of foreign-born migrants, partial restoration of documents for migrants' descendants who had previously had *cédulas*, and registration of migrants' descendants without birth registration in a special foreigners' book. At the time of writing, these processes had just concluded, with many in Dominican labor and human rights movements doubting that they have been successful in remedying ongoing problems of disregard for Haitian migrants' labor and human rights.

Labor laws complete the surreal picture in which Haitians and Dominicans of Haitian descent find themselves. There is no law in the DR that explicitly prohibits the unionization of foreign workers (documented or undocumented), but the Ministry of Labor, by administrative order, requires workers to show national identification in order to join a union. In addition, labor law requires a minimum of twenty workers to form a union and 50 percent plus one to be able to engage in collective bargaining.[27] Workers without identification papers cannot show unions or government officials documents they do not have, a situation that could potentially be improved through the regularization process described above.

Informal Economy Worker Advocacy and Organizing

CNUS is an alliance of three of what were five main labor confederations. The Solidarity Center (SC) staff in the DR invested a great deal of effort in unifying the confederations and reducing the chronic fragmentation of the labor movement and its attendant institutional weakness in the DR. During this process, Cathy Feingold forged a strong working partnership with Eulogia (Gina) Familia, a leader of one of the three confederations that had joined together to form CNUS.

Familia, an unusual figure in the Dominican labor movement, had been involved since 1984 and had risen to the presidency of the CUT, a public-sector labor federation. She was one of the few women leaders of a labor federation in the DR. Familia was also a politician, the only elected labor leader in Congress, having run for office on a platform that included working women's issues. While most labor leaders had not been involved in migration issues and had not spoken out about the plight of Haitians in the DR, Familia had a history of doing so. As a young woman in the early 1980s, she had worked with Haitian sugar cane workers to ensure they received their proper wages as well as to help build opposition to the Duvalier dictatorship in Haiti.[28] Perhaps her empathy with these workers stemmed from her personal experiences of discrimination when she was asked to produce her papers when traveling abroad. When Familia took on the role of director of CNUS's migrant worker department, she brought a great deal of passion and credibility to the effort.

In contemplating their strategy, Feingold and Familia perceived the key obstacle to be overcoming the generalized hostility to Haitian migrant workers. They brought in Ana Avendano, the main architect of the AFL-CIO's collaboration with the worker center movement as well as its more progressive and activist approach to immigration policy. In her presentation and follow-up conversations with CNUS and its affiliates, Avendano reinforced the argument that migrant workers' issues were labor issues.

The SC staff also leveraged the US State Department's interest in human trafficking to forge a conceptual link between forced labor and migrant worker exploitation.[29] The SC began to highlight the link between labor trafficking and migrant worker rights in general and obtained funding from the US State Department for its informal economy work in Indonesia and the Dominican Republic through the Office to Monitor and Combat Trafficking in Persons (G/TIP)[30] program.

The Solidarity Center hired Familia to run CNUS's antitrafficking network that had been launched prior to Feingold's arrival in the DR. The network was made up of organizers and second-tier labor leaders from unions in the five sectors in which they considered migrants to be most vulnerable: sugar, construction, free trade zones, hotels and tourism, and agriculture domestic work and market vending. Through surveys of construction, domestic, and agricultural workers, Solidarity Center and CNUS identified 314 cases of suspected trafficking, involuntary servitude, or forced labor and became respected authorities on antitrafficking efforts. They also developed teams of trained worker activists to learn methods to reach Haitian workers and train their peers on identifying trafficking victims.[31] By placing migrant workers' experiences in a trafficking framework, CNUS was able to begin to reframe Haitian workers in the eyes of Dominican labor leaders and members, as well as in the eyes of Dominican and US policy makers.

In the first few years, the organization created educational programs and materials for workers, labor lawyers, and union representatives. The network helped to develop the expertise of its participants who became involved in identifying cases of human trafficking and in testing the capacity of various agencies within the Dominican government to hold traffickers and abusive employers responsible for their violations. It also established a network of labor lawyers to represent migrant workers in labor courts and before the Labor Ministry in cases when employers refuse to pay them. CNUS and FEDOTRAZONAS (The Dominican Federation of Free Trade Zone Workers) used a case of twenty young Dominican women being trafficked by illegal labor contractors to Turkey to help hone a strategic approach of linking the defense of labor rights and the defense of decent work in the country to migrant worker rights and to define the trafficking in persons as an extreme case of labor exploitation.[32]

The SC and CNUS developed a survey and recruited Haitian and Dominican workers to administer it together in Spanish and Creole. The logic of creating mixed teams was that Haitian migrant workers would be more likely to discuss their situation with another Haitian while a Dominican could help in case the authorities came, and it would also sensitize the Dominicans to the plight of the Haitian workers. The first survey project was undertaken in partnership with FENTICOMMC and will be discussed in greater detail in the next section on sectoral strategies. As the survey work unfolded, Familia felt the teamwork approach led to a moving process of integration and overcame entrenched issues of xenophobia.[33]

Based upon what they learned about the situation of migrant workers, CNUS and the antitrafficking network created workshops, organized forums, and designed posters and brochures in Spanish and Creole about migrant workers' rights in particular sectors. Early on, CNUS also began creating presentations for Dominican workers on the dynamics of labor competition so they would begin to hold employers, rather than Haitian workers, responsible for the decline in conditions. CNUS, with the support of the SC, has built its internal capacity to engage on migrant worker issues. The SC and Familia decided early on that they did not have the capacity to take on individual immigration cases but would refer these cases to other NGOs, including Centro Bono, a key Jesuit NGO, that were focusing on migrant rights.[34]

In 2009, as a natural outgrowth of its migration work, CNUS made an official organizational decision to "open the doors" to the informal economy. Within the confederation, the inclusion of workers who were excluded from a formal labor contract was viewed as the next logical step in a process intended to strengthen workers' ability to respond to neoliberalism.[35] Also that year, the Department of Gender Equity Policy at CNUS decided to focus on organizing women in the informal economy, which led to a close partnership with the Association of Domestic Workers (ATH), a twenty-year-old organization that had initially been funded by the Ford Foundation but had largely fallen apart after its funding ended. ATH was already allied with CNUS but had very limited resources to engage in organizing.

Organizing in Two Sectors

Construction

Virtually all construction workers in the DR are informally employed due to the lack of employment-based social protections. FENTICOMMC has set collective bargaining for construction workers and their inclusion in the state social security system as its ultimate goal.[36] While agriculture and construction have been historically the two most important labor sectors for Haitian men in the DR, Haitian agricultural workers in recent years have shifted in large numbers to construction work. Research studies have documented that Dominican construction contractors prefer Haitian workers because their labor is cheaper and they are more flexible about the work they are willing to carry out.[37]

While some on construction sites are hired directly by the company, the majority of Haitians work as day laborers for subcontractors. Generally speaking, companies hire the *maestros* or foremen and *ajusteros* or subcontractors, who are predominantly Dominicans but also some Haitians with legal documents, and pay them by the job or the product. The *maestros* and *ajusteros* then hire their own laborers who are usually Haitians and work for a daily rate.[38] A 2012 study conducted by the US Department of Labor (US DOL) through the Bureau of International Labor Affairs (ILAB) found that while most of the skilled construction work is carried out by Dominicans and the unskilled work by Haitians, Haitian construction workers are becoming more skilled and graduating to more specialized occupations including finishing, carpentry, rebar installation, ceramics, and plastering.[39]

The SC staff initiated a series of conversations with the leader of FENTICOMMC about the struggle to defend the unionized construction sector and the evolving role of Haitian workers in the industry. FENTICOMMC's president, Pedro Julio Alcantara, was another Dominican labor leader who gradually came to understand the importance of organizing migrant workers. Alcantara had been a construction worker for forty-five years, beginning at the age of fourteen, and involved in unions for almost all of that period. Although he has served as president since 1996, it is not a paid position and he still works "in the tools." While initially skeptical of SC because of the role the US government and earlier SC staff members had played in the country's politics, Alcantara became committed to the collaboration due to SC's political transformation and its vision of organizing in the informal economy. Like Familia, Alcantara was a protégé of Francisco Peña Gomez—the first Dominican of Haitian descent to become prominent in politics—and he also had personal experience of discrimination, having been mistaken for a Haitian laborer on a construction site and jailed until the police realized their mistake.

Membership in the leadership group for Latin America and the Caribbean in the Building and Woodworkers International (BWI), a global union federation (GUF), also raised Alcantara's consciousness about the impact of globalization and the importance of taking on migrant workers' issues. In describing this trajectory he said, "The labor movement had come to understand that capital is mobile, but we recognize that workers are not and that we all have to work together, Dominicans and Haitians."[40] BWI had experimented with creating a workers' passport and although it had not gotten off the ground, these discussions had deepened the GUF's commitment to organizing with migrant workers. Alcantara felt strongly that Haitian workers needed a union in order to improve their situation, but he also knew that many union members blamed Haitian workers for eroding conditions in the sector. "At first there were union members who did not see it in their interest to represent Haitian workers, but they started to analyze the situation," Alcantara recounted. But, he continued, "They realized employers were using migrant workers to lower native workers' salaries, skimp on workplace safety, and avoid having to pay social security or double salary at Christmas time."[41]

The SC and Alcantara pulled together some workshops with FENTICOM-MC's members to explore their perceptions of the migrant workforce. "They were exactly like the US labor movement twenty years ago," Feingold observed. Union members said things like, "They are taking our jobs" and "They are willing to work for nothing and to do it without safety apparatus." But Feingold pushed back. "What do you think people say about Dominicans in the US?" she asked, referring to the high number of Dominicans who had migrated to the United States, and then replied to her own question: "That you are taking our jobs!" One thing that became clear was how little union members knew about Haitian workers in the industry and how important getting to know them would be to move forward. SC and FENTICOMMC recruited a team of Dominican and Haitian or Haitian-Dominican construction workers to design and conduct a survey of Haitian immigrant workers in the construction industry in the five zones within the eastern region of the country where tourism was centered.[42] By using a participatory research methodology in which workers were interviewed by other workers, FENTICOMMC hoped to be able to gain the trust of those being interviewed, raise the consciousness of union members about the problems immigrant workers were facing, and build the internal capacity of the union to conduct research. In July of 2008, teams of workers interviewed 498 Haitian migrant workers.[43]

Through the surveys, FENTICOMMC and SC were able to amass a great deal of information about the terms and conditions of employment for Haitian workers as well as their living conditions. Eighty-two percent of workers surveyed stated that they had to pay bribes to the authorities in order to enter the country.[44] Haitian workers were not being compensated for the overtime they worked and wages were too low to meet basic needs and to regularly send money back home to their families. Additionally, employers often paid workers late and frequently did so in "tickets" that served as money in their workplaces. They were often required to use the tickets to patronize high-priced, company-controlled shops where they would rack up debt. When workers refused to use the shops, they were threatened with dismissal. After accidents, employers did not provide Haitian workers with health care or workers compensation. Although undocumented workers are ineligible for government health care and pension programs, 68 percent of workers were having money deducted from their paychecks by employers anyway, and they did not receive documentation showing that they had paid into health care, workers' compensation, or pension funds. The Haitian workers lacked written contracts and feared they would be dismissed if they complained about working conditions or pay. It was also clear there was a division of labor, with Haitians occupying the bottom-level positions and being assigned the most difficult physical labor.[45] Disturbingly, employers were relying on the general foremen of the jobs, often FENTICOMMC members, to turn a blind eye to the treatment of the Haitian workers.

The survey helped FENTICOMMC and CNUS to understand the demand for migrant workers, the massive incorporation of Haitian laborers into the sector, and the workers' needs.[46] The report was released in Creole and Spanish, and Alcantara, Feingold, and Familia traveled together to Haiti to launch the report and to begin to build relations between the Dominican and Haitian labor movements. As Feingold recalls, Alcantara was shocked when he saw conditions in Haiti. The press conference and report helped reconnect labor leaders from both countries.

While the vast majority of Haitian workers expressed strong interest in becoming members of a union, only 20 percent had had any contact with FENTICOMMC. Despite the rule that migrant workers were barred from becoming union members if they did not have documentation, FENTICOMMC resolved to organize them, with financial support from the SC to pay organizers. The organizers say that they visit construction sites, recruit workers to join the union, and help bring anyone interested in technical training to the union's training institute. Alcantara says that the union welcomes Haitian workers to the institute. Additionally, the organizers sometimes go with labor inspectors from the Ministry of Labor to visit project sites.[47] "We cannot give workers who do not have papers formal membership," said Alcantara. "But we do recognize that they must be protected, we have committees of undocumented workers, which is more a measure of solidarity than any formal mechanism." The organizers say that they are signing up migrant workers, reporting to SC that out of fifty-six workers affiliated by FENTICOMMC in the month of October 2012, twenty-six were migrants.[48] The union says it provides legal support to migrant workers about labor violations but the new migration law has made it difficult for them to apply for status because most employers in construction are unwilling to go through the process. For this reason, FENTICOMMC is active in the migration policy debate, working with CNUS to advocate for all workers, regardless of their migratory status, to have opportunities to receive technical training, access to social security, decent work, and adequate protections against workplace accidents.

In addition to paying the organizers, SC has provided other kinds of support to FENTICOMMC, including the organization of seminars around the country regarding the Labor Code, safety and health, support for negotiations with employers to pay into the retirement fund for construction workers, and financial support for union conferences. Alcantara says he has seen a transformation in the attitudes of his members toward Haitian migrant workers; they no longer complain about sharing space and resources with Haitian coworkers and agree that it is just as important for Haitian workers to acquire technical skills as it is for Dominicans. Along with their efforts in the construction sector, SC and CNUS also became increasingly involved with domestic worker organizing.

Domestic Work

As Isis Duarte describes it, between 1970 and 1980, women migrated to urbanized areas within the DR for work in the export manufacturing industry and domestic service.[49] In the DR the percentage of the economically active urban female population in domestic work has risen from 8.7 percent in 1992 to 12.5 percent in 2010.[50] Studies estimate that between 7.2 and 16 percent of female Haitian migrant workers were employed in domestic work.[51] Although it is difficult to estimate what percentage of the sector as a whole is made up of Haitian migrant women workers, there are indications that this percentage is likely much higher, up to 25 percent according to a 2010 regional study by the Consejo Ministral de la Mujer de Centroamérica del Sistema de Integración Centroamericana (COMMCA/SICA) (which grouped together both Haitian migrants and Dominicans of Haitian descent).[52]

Although they do possess Haitian birth certificates or passports, most domestic workers come without legal authorization and do not know their rights. They have not worked as domestic workers in Haiti and they say that the status of domestic workers there is extremely low.[53] Feingold recalled her shock upon arrival in the DR and observing the anachronistic social expectations of domestic workers: "It was out of an era I didn't know still existed . . . starched uniforms and women carrying lunches."[54] Nevertheless, Wooding and Sangro find that part of the reason Haitian domestic workers in the DR can be exploited so terribly is because they come from an even more exploitative system in Haiti, where it is even more difficult for them to assert their rights, if they even have a concept of having rights at all.[55]

In 2009, Familia became acquainted with Victoria Garcia, the leader of Asociación de Trabajadoras del Hogar (ATH), the then twenty-year-old domestic worker organization in Santo Domingo, which had accomplished important reforms during the 1990s. ATH was founded in 1989 after the DR had been condemned by the ILO for slave-like practices with regard to the treatment of Haitian workers. The organization urged the ILO to look into the situation of domestic workers as well. Under the Trujillo labor code at that time, domestic workers had only one half-day per week free, which began at 2 p.m. on Sunday afternoon. As a result of workers' participation in public hearings at the Congress and their grassroots organizing efforts, the Dominican government included domestic workers in the 1992 Labor Code, stipulating that they get thirty-six hours of rest rather than the half-day, as well as fourteen paid days off and inclusion in the Christmas bonus system. Later, the 1999 Law on Domestic Workers (no. 103–99) built upon these improvements by stipulating that they be guaranteed fourteen paid days off, inclusion in the Christmas bonus system, and granted permission to attend school and medical appointments.

During its initial period of activism, the ATH had no relationship to the labor movement. As Victoria Garcia recalled, "Traditional unions practically had their back turned to us. They didn't consider us an important group. We had cordial relations but there was no commitment on their part."[56] By Garcia's account, the association continued to organize and recruit members, coordinating Sunday get-togethers in the parks around Santo Domingo, carrying out literacy courses, and organizing cultural events. But other knowledgeable observers felt that ATH was much less active and much less visible for most of the 1990s and 2000s. When CNUS and the SC began working with ATH, it began organizing on a much larger scale.[57]

With financial and technical support from the SC and CNUS, ATH began actively organizing again, going to bus stops, distributing fliers, offering women hot chocolate as they waited to go to work, and establishing small organizational nuclei in a number of communities. Hundreds of domestic workers packed into meetings around Santo Domingo and in other regions as well. SC found that organizing in this way, independent of political parties and without any promise of reward, was extremely uncommon in the party-dominated patronage culture of the DR. SC staffers often felt compelled to begin meetings with domestic workers by joking about it in order to defuse the tension and to communicate that no individual financial help would be forthcoming.

SC worked with ATH to send representatives to the negotiations on the Decent Work for Domestic Workers Convention (Convention 189) at the ILO. The leader sent to Geneva to testify, Maria Jean Louis, had been a domestic worker from the age of twelve. Maria was the perfect representative of the compound problem of the "informal economy and migrant worker" in the DR. Even though she had lived in the country since she was twelve and her three children had been born in the DR, they struggled to be able to attend high school and were not allowed to go to university because they did not have documents.[58] Maria described how important her experience with ATH has been:

> Women who worked in housework were practically invisible . . . so it caught my attention that yes we could struggle for something that we wanted because we are people like any other employee, we are workers. . . . I began to participate in some workshops learning and gaining new knowledge and for me it went really well because when I first started I didn't even know how to write my name and now I can read and write and participate in some workshops. . . . Through the medium of our being organized, we can speak and be heard . . . before I had a lot of friends who felt ashamed to say they were domestic workers, but not anymore. Now we feel proud because we know that we have an institution that struggles with us and helps us to know that we are also human beings and we are also important.[59]

Another Haitian domestic worker, Tamara Normil, became one of ATH's paid organizers. She worked as a domestic worker during the week and then spent her weekends working for ATH because that is when domestic workers are usually at home. Normil had a goal of recruiting ten women a month, and by December 2012 she had recruited more than a thousand women in her region to join ATH, about half of them Haitian. She felt strongly that ATH's partnership with SC had helped with the recruitment: "When I ask them to sign up they ask for a phone number to call if they have a problem, but I have an advantage to say I have a lawyer who can help them if they need help and that I can send them to the SC." Normil was afraid of public speaking until SC sent her to a workshop, and now she says she has no fear: "I will talk to anybody. If you had seen me before I would not have spoken to you because I would have felt ashamed."[60]

As they had done with FENTICOMMC, SC helped to organize a participatory survey of domestic workers in the DR that was published in 2010.[61] Also by 2010 SC was funding organizers to help build the leadership and membership of ATH. As Victoria Garcia recounted, "The Center gave us financial support and we began to grow."[62] With SC's support, ATH mounted two campaigns. The first was a national education drive intended to assert that domestic workers were in fact workers, in synch with the global push to get the ILO to adopt Convention 189. The campaign was intended to educate domestic workers and their employers on domestic workers' rights and to encourage women to identify themselves as workers.[63] Fliers and posters were printed up in Spanish and Creole titled "I Am a Domestic Worker and I Have Rights" and listing the specific rights domestic workers have. The fact that the fliers were in Creole was extremely unusual. Within a single weekend, according to Garcia, membership in ATH grew by 150 members. Along with the outreach campaign, ATH partnered with several NGOs that provided legal support, helped to elaborate a legislative proposal to include domestic workers in the DR Labor Code, and provided cooking courses for professional advancement.[64] SC also worked with the regional network of domestic workers, CONLACTRAHO (Confederación Latinomericana y del Caribe Trabajadoras del Hogar) to organize an exchange between the Dominican and Mexican domestic worker organizations. From SC's perspective, the exchange helped build regional connections more broadly and also was key to showing ATH the importance of organizational self-sufficiency, which was much stronger in Mexico than in the DR.

Following on the "I Am a Worker" campaign that had as its goal having domestic workers assert their status as workers, SC and CNUS worked with ATH to mount a campaign in which domestic workers would assert their employment rights to their employers. Labor law requires that workers be paid a Christmas bonus or "thirteenth month bonus" of one month's salary, but domestic workers were seldom receiving it from their employers and many were not comfortable even asking for it. According to Elena Pérez Garcia, Victoria's daughter and a strong leader in the ATH, "The campaign was aimed at both the domestic worker, so she knows she has a right to the bonus, and the employer, so that they know they must comply with the law."[65] The organizations printed up fliers and posters in Spanish and Creole picturing a domestic worker standing beside a Christmas tree with the caption: "*En Navidad, todo es limpio y brillante en tu casa. ¿Pagaste a la trabajadora doméstica su Regalía? Ponte a tono con sus derechos, ¡Pagale la regalía!*" (On Christmas, everything is clean and shiny in your house. Have you paid your domestic worker her bonus? Get in tune with her rights and pay her the bonus!) ATH members made the decision to begin with the social classes they knew had the funds to pay the bonus. They posted the fliers in middle- and upper-middle-class communities across the country and got their message out through the national press.

Along with the successful campaign for the Christmas bonus, from ATH's perspective, one of its greatest achievements has been the growth of the organization itself. As of December 2014, it had 4,140 members. Enlisting migrant domestic workers such as Maria and Tamara as organizers has also paid off. In December

2012, ATH created a network of migrant domestic workers that includes both Haitian migrant and undocumented Dominican-Haitian women and has a membership of approximately seven hundred domestic workers, primarily from the *batey* communities in the East. In the organization's new statutes, the leadership made a conscious decision to employ more inclusive language to avoid the de facto exclusion that may have characterized organization efforts in the past; eligible members must be "domestic workers in the Dominican Republic" instead of "Dominican domestic workers." ATH coordinates the network, provides legal orientation and support for members, and holds regular training workshops on labor and union rights and migration issues (especially the importance of documentation and regularization). Regarding the latter, since mid-2014 ATH has been collaborating with Centró Bonó, SC, and other migrants rights and labor organizations in a working group called Justicia Migratoria, which has banded together to educate migrant workers on how to regularize their migratory status through the National Regularization Plan. Regularization has proven quite difficult for migrant domestic workers, whose employers often refuse to provide letters of employment or give permission for them to miss work to obtain necessary paperwork; this on top of existing difficulties due to costs involved, low education levels, and requirements that have been deemed excessive in comparison to other regularization plans in the region.[66]

Victoria García and Elena Pérez García credit SC for transforming ATH's relationship to the labor movement. She and others in ATH believe that the labor movement in the DR became more involved in domestic worker issues when Convention 189 became a serious possibility because this "signaled to the labor movement that it was a labor issue."[67] ATH saw the need to get closer to the labor movement in part because they wanted to have a voice within the ILO as it began considering the new convention regarding domestic workers, Convention 189, a draft of which was circulating around the world at that time.[68] By 2010, ATH was officially part of a domestic worker federation affiliated with CNUS.[69] ATH participates fully in CNUS and believes that the confederation's leaders are extremely supportive of ATH. As Maria put it, "CNUS is a part of us. We always say we are also affiliated to CNUS."[70] They have been actively involved in Convention 189 deliberations and have adopted ATH's leaders as their own.

In 2013, ATH succeeded in ratifying Convention 189 in Dominican law.[71] But to the labor movement's consternation, as of March 2015 the executive branch had yet to notify the ILO. ATH, with the support of its national federation and all three labor confederations, has been campaigning yet again, enlisting the support of the Ministry of Women on the occasion of International Women's Day, to exhort the president and Ministry of Foreign Relations to register the DR's ratification of the convention in Geneva. Once Convention 189 is actually implemented in the DR, ATH and CNUS recognize that further battles lay ahead in terms of bringing domestic workers' rights into line with other workers. For instance, ATH has been campaigning for inclusion in the social security system since 1991. Domestic workers do not have an official payroll from which social security can be deducted, but ATH and its allies have been pushing for mechanisms for domestic workers, their employers, and the state to be able to pay in to the system, changes that require reforms to the Labor Code. On February 27, 2015, President Medina announced as part of his Independence Day speech that the government would be affiliating up to 50,000 of the country's 260,000 domestic workers with the subsidized social security regimen, which includes health insurance, workplace accident insurance, and pension.

ATH's longer-term goal is to become a union so it can take advantage of the possibility of tripartite dialogue on the implementation of Convention 189 and Labor Code reform more generally. In the short to medium term, it continues to collaborate with CNUS and SC, as well as other bodies such as the Comité Intersindical de la Mujer Trabajadora (CIMTRA) and the Gender Studies Center at INTEC University, to promote women workers' proposals as part of the Labor Code reform process. As of spring 2015, negotiations were still under way, with their main claims being the establishment of a minimum wage, work day, and of course access to social security for all domestic workers.

Becoming Advocates for Immigration Policy Reform

As engagement with national and migrant workers in informal employment arrangements intensified, CNUS became more and more deeply engaged in the migration policy debate and emerged as an important voice in opposition to the country's draconian policies. From CNUS's perspective, starting from the premise that the DR is a country that receives as well as sends migrants has made a difference in terms of how unions perceive the issue. Familia argues that many trade unionists have changed their tune regarding Haitian workers: "It wasn't a strange thing to hear a unionist speak out in the media that a Haitian was taking employment from Dominicans, but it has been a little while now where they don't do it and understand that it is the employers who look for vulnerable people that they can pay less." While there will undoubtedly always be unionists who say that migrants are the problem, Familia says this is no longer the position of the labor movement.[72] Additionally, while it used to be commonplace for unions to assume that undocumented migrant workers had no rights, there is a growing understanding that they do have rights that can be protected.[73]

Through Familia's leadership and the support of SC, CNUS has become quite involved in the national policy debate. In 2012 it launched a campaign for ratification of ILO Conventions 97 and 143 on migrant workers[74] and helped to bring together civil society organizations to develop a consensus document on managing migration. The organization's position has been evolving over time, and like national federations and unions in the United States and Europe, it has had to balance concern for the rights and conditions of migrant workers on the one hand with concern for the preservation of decent jobs for national workers on the other.[75]

In a February 2011 communiqué to the national government and employers, CNUS and its member unions articulated a detailed policy position.[76] While acknowledging that the Dominican government had a right to repatriate Haitian nationals lacking authorization to remain in the DR, the communiqué said it had to be done with respect for their labor and human rights. The statement went on to insist that the larger issue of migration policy needed to be addressed proactively and comprehensively, not just when a crisis presented itself. It called for several steps to be taken by government authorities including cracking down on corrupt border officials and those who engage in human trafficking and pursuing exploitative employers who, to keep production costs low, employ undocumented migrant workers under poor conditions.

This gradual shift in consciousness has meant that CNUS was well-positioned to lead lobbying efforts around the much-criticized National Regularization Plan and against ongoing deportations in 2014 and 2015. CNUS, for instance, participated in a successful effort to protest the high costs and inefficiency of the Haitian consulate, which were preventing migrant workers from obtaining the necessary identity documents to benefit from regularization.[77] At the time of writing (spring 2015) the regularization period was drawing to a close, and the three labor confederations held a forum in which they took the historic step of developing a public joint position calling for the extension of the plan.

CNUS also held activities to empower and inform workers on the regularization plan focusing specifically on migrant workers' rights, and it collaborated with the SC on flier distribution and referrals. The SC has also been financially supporting the work of coordinators and monitors at multiple points along the Dominico-Haitian border who are documenting cases of deportations and human rights abuses. Dominican labor confederations have enlisted the support of international counterparts ITUC and the Trade Union Confederation of the Americas (TUCA) to pressure the Dominican government regarding both the deportations and faulty regularization process, calling for protests at Dominican embassies around the world.

Accounting for the Shift in the Position of Formal Labor Unions toward Informal Workers in the DR

From 2007 to the present, CNUS and its affiliated unions have pivoted dramatically in the direction of informal economy organizing and protection and regularization of Haitian workers and Dominicans of Haitian ancestry in the DR, two goals that are inextricably linked. Given the country's long and virulent anti-Haitian past and present, the transformation of one of the nation's largest labor confederations requires an explanation. As described below, four factors taken together have resulted in CNUS's enduring shift: institutional change, availability and strategic use of resources, global links, and a powerful focusing event.

Institutional Change in Labor: Organizational Learning and Leadership Experience

Major changes took place in the labor movements in both the United States and the Dominican Republic that contributed to an opening to the informal economy and migrant workers. When John Sweeney was elected president of the AFL-CIO in 1995, he set in motion a chain of changes, including a reorientation of its international work away from the staunch anticommunism of previous administrations[78] and its restrictionist immigration policy stance toward the undocumented.[79] The institutional reorientation of the AFL-CIO, a shift in staff, and alliance building all contributed to a new openness to migrant and informal economy organizing at the Solidarity Center.

Just as central to these developments in the United States were those in the DR, where labor leaders had been engaging in strenuous efforts to unite and revitalize their movement. In a country in which the labor movement has historically been fragmented, CNUS represented an important attempt at unification when some of the most important unions and union federations in the country came together to form a single institution. Part of the *auto-reforma* (self-reform) movement throughout the Americas, the unions that formed CNUS were united in the conviction that internal union practices, including lack of unity and coordination between them, were contributing to labor's decline. Some of the key leaders who emerged in this process were also among the most open to expanding the ranks of their organizations to include migrant and informal economy workers.

Organizational leadership always plays a central role in shaping strategy and outcomes, and in the case of SC and CNUS opening up to the informal economy, it was terribly important. Ganz argues that there is a strong relationship between leaders' personal backgrounds and the likelihood they will engage in effective strategy.[80] He posits that innovative or creative thinking derives from three sources: *salient knowledge*, or a strong familiarity with the domain in which a leader is working; *heuristic processes*, which is the ability to use one's salient knowledge to imagine many possible interpretations and pathways and respond creatively to changing circumstances; and finally, *motivation*, which he argues is instrumental to creative output because of the focus it leads actors to bring to their work.[81] The leaders of CNUS, SC, and to a certain extent FENTICOMMC all had important experiences that shaped the way they viewed the labor movement in the DR as well as the potential role of migrant and informal economy workers.

Availability and Strategic Use of Resources

Social movement scholars have long argued that one of the most important contributing factors to a movement's success is its ability to access external resources (skills, relationships, time) and in particular financial resources.[82] The SC was able to bring financial resources and staff positions to CNUS, FENTICOMMC, and ATH. During the regularization plan, it provided stipends for seventy-nine organizers who accompanied migrant workers at strategic locations around the country (*bateys*, cities, border provinces) to ensure as many workers as possible could benefit from the plan.[83] Having a full-time staff engaged in the work led to a deepening level of engagement, which led in turn to strong buy-in to migrant worker and informal economy issues on the part of the participating unions. In an environment like the DR in which union resources are scarce, it is doubtful that vision and strategy alone would have been enough for the organizations to embrace more of an aggressive organizing approach in general and to have taken on informal economy and migrant worker issues.

Global Links

CNUS's close relationship with the SC was instrumental to its more inclusive vision and, as stated above, to its capacity to build programs around it. In addition to the SC, CNUS participates in TUCA, which has been an important forum for discussion of the need for trade union self-reform, including the unification of the labor movement, development of alliances, and prioritization of precarious workers in outsourced, subcontracted, or temporary arrangements in both formal and informal enterprises.[84]

For both ATH and FENTICOMMC, relationships to global organizations have also been critical. ATH was growing and taking action in the DR at just the moment when a global domestic workers movement emerged, bringing new focus and excitement to the issue and linking them to a larger fight around

Convention 189. Alcantara of FENTICOMMC credits the union's relationship to its global union federation, the BWI, for raising the union's consciousness around the connection between neoliberalism, migration, and the growth of the informal economy.

Focusing Event

Political scientists define a focusing event as a sudden and dramatic occurrence, like a natural disaster or some other kind of external shock to the status quo.[85] The Haitian earthquake in January of 2010 had a catalytic effect on some quarters of Dominican society and certainly on the Dominican labor movement. Wooding described it as a kind of "tectonic shift in terms of solidarity at all levels."[86] Dominican unions raised money, contributed goods, helped Haitian workers desperate to contact relatives, and traveled to Haiti in brigades to provide direct support. Familia, along with other labor leaders, noted a dramatic shift: "Haitians began to see us in a different manner because although the DR had discriminated a lot against Haiti and there had been tragedies, the Haitians also had prejudices towards us. . . . [B]eginning then relationships have improved and gotten a lot less tense." On the other hand, the earthquake also touched off a wave of migration to the DR, although much of it was temporary. Unfortunately, much of the sentiment of solidarity has since been clouded by a resurgence in anti-Haitianist attitudes in the DR.

Emerging Challenges

Two final issues having to do with organizing and sustainability and the nature of the organizing itself are important to explore briefly. First, although there is more openness to organizing migrants and informal economy workers, in the DR, as in so many other parts of the world, the route to building powerful and financially sustainable labor organizations is not yet clear. In 2013, the SC no longer had funding available to support the ATH. Yet both, ATH and FENTI-COMMC, claim to charge only nominal, largely symbolic dues to their members (and even these claims of some dues requirements were not entirely credible). The SC has not ignored sustainability questions and has taken some steps toward pushing the domestic workers at least to support their own organizations. Geoff Herzog, SC director in the DR at the time of this writing, estimates that FENTICOMMC has always maintained a voluntary dues base of about 30 percent of its members. "They go around on pay day raising consciousness and asking people to pay their dues," but he says, "When people don't have work they don't ask them for money."[87]

The SC funding has helped to jump-start the organizations into organizing, but it does not seem that the organizers have taken advantage of the period during which they have had funding to develop a longer-term strategy for financial sustainability.[88] Should the SC require organizations, in return for receiving funding and support, put membership dues systems in place that charge enough money to significantly contribute to the cost of retaining organizers? A second set of tensions nested throughout the research for this chapter concerned the approach the DR union organizers were taking to organize migrant workers and whether questions of labor rights can really be taken up separately from immigration status for Haitians. Every day in the DR, undocumented Haitian migrants and Dominican Haitians are blocked from registering their children's birth, sending their children to school, and other basic rights because of their status. As workers, they are unable to participate in the social security system or to form and join unions. Fearing they would be overwhelmed by the legal issues and taking on individual cases, the SC made a decision that it would not take on individual immigration cases and would focus on organizing, and CNUS decided it would address migration issues through trying to move forward on migration policy. But it is not clear that these issues are really separable for Haitian workers.

The general approach taken by FENTICOMMC has been to focus on labor issues in the informal economy and to invite Haitian workers to participate in the organization. It is quite difficult for the Haitian workers to join FENTICOMMC, however, given that most do not have Dominican *cédulas*. Given this formal barrier to their membership, what does it mean practically to say that "our doors are open"? It is important to ask the question of whether the existing union model serves undocumented Haitian workers or whether there might be some other approach that works better.

One such model exists in the Association of Haitian Construction Workers (ATHIC), an organization that has existed informally since 1990 and received formal registration from the state in 2008 with the objectives of organizing, recruiting, and defending the rights of Haitian construction workers. ATHIC strongly disagrees with FENTICOMMC's approach; it says that Haitians have specific problems that overwhelmingly have to do with their irregular migration status. In ATHIC's view, their union brothers and sisters do not recognize the importance of the underlying issue of documentation. ATHIC says that its top priority is to help Haitian workers devise strategies individually and collectively to get their employers to support their application for regularization of their status.

The differing priorities of the two organizations were apparent during the implementation of the National Regularization Plan. While ATHIC hit the streets providing continuous training and accompanying Haitian construction workers in the two major cities, Santiago and Santo Domingo, and assisting 1,500 workers to fill out and submit their documents to apply for regularization, FENTICOM-MC's involvement was much more passive. The federation basically responded to requests for copies of technical course completion certificates and certifications of diplomas from their training institute from workers seeking to demonstrate time in country and technical qualifications. Not surprisingly, the relationship between the two organizations is tense.

This case points to the inextricable link, in the Dominican context and beyond, between informality and immigration status. Four factors appear to have contributed to the union confederation's shift in stance regarding Haitian immigrants and informal workers: institutional change, availability and strategic use of resources, global links, and a powerful focusing event. At the same time, questions remain about both the sustainability of work that has largely been funded by the SC and about the desirability of a model that has emphasized labor issues rather than immigration status.

As this chapter goes to print, SC, CNUS and to a lesser extent the other union confederations are pushing for the regularization plan to be extended, while President Medina makes declarations to UN General Secretary Ban-ki Moon that the DR "cannot harbor two poor nations," has done everything possible to regularize migrants, and is prepared to fully apply its migration norms following the conclusion of the period in mid-June 2015[89] (read: deport all those who did not benefit from the plan). The fact that all three union confederations came together to issue a joint statement on regularization of migrant workers speaks to how far the historically weak but increasingly dynamic Dominican labor movement has come in its understanding of the linkages between informal employment and migrant workers' rights.

DOMESTIC WORKERS IN URUGUAY

Collective Bargaining Agreement and Legal Protection

Mary R. Goldsmith

Uruguay is the only country in Latin America and one of the few in the world that has collective bargaining for domestic workers. This and its labor legislation, social security coverage, unionization of domestic workers, and general working conditions of private household employment were the reasons Uruguay was chosen by the International Labor Organization (ILO) as a model of good government practices regarding domestic work. This chapter analyzes why and how collective bargaining for domestic workers began in Uruguay in 2008, three years after the rise to political power of the leftist coalition Frente Amplio (FA)[1] and two years after the adoption by the Uruguayan legislature of Law 18.065, which recognized virtually the same rights for domestic workers as other workers, including the right to collective bargaining. It provides a brief history of domestic workers' organizations and an overview of the representatives for domestic workers, the Sindicato Único de Trabajadoras Domésticas (SUTD), and employers, the Liga de Amas de Casa, Consumidores y Usuarios de la República Oriental del Uruguay,[2] on the wage council. It describes the bargaining process of the first two collective agreements on the wage council, which were signed respectively in 2008 and 2010; it briefly touches upon the third collective agreement that was subscribed in 2013 and is currently in effect. Finally, it analyzes the outcome of this process in terms of the recognition of domestic workers' rights and the relations of domestic employment in Uruguay as well as outlining lessons to be gleaned from this experience and which can be replicated elsewhere.

Background

An Overview of Uruguay

Uruguay is located on the southeastern Atlantic coast of Latin America, sharing borders with Brazil to the north and with Argentina to the west. With a population of approximately 3.3 million, it is one of the smallest countries in the region. The overwhelming majority (94.6 percent) of its inhabitants reside in urban areas; 40 percent live in Montevideo, the nation's capital. Uruguay's population is rapidly aging (more than 14 percent is sixty-five years of age or older), which is particularly relevant to the issue of care work.[3] Uruguay is a middle-income country with lower poverty rates and less income inequality than most other countries in the region. The nation has one of the highest levels of education in Latin America and ranks fourth in the United Nations Development Program's (UNDP) Human Development Index and the Gender Inequality Index in the region.[4]

Uruguay is a constitutional republic and, with the exception of the period of military rule between 1973 and 1985, has been governed since independence (1828) by two parties, the Colorado (Red) and the Blanco (White, or, as it is officially called, Nacional). In 2004, however, the FA, a leftist coalition party[5] founded in 1971, ran a campaign that emphasized economic growth, decent employment, and social justice and won the presidential and congressional elections. Tabaré Vázquez, who took office as president in 2005, sought justice for the poor, the workers, and the victims of the military dictatorship.[6] The FA won a second and third presidential race in 2009 and 2014 with, respectively, José Mujica and Tabaré Vázquez as its candidate. During the FA administrations, there generally has been a good relationship between the government and the Plenario Intersindical de Trabajadores—Convención Nacional de Trabajadores (PIT-CNT),[7] the nation's only labor federation.

When the FA government took power, it immediately implemented measures against unemployment, which had peaked in 2002 at 17 percent, and in favor of better working conditions. Income inequality began to decline in 2007—a trend that continues to date—which is related to the increase in the general minimum wage that applies to workers not covered by sector- or occupation-specific measures and periodic wage adjustments,[8] the return of collective bargaining, the strengthening of unions, and the implementation of redistributive fiscal reforms in 2008.[9]

Since 2005, informal employment, defined in Uruguay by a lack of social protection, has decreased significantly. The percentage of workers who do not contribute to the Banco de Previsión Social (BPS)[10] has dropped from 38.7 percent in 2005 to 25.6 percent in 2012.[11] This decline is related to the adoption of public policies, including tax and social security reforms, investment incentives to create jobs, and the resurgence of collective bargaining in the context of sustained economic growth.[12] Still, a large portion of workers in some occupational categories and economic sectors are not enrolled in social security. Worth noting is that two-thirds of the working poor hold informal jobs. The government has taken steps to encourage street vendors, car washers, tourist guides, and sex workers to enroll in a simplified social security scheme through the BPS.

Some informal workers are organized in associations and unions, which dispute urban space and notions of justice, cleanliness, and economic worth. For example, roughly 1,200 sex workers are members of the Asociación de Meretrices Profesionales de Uruguay (AMEPU)[13] and an undetermined number of street vendors belong to the Asociación de Tortafriteras and the Sindicato Único de Pancheros.[14] The Unión de Clasificadores de Residuos Urbanos Sólidos (UCRUS) is affiliated to the PIT-CNT and has engaged in negotiation with the Ministerio de Trabajo y Seguridad Social (MTSS)[15] regarding pay rates for solid waste products, job training, and social protection.

Methods

This chapter is based primarily on fieldwork carried out in November 2012 in Montevideo, during which I interviewed members of the SUTD, the Liga de Amas de Casa, and the MTSS, who had been directly involved in the process of tripartite collective bargaining. In addition, I interviewed officials from the PIT-CNT, participants in nongovernmental organizations (NGOs), lawyers who worked with the SUTD and the Liga, and researchers who had studied domestic work. A list of interview subjects is presented in Appendix I.

In addition to interviews, I observed the activities of the legal aid clinic at the SUTD and a training workshop about computer skills for migrant domestic workers at Cotidiano Mujer. I consulted the minutes for the sessions of the tripartite bargaining of the first two collective agreements at the legislation,[16] government statistics, and other studies on paid domestic work and the political economy of Uruguay. During January 2013 and spring 2015, I carried out follow-up interviews regarding collective bargaining by phone and e-mail with members of the SUTD and the Liga. The present chapter also draws upon prior fieldwork in Montevideo in November 2011 regarding good government practices and domestic work, as well as interviews with delegates from Uruguay in June 2011 at the 100th International Labor Conference at the adoption of Convention 189 concerning decent work for domestic workers. The documentary research includes review of local newspapers,[17] theses, government studies, and other publications regarding paid domestic work and the political economy of Uruguay.

The Case Study

The Conditions of Paid Domestic Workers in Uruguay

Slightly more than 15 percent of all employed women in Uruguay are domestic workers.[18] This figure has remained fairly constant since 1998[19] and is the most common occupation for women, followed by office work and retail sales. In 2012, there were 109,220 domestic workers, with 33 percent living in the capital Montevideo, 16 percent in the adjacent department of Canelones, 7 percent in Maldonado (a department on the Atlantic coast and home to the beach resort Punta del Este), and the other 44 percent in the remaining sixteen departments. This distribution coincides largely with that of the general population.[20]

Approximately 99 percent of all domestic workers are women.[21] In 2012, 7.7 percent of domestic workers identified as black or of African ancestry, and domestic work accounted for almost one-fourth of all employed black women. Slightly fewer than 2 percent of domestic workers declared that they were of indigenous ancestry.[22] There is also a small but undetermined percentage of women who have migrated from Peru and Bolivia to work in domestic service because wages are much higher in Uruguay than in their home countries. Domestic workers of African and indigenous ancestry face additional discrimination in Uruguay, and migrants are even more vulnerable than local workers to exploitation and human rights violations.

In 2012, 9 percent of domestic workers were caregivers for the sick, 15.2 percent were child caregivers, and 75.9 percent were cooks, cleaners, and general domestic personnel. It is important to underscore that the experience of most workers is that occupational categories are not treated with such precision on the job, meaning they are often burdened with additional tasks for no extra pay. In 2007, roughly one out of twenty worked on a live-out basis.[23]

Domestic workers on the whole work fewer hours than other women in the labor force, which probably reflects that many are hired on a part-time basis. In 2012, 47.6 percent of domestic workers were employed for twenty hours or less per week, whereas 6.1 percent worked forty-eight or more hours. Caregivers for children and the sick tend to have much longer workweeks, but they generally earn less than other domestic workers. In 2012, the average monthly wage for domestic workers was 46.1 percent of that of other employed women, and the average domestic workers' hourly wage was 70.1 percent of that of other working women (a substantial improvement from only a few years before). There is regional variation in wages and working conditions; workers outside Montevideo tend to earn less and have longer hours than workers elsewhere, and there are still cases of women who earn approximately one-third of the minimum wage and work from dawn until dusk.

Approximately 63,000 domestic workers are registered with and pay into social security. Since 2006, the number of domestic workers who make contributions has increased by 45.6 percent, largely due to the media campaign by the BPS. Still there is a very high evasion rate, and less than 60 percent of domestic workers make social security payments. In 2012, 20.3 percent of domestic workers received holiday pay, a rise from only 14.4 percent in 2009, and 52.7 percent received a semiannual bonus.

Uruguay does not have a general labor law nor labor code. Instead, the labor legislation consists of a series of laws referring to specific workers and topics and is guided largely by jurisprudence.[24] Until 2006, with the government adoption of Law 18.065, there was no specific labor law for domestic workers. Law 18.065 defines domestic work "as that performed in a household by a person in a dependency relationship in order to provide care and housework to one or various persons or one or various families, without these tasks resulting in a direct economic profit for the employer." It sets a minimum work age of eighteen years and recognizes domestic workers' rights to an eight-hour work day, forty-four-hour workweek, nine-hour rest period during the night for live-in workers, rest periods during the workday, a thirty-six-hour weekly rest, tripartite negotiation both of wages and job categories, severance pay after ninety days of work, additional compensation in the case of dismissal during pregnancy, the issuing of a pay slip, unemployment insurance, labor inspection, and a choice between private and public health institutions for medical care.[25] Finally, it states that domestic workers will have the same general labor and social security rights as enjoyed by other workers.

In June 2007, the regulatory Decree 224/007 was issued, which provides overtime pay, paid sick leave, the right of live-in workers to food and lodging, and the right of employers to deduct a maximum of 20 percent from wages for room and board and a maximum of 10 percent where only meals are offered.[26] Domestic workers in Uruguay have had access to disability, old age, and survivor pension since 1942, maternity benefits and family allowance since 1980, medical coverage and sick pay since 1984, and unemployment insurance since 2006.[27]

In 2008, domestic workers were incorporated into tripartite collective bargaining with the creation of a specific wage council for this occupational group. In 2009, the BPS implemented an innovative publicity campaign to raise awareness about domestic workers' rights and to increase their registration for social security. Some of the most outstanding examples of this campaign were information pamphlets (aimed at employers) in the form of tags to hang on the doorknobs of employers' homes, with the message, "The domestic worker in this house is enrolled in the Social Security Institute," television spots ("*Desorden*" won the Balero de Bronce), and sociodramas on buses.[28] In 2010 and 2011, labor inspectors visited more than nine thousand homes to find out whether domestic workers were registered for social security.[29]

In recognition of these efforts, the ILO chose Uruguay as a model for good government practices regarding domestic work. On June 14, 2012, it became the first country to adopt ILO Convention 189, "Decent work for domestic workers."

Background of Domestic Workers' Organizing in Uruguay

Domestic workers' organizing dates back at least as far as 1964, when workers started to meet in various parishes in Montevideo, encouraged by progressive clergy of the Catholic Church.[30] This served as the groundwork for the Asociación Nacional de Empleadas de Casa Particular (ANECAP),[31] which was founded three years later, in 1969, by domestic workers who belonged to the Juventud Obrera Católica (JOC).[32] In 1975 ANECAP formed the Asociación Laboral de Empleadas del Servicio Doméstico y Afines (ALESA),[33] which later expanded its area of intervention to the provinces.[34] These developments were possible because although union activity was prohibited, the workers used other forms of organization such as professional associations, which were granted legal status in 1981.[35] With Uruguay's return to democracy in 1985, the ban on union activity was lifted and the SUTD was founded. At one point, it was said to have two thousand members, but it then entered a fifteen-year period in which it was dormant.[36] Nonetheless, during the following years, various reform bills to extend domestic workers' rights were presented to congress by legislators from the FA, none of which were enacted.[37]

A New Phase for the SUTD

In 2002, Mariselda Cancela, a lawyer who would later collaborate pro bono with the SUTD, and other members of the Gender Department of the PIT-CNT began to organize domestic workers. Cancela played a key role in the PIT-CNT campaign to involve domestic workers in drafting a list of demands that they planned to present to the FA for inclusion in their platform for the upcoming presidential elections. Cancela describes the snowball technique that they used in the PIT-CNT:

> As election time approached we started to work with the *compañeras* and we had a voice. We talked with the domestic workers we knew and

they told us where to locate others; some of these came to the Gender Department to work on the campaign and contact the wives and relatives of members from the PIT-CNT. We leafleted in the markets, near the churches in residential areas around Montevideo, like Pocitos, Punta Gorda, and Carrasco, where we knew a lot of them worked.[38]

This laid the groundwork for the inclusion of domestic workers in the platform of the FA and the reorganization of the SUTD in 2005.

As mentioned above, in 2004, the left won the presidential election for the first time in Uruguayan history. When Vázquez took office in 2005, he announced in his inaugural address that his government aimed to create a wage council for domestic service.[39] The Vázquez administration, during which a series of labor laws were approved that reinstated rights and practices that had been suspended by prior governments, was supportive of labor;[40] Eduardo Bonomi, the new minister of labor and social security, publicly stated, "I am aware that the balance must be inclined one way or the other and I have decided to take the side of the workers."[41]

Many of the women garment workers who lost their jobs during the 1998–2002 economic crisis sought employment in domestic work. They brought their union experience and expertise and tried to construct a new kind of labor relations, quite different from the feudalistic relationship that had characterized domestic service in much of Uruguay.[42] Many of the other domestic workers had started in this occupation as young girls, in exchange for room and board. Current domestic workers recall that their mothers were often expected to sleep on the floor or eat leftovers from their employers' plates.

Some of the former militants from the garment workers' union, who then worked as domestic employees, were invited by the Gender Department of the PIT-CNT to help revive the SUTD. Cristina Otero, Matilde Castillo, and Nora Pacheco, former garment workers, joined forces with María Salas, María Esteban, and a few other women who had been in the SUTD during the 1980s to rebuild the organization. There already was a network of domestic workers who had been contacted during the presidential campaign by the Gender Department, and many were the partners of members of the Sindicato Único Nacional de la Construcción y Anexos (SUNCA),[43] which would later be an important ally to the SUTD, providing them with space to meet and even making financial contributions.

By mid-2005 the SUTD was active again, both internationally and nationally. A delegate attended the ILO seminar about migrant labor and domestic work in December 2005. The domestic workers and trade union activists who participated then issued the Declaration of Montevideo, which called for recognition of the value of domestic work, respect for domestic workers' rights, and the inclusion of their demands in the agendas of labor unions and federations.

The union members contributed to the campaign for legal reform for domestic workers, which would grant them the same rights as other workers. The new labor law for domestic workers was drafted by the Comisión Tripartita para la Igualdad de Oportunidades y el Trato Igual en el Empleo (CTIOTE) with the participation of the MTSS, Instituto Nacional de las Mujeres (INAMU), PIT-CNT, and la Cámara de Comercio e Industria.[44] Although the members of the SUTD union initially were not consulted, they later fought for the incorporation of their observations into the new law, which was based largely on previous legislative proposals. Law 18.065 was adopted by the Uruguayan legislature on November 27, 2006.[45]

The Representatives of Domestic Workers and Their Employers

The Sindicato Único de Trabajadoras Domésticas

The SUTD is the only membership-based organization that represents domestic workers in Uruguay. There are a few NGOs—notably Cotidiano Mujer and to a lesser extent Casa de la Mujer de la Unión—that have had projects aimed at empowering domestic workers. Former members of the SUTD created the Agrupación María Goretti (with the support of Cotidiano Mujer) for the dissemination and promotion of domestic workers' rights. All these groups recognize that the only representative per se of domestic workers at the bargaining table and in the media is the union.

All members of the SUTD must be employed in domestic service. If a member changes to another line of work or retires, she must withdraw from the union. The same criterion operates for members who participate in any commission or secretariat. The women argue that full-time activists lose touch with the day-to-day reality of work life and there is consensus that it is morally and politically incorrect for leaders to leave their jobs and dedicate themselves exclusively to the organization. All members must pay dues, contribute to the unity and development of the union, respect the decisions of the assembly, vote in elections, and discharge assigned responsibilities. Currently there are more than 1,300 members, of whom slightly more than 700 pay their dues regularly. The union's membership has roughly doubled over the past six years and they have campaigned to create branches outside Montevideo. This resulted in the creation of local branches in eleven of Uruguay's nineteen departments and broadened the union's base numerically, socially, and geographically, although the majority of the members are from Montevideo.

The SUTD de-emphasizes formal hierarchy and until quite recently did not have a general secretary or a president. From 2005 to 2012, the core group of members planned and carried out their activities via three commissions (organization, communication, and finance). In November 2011, it revised its constitution, and in October 2012, it held elections for the first time in the union's history. The revised constitution and bylaws call for a general secretariat composed of seven secretariats (organization, propaganda, finance, public relations, health and hygiene, acts, and interior, each with two members) and a fiscal commission (six members). The general assembly is the highest authority of the union. Since 2006, it has held six national meetings, which include members and nonmembers.

The union's activities are coordinated from the office in Montevideo. On Fridays they provide legal aid for members. Workers are interviewed by a member of the secretariat and can be referred to a legal team from the national university. The union is an affiliate of the PIT-CNT, where it has a small, simply furnished office, and the PIT-CNT allows the union to use its phone and its auditorium for the assemblies and larger meetings and other rooms for the legal aid clinic. The PIT-CNT and the Instituto Cuesta Duarte (the research and training center associated with the PIT-CNT) provide them with advice and guidance throughout the year. They help SUTD calculate the demands for the wage increases, and the PIT-CNT leaders accompany SUTD representatives to the collective bargaining meetings. A representative from SUTD participates in the Gender and Diversity Secretariat of the PIT-CNT. The relationship with the PIT-CNT has, however, not always been smooth. A few SUTD members have had grievances with PIT-CNT members who are their employers, and once in a while a member of the PIT-CNT refers to the domestic workers in a derogatory fashion. In 2010, there was a rift between the SUTD and the PIT-CNT because the federation sent the head of the Gender Commission, not a member of the SUTD, to the 99th International Labor Conference, focused on domestic work, on the grounds that the members of the SUTD lacked experience. The SUTD members, who had spent months preparing for the conference with the support of the ILO, were furious and presented a letter to the general board of representatives of the PIT-CNT. Nonetheless, the PIT-CNT is undoubtedly the SUTD's main political ally.[46]

The Liga de Amas de Casa, Consumidores y Usuarios de la República Oriental del Uruguay

The Liga de Amas de Casa was founded in 1995 to represent consumers. The Liga is a membership-based organization, but it is difficult to calculate the precise number of its members since this fluctuates monthly by the number who pay their dues. At its peak, Liga membership was approximately eight hundred. Every two years, the membership elects its authorities; Mabel Lorenzo de Sánchez has been re-elected repeatedly as president. It celebrates July 22, international housework day.

The Liga originally had two objectives: to dignify women as housewives and to defend consumers' rights. The Liga has disseminated information regarding the contribution that housewives make to society and has fought for their rights to a pension (which is recognized in the neighboring countries of Argentina and Brazil). Since 2008, the Liga has had a third objective, namely the representation of employers of domestic workers in the tripartite wage councils. The minister of labor invited the Liga to participate in the wage council for domestic workers. The invitation created a great deal of controversy; although the majority of the Liga's assembly voted in favor, several members abandoned the Liga over the issue. Not all of its members are employers of domestic workers, and in fact a few are domestic workers.

Representation of employers for collective bargaining is a large responsibility, given that approximately 9 percent of all households hire a domestic worker.[47] President Lorenzo de Sánchez has recognized on numerous occasions that this was a tremendous challenge because neither she nor other Liga delegates to the council had experience in labor relations, though they were employers of domestic workers. Currently, her organization disseminates information on employers' rights and obligations and provides legal advice to employers on a broad range of issues such as how to write out a pay slip, how to calculate wage increases, and how to resolve labor conflict. Lorenzo de Sánchez attended the 99th and 100th International Labor Conferences as an employer representative, one of the few such delegates to have expertise in collective bargaining with domestic workers.

The stark contrast between the offices of the SUTD and the Liga is eloquent. The Liga has a spacious two-story office located in the center of the city, with a large meeting room in the basement and a computer and telephone. The walls are covered with photos and news clippings that tell the story of the Liga. Both the Liga and the SUTD have copies of the Convention 189 that they proudly distribute.

The Inclusion of Domestic Service in the Wage Councils and the Tripartite Negotiation of the First Collective Agreement (2008)

Until 2008, there were two channels for setting wages in Uruguay: tripartite negotiation in the Consejos de Salarios[48] and, for those occupational groups that did not participate in the wage councils, presidential decrees. The minimum wage was introduced in Uruguay in 1969 and was set by presidential decree 1534/969. Domestic workers were explicitly excluded from the minimum wage until 1990 when, for the first time, a minimum wage was set for them by executive decree 246/90. The decree set one minimum wage for Montevideo and a lower one for the rest of the country. Both minima were slightly higher than the national general minimum wage. The decree also permitted employers to deduct 20 percent from wages if housing and food were provided to the workers, and 10 percent if only meals were provided.[49] The FA eliminated these geographic differences between the minimum wages for domestic workers in order to promote greater social and economic equality.

Even after the adoption of Law 18.065 and the enactment of Decree 224/007, which stipulated that domestic workers' wages should be established through tripartite negotiations, wages continued to be set through presidential decree in 2007 and 2008. In February 2008, the minimum monthly wage was increased to UYU 3,550 (US $160) per month and by the hour to UYU 18 (US $0.81). The SUTD rejected the establishment of domestic workers' wages via presidential decree because this was reminiscent of the period of the dictatorship. It demanded their right to tripartite negotiation like other groups of workers. Cristina Otero recalls the following:

> We went to the Ministry of Labor time after time, and sat there hours on end, waiting for a response: when were they going to convene the wage council for domestic workers. On Christmas Eve, we met at midday in the Ministry to ask the authorities to convene a wage council for domestic workers. The date nor the time mattered to us. They would tell us to be there at 10 o'clock at night, and there we were, at 10 p.m. We told them "We do not want to regulate our work, rather we want to regulate our salaries."[50]

The primary obstacle to forming a wage council for domestic service was the lack of an employers' organization. It was at this point that the Liga was invited and agreed to represent the employers of domestic workers on the wage council.[51] From the onset, the Liga requested technical assistance and training from the MTSS in order to grapple with tripartite negotiation.[52]

The wage council for domestic service was created on July 7, 2008, and because it was the twenty-first council to be formed, was named the Grupo 21 (Group 21).[53] As in the case of most other wage councils, each party named three to four delegates. The government had three representatives: the council president, Nelson Loustaunau (deputy minister of labor and social security) and two full delegates. The SUTD chose as its delegates Cristina Otero and Mariela Burlón Rodríguez and, as substitutes, Matilde Castillo and Nora Pacheco. Burlón

Rodríguez had been employed most of her life as a domestic worker, and, as mentioned earlier, the other representatives were former activists of the needle-workers' union. The Liga members selected its president, Mabel Lorenzo de Sánchez, and other employers of domestic workers to represent them. Mariselda Cancela provided legal advice for the SUTD, and the Liga also brought a lawyer for the first few sessions.

The government played and continues to play a lead role in the negotiations. Each year, the Ministry of the Economy and Finance and Ministry of Labor and Social Security prepare general guidelines for all the wage councils concerning the duration of agreements, the criteria for wage increases and periodic adjust-ments, and the time line for wage adjustments. These written recommendations set the framework for the wage councils.[54] The workers and employers negotiate, taking these guidelines into account, but they may also introduce other issues regarding salaries, labor conditions, and benefits. The MTSS convenes and pre-sides at the meetings and in the case of deadlock can call for a vote.

The wage council for Group 21 met for the first time on August 19, 2008. The SUTD proposed a minimum wage of UYU 8,500 pesos (around US \$410) per month, an increase of almost 150 percent. In addition, the SUTD used a wage-scale approach, asking for a 4 percent increase for those women already earn-ing between UYU 8,501 and UYU 9,500 (US \$411 and US \$459) and 2 percent for those earning more than UYU 9,500 (US \$460). These proposals were well above the government guidelines regarding wage increases, but the SUTD justi-fied the demand on the basis of the decrease in the real value of domestic workers' wages; workers contend that their own experience contradicts the government figures for inflation and cost of living adjustments. The SUTD also presented a list of thirteen additional demands that had been formulated after consultation with workers from various areas of the country and discussed in assembly. These demands included Domestic Workers' Day (August 19) as a paid legal holiday; protection from dismissal for claims made by workers in respect to Law 18.065, regulated in July 2007, or salary increases; paid time off for family or education reasons; paid union leave; seniority pay; work clothing; compensation for reduc-tion in working hours; equal pay for equal work; and nondiscrimination.

Over the two and a half months of negotiation, Group 21 held approximately ten bargaining sessions in an area designated specifically for collective bargaining within the Ministry of Labor and Social Security. Other union members pro-vided moral and political support, waiting outside the sessions and occasionally accompanying the delegates from the SUTD. This served also as a show of politi-cal clout to the government and employers. The proceedings were coordinated by the representatives from the MTSS, one of whom later filled in a very short form by hand recording the minutes of each session. Occasionally between sessions, there was communication via phone and e-mail to exchange proposals and counterproposals. Throughout this period, the SUTD delegates discussed the negotiations with their commissions that met once a week and convened assemblies:

> As we negotiated we convened meetings. We invited members and nonmembers to the meetings. It was very important to invite domestic workers who were not in the SUTD, so that they open up their minds. They needed to know why a union is such an important tool and that we must be united and present a common front.[55]

Through the give and take of the negotiation process, the union clung to some of its demands while letting others go. The demands the union held onto had special meaning to the SUTD, such as using a wage-scale approach in order to benefit those women with the lowest wages, most of who lived outside Montevideo; designating August 19 as Domestic Workers' Day, signifying the acknowledgment of the Sindicato Único de Trabajadoras Domésticas and recognition of domestic labor; and workers' right to union leave not only because it was their right as with other workers, but also since it would allow them to build their union both numerically and politically.

Many of the SUTD demands were included in the collective agreement, most with amendments. For example, the monthly minimum wage for the rest of 2008 was fixed at UYU 4,260 (US $206), roughly half of the level proposed by the SUTD. This in turn affected the salary scales and adjustments projected for this same period as well as for 2009 and 2010. A one-off bonus was introduced into the agreement to offset the limited wage increase. After some debate, the employers acceded to seniority pay (but at a lower rate than that demanded by the union) and August 19 as a paid holiday. The provision of work clothes and equipment (but with no description) by the employer at no cost to the worker, overtime pay, a bonus for working at a location other than the normal household (though the amount remained undefined), and compensation in the event of a reduction in the number of workdays or hours were included. A special tripartite commission was set up to analyze the issues of union leave, a written contract, and job categories. The agreement incorporated the principle of equal opportunity and treatment and the commitment of the parties to create decent working conditions, to build social awareness about the need to formalize domestic work, and to implement initiatives to disseminate this agreement, a concern displayed by workers and employers alike during the negotiation. Overall, the workers did not encounter a great deal of opposition by the employers during the negotiation. This was in part because many questions, such as additional compensation for night work, care of the elderly or children, categories of work, and union leave were left for future discussion.[56]

On November 10, 2008, the government, employer, and worker delegates signed the first collective agreement for domestic service not only in Uruguay but also in the entire region of Latin America. The agreement was effective until June 30, 2010, and one of its most important features was that it had national jurisdiction and applied to all domestic workers and their employers, regardless of whether they were affiliated with the SUTD and the Liga de Amas de Casa.[57] During 2009 and 2010, in accordance with the first collective agreement, the wage council of Group 21 met to sign periodic wage adjustments and to discuss written individual contracts, work categories, and union leave. The SUTD and the Liga had different priorities: the first, union leave, and the second, the written contract. The employers were looking for a standard employment contract with concrete details regarding tasks, requirements, and penalties (for example, repercussions for workers' absences and late arrival). The workers also proposed a fairly simple individual contract with the names of the worker and the employer, the total number of working hours, and the tasks the worker was hired to perform. In July 2009, the SUTD presented a proposal for union leave that called for two hundred hours per month with full pay for workers who had to fulfill union responsibilities, hours that would be distributed among its membership. After months of suspended negotiations, the tripartite commission reconvened in March 2010. The Liga stated that its membership did not consider the SUTD's proposal regarding union leave viable. In response, the MTSS explored options regarding how to organize and finance union leave. It suggested that a fund be set up through the Social Security Institute to which all employers of domestic workers would contribute, and not simply those whose workers had union responsibilities, thus distributing this expense. The SUTD and Liga agreed to the MTSS's proposal, but when the SUTD submitted a draft of the law that such a proposal required, the Liga did not respond.

The Bargaining Process of the Second Agreement (2010)

On August 20, 2010, negotiation of the second agreement began; it lasted four months and included fourteen meetings. As in 2008, all of these were held in the MTSS following the same protocol. There was almost no variation in the composition of the worker, employer, and government delegations with the exception that the main leader of the SUTD, Cristina Otero, had abandoned the union in late 2009 and did not participate. The delegates from the MTSS presented the executive branch guidelines for the wage council negotiations in July 2010. These recommendations included a three- to five-year duration for agreements, annual wage adjustments based on projected inflation and other macroeconomic considerations that would promote "distribution of the fruits of economic growth," and a guarantee of the stability of real wages. These would be complemented by later corrective measures that would take into account real inflation and any reduction in purchasing power.

The SUTD presented a platform of fourteen demands, some of which had originally been proposed in the first round and some of which were new. The demands included items such as holiday pay, a perfect attendance bonus, notice prior to dismissal, payment of full wages in the event that the employer suspends the workday, additional pay for night work, and substantial paid time for breastfeeding. The Liga eventually only accepted (at least in part) four of the union's demands: additional pay for night work (but at a rate of only 15 percent), full pay to the worker when the employer suspends the workday, the creation of a tripartite committee for occupational health, and that none of the provisions in the agreement could be used to undercut workers' conditions. All of these were included in the second collective agreement.

Union leave and wage categories were also still on the bargaining table from the earlier round of negotiations. There was serious conflict over these and the issue of wage increases. The issue of union leave was particularly difficult. The Liga focused on the disruption the leave would create in their households, while the union emphasized the legal right to union leave under Law 17/940. Exasperated by the lack of headway, the SUTD took union leave off the bargaining table on September 15 and demanded that the MTSS present a law to congress establishing the mechanisms for implementing union leave for domestic workers. The government voted in favor of this proposal, and the Liga abstained on the grounds that it needed legal advice.

The SUTD expected to make progress regarding job categories. On September 6, 2010, it submitted a detailed proposal for fourteen categories of workers with varying degrees of specialization, knowledge, responsibility, and different monthly wage levels. At the bottom of the scale were common cleaners, bedroom cleaners, and child care providers, all at UYU 7,000 (US $338). Next came care providers for the elderly, caretakers of grounds and houses, and common cooks at UYU 7,700 (US $372). From there, with escalating pay rates, came cleaner (category 1), maintenance worker, housekeeper (category 2), housekeeper (category 1), specialized cook, cook of meals for freezer, cook for special events, and finally, at UYU 15,000 (US $725), cook of international cuisine.[58] The SUTD also demanded that in the event a person carries out several activities, she should be paid according to the one with a higher salary. The employers objected but did not present a counterproposal, arguing that they needed legal advice. Further discussion of categories was postponed.

There was heated discussion back and forth regarding the wage increases and later adjustments for the different wage levels. Almost three months into negotiation, the SUTD decided to distribute leaflets in the residential neighborhoods criticizing the president of the Liga for being tight-fisted and "starving" the domestic workers. This was aimed at undermining her image among employers and to pressure the Liga to come up with a more reasonable offer. Instead, the employers demanded an apology and asked that the government present a proposal that would be voted on. The MTSS attempted to ease the tension, indicating that the SUTD's actions were normal in politics. The Liga demanded that the government submit a final proposal and take a vote. After discussing the situation during its National Assembly, the SUTD decided not to attend the next bargaining session because it knew that if a vote were taken, it would lose. It sent a formal protest in rejection of the government proposal and demanded an interview with the president, the minister of economy and finance, and the minister of labor and social security.

On December 6, the Liga submitted an offer that exceeded the SUTD's expectations, because they believed it was better to yield on this issue and to maintain a more harmonious relationship: effective December 1, 2010, to June 6, 2011, the offer consisted of a 37.6 percent wage increase for those workers at the lowest pay level, 26.6 percent for those at the second level, and 13.7 percent for those earning the highest wages. Minimum wage for domestic work was set at UYU 6,591.40 (US $297),[59] which equates to an hourly wage of UYU 34.67 (US $1.56).[60] The SUTD accepted the offer immediately and, after some further back and forth on the length of the contract, the union prevailed on its demand for a two-year agreement. On December 17, 2010, the representatives of the wage council for Group 21 signed the second collective agreement and decided to resume negotiations in March 2011 in order to resolve the issues that remained pending. Like the previous one, the second agreement had national jurisdiction and applied to all domestic workers and their employers. During 2011 and 2012, representatives from Group 21 met four times to formalize the wage adjustments for domestic workers that had been provided for in the second collective agreement. At the final meeting, the minimum monthly wage as of July 1, 2012, was increased to UYU 8,534 (US $384). For those workers at the lowest wage level, there was a 7 percent increase, and 6 percent and 5 percent for the higher wage levels.

The Third Agreement (2013)

On November 27, 2012, the delegates met to discuss the terms of the next agreement.[61] As in the past, Mabel Lorenzo de Sánchez led the representation from the Liga, but there was a slight change in the composition of the SUTD delegation.

A few of the main negotiators had abandoned the union because of political and personal differences; therefore most of the delegates, elected by the secretariat, were new to the wage council. As on prior occasions, the central issue was the increase in wages, once again with a wage-scale approach. From the onset, the SUTD decided not to include union leave within its demands because it did not believe it would make headway with the Liga de Amas de Casa and because it was the government's responsibility to protect this right. The SUTD had pressured the government regarding the issue of union leave, but thus far it had not presented any initiative to congress. The SUTD included within its demands paid time off for uterine and breast cancer scanning. The time off for cancer screening was an example of how the union often included rights that had already been recognized legally but which had not been enforced.[62] In addition, various issues were still on the bargaining table (including occupational health and paid free time for breastfeeding). The most contentious were those regarding a written contract, categories of work, and related wage rates.

On April 10, 2013, the government, Liga, and SUTD delegates to Group 21 signed the third collective agreement. In addition to one day off per year for uterine and breast cancer screening, the agreement provided for continued discussion within the wage council regarding job categories and the written contract with results prior to August 2015. It also declared that the parties would closely follow any advances regarding the National System of Care, particularly those concerning professional training that could be relevant to domestic workers and certain job categories.[63] Finally, it provided for increases to the minimum monthly wage of UYU to 9,544.43 (US $465),[64] which equates to an hourly wage of UYU 50.21 (US $2.45), and wage increases every year. As in the prior two agreements, a wage-scale approach was utilized, with larger percent increases for those earning less; these increments, however, were far less substantial than those in the past. As a measure to compensate for the less dramatic and more infrequent wage increases, a bonus for perfect attendance was included in the 2013 agreement. This agreement has national coverage and a three-year duration. There has been no progress in the discussion with respect to the issues of categories, wage rates, and the written contract. Following the adjustments of January 1, 2015, the current minimum wage for domestic workers in Uruguay is UYU 11,945.35 (US $468) per month or UYU 62.84 (US $2.46) wage.[65]

Enforcement

While the SUTD has been successful in improving the collective bargaining agreement for domestic workers, a key question is whether the agreement is enforced or enforceable. Domestic workers are often still unaware of their rights and, if they are aware, cannot exercise them fully because of employers' opposition. After each wage adjustment, domestic workers are fired and others face the same fate if their employers find out that they belong to the union. A few employers, in a desperate attempt to avoid compliance with the law and safeguard their privileges, hired Bolivians and Peruvians through employment agencies in those countries. Although these workers are covered by the same laws and collective agreements as their Uruguayan counterparts, they often do not know this. Hence they are sometimes preyed upon by their employers, who confiscate their passports, impose humiliating conditions that are in flagrant violation of their human rights, and threaten to throw them out on the streets if they protest. The SUTD and feminist organizations have denounced these situations and have demanded that the MTSS pinpoint for inspection residential neighborhoods known to concentrate migrant domestic workers.

The 2006 Uruguayan law for domestic workers is exceptional in the sense that it includes a provision for labor inspection. Worth noting in this regard is that approximately 130,000 households employ at least one domestic worker; therefore, routine inspection is a formidable challenge. The SUTD has collaborated with the Inspección General del Trabajo y la Seguridad Social (IGTSS)[66] by informing employers that they should not violate workers' rights and if they do, inspectors may go to their homes to investigate. Between 2010 and 2011, the IGTSS dedicated additional resources to routine inspection of households that employed domestic workers. Over this period, inspectors visited 9,200 households.[67] During the first year, the IGTSS limited the campaign to Montevideo and Canelones and focused on registration with and payment to the BPS. During the second year, it expanded the campaign to four other departments and covered other issues such as payment of wage increases, holiday pay, yearly bonus, and the availability of work clothes and equipment. The inspectors did not enter the households, so they did not require a judicial order. They asked the employer (and if he or she was unavailable, the worker) to answer a series of questions regarding work conditions and benefits and to show pay slips and documents from the BPS that would allow them to detect violations. They found that there was at least some degree of lack of compliance in 80 percent of the cases, most frequently regarding some aspect of social security. The IGTSS officials have emphasized that rather than utilizing inspection to sanction employers, they use it as an opportunity to educate them about their obligations and workers' rights, thus encouraging them to comply with the law.

In regard to education, an additional benefit for both the SUTD and the Liga associated with the experience of collective bargaining has been the legal service provided by members of the Law Faculty from the Universidad de la República. In

August 2011, the BPS signed an agreement with the Universidad de la República in which the Law Faculty would designate two lawyers to provide legal consultation to the SUTD and the Liga in exchange for payment by the BPS. A lawyer and a group of students from the university participate in a legal aid clinic at the union that meets weekly; they found that workers' most frequent complaints were with regards to unpaid overtime, retention of holiday pay, lack of compliance with wage increases, and problems with social security. The legal aid clinic has contributed to compliance because it educates workers regarding their rights and assists them in formulating and placing grievances. The BPS agreement with the university has also provided the Liga the legal counsel that it demanded during negotiations and legal services to employers on a drop-in basis at the Liga office. The lawyer from the university and the Liga believe that the education of employers regarding their rights and obligations is key to formalization of domestic employment. The lawyer offers information and assistance to employers, who usually lack the knowledge and managerial skills needed to keep track of records, fill out forms, and calculate BPS payments, premiums, wage increases, overtime pay, and additional compensation. An important outcome of this collaboration between the BPS, the SUTD, the Liga, and the Law Faculty has been the publication and dissemination of a manual with information about the rights and obligations of domestic workers and employers, the legal framework, BPS procedures, accident insurance, and occupational health and safety and other issues.[68]

Reflections about the Negotiation Process

The current leadership of both organizations emphasizes the cordial relationship they share. According to personnel at the MTSS, the climate of bargaining within Group 21 is atypical and less conflict-ridden than that involving other sectors.[69] This is attributed to the character of the domestic work relationship, namely that it is between women, home-based, care-oriented, and not geared toward the generation of profit.

Given that the SUTD is part of a workers' federation, it is to be expected that their bargaining tactics will be fairly traditional. SUTD representatives indeed used such traditional tactics as leaving a session if the other party makes a totally unacceptable (offensive) offer, leafleting during the negotiations to build public support and undermine the other parties when there is a conflict, and threatening to strike. Yet the negotiations were also influenced by the dynamics of domestic employment. For example, the importance of polite demeanor cannot be extrapolated from the class and gender relations that are entrenched in notions of respectability and which are so evident in domestic employment. The preference for inclusion of domestic workers with years of job experience and seasoned activists on the bargaining team implicitly acknowledges the exceptionality of domestic work in terms of its content, relations, and workplace. Finally, the reference to a possible strike evokes a powerful image that underscores that domestic work is absolutely fundamental to society.

The negotiation process has been informed by the underlying principle that domestic work is vital to society.[70] From the standpoint of Mabel Lorenzo de Sánchez, the household is at the heart of the negotiation. It is not simply a physical sphere; rather it is basic to the domestic economy, family relations, and well-being. Consequently, formalization of domestic work and compliance with the law are considered positive for everyone in the sense that they contribute to harmonious, orderly workings of the home and to a more just society. The members of the SUTD know that their work is essential, like the domestic workers who argued that they were the "oil in the wheels" of society in their struggle for a convention at the 99th International Labor Conference. At the same time, the exceptionality of domestic work has also been used by the Liga as an argument against the right to union leave, because it would be a burden to the individual household, which would pay for services not rendered.

If one considers that in 2005 there was not even a law regulating domestic work in Uruguay, the change over the past decade has been extraordinary. Although this certainly reflects the commitment of the FA government to improve domestic workers' conditions, this change started four decades ago when domestic workers began to organize. The election of the FA government provided the political opportunity, but the extension of labor rights, including collective bargaining, would not have happened absent the organizing of domestic workers into the SUTD. In turn, that organizing would not have happened without the support of the PIT-CNT and in particular the federation's Gender Department. Nor was the adoption of the law the end of the story. The establishment of the wage council, workers' inclusion in the wage council, the implementation of measures that enforce the law, and the collective agreements are products of domestic workers' political work, not simply a gift from the government. Therefore, the Uruguayan experience illustrates the importance of the participation of organized domestic workers in defining the terms of their work life and of transforming their reality.

Through the collective bargaining process, the SUTD has been able to win rights that were not included in the 2006 law nor the 2007 regulatory decree: work clothes and equipment, a seniority bonus, premium for perfect attendance, additional compensation for night work, a bonus for work done in a location other than the normal household, compensation for a reduction in work hours or workdays, full payment of workdays that are suspended by the employer, and an additional paid holiday, August 19, designated as Domestic Workers' Day. All these formed part of the platforms of demands that the SUTD presented.

There are other provisions in the collective agreements that strengthen clauses in the 2006 labor law and the 2007 regulatory decree (such as overtime pay) or other recent laws that theoretically covered domestic workers (Law 18.345, special paid leaves for study, family deaths, adoption, marriage). Their inclusion in the collective agreement reaffirm that domestic workers have these rights. In particular, the SUTD hoped that the collective agreement would help to increase compliance with legal requirements to pay for overtime. In fact, members of the SUTD note that live-in work has actually declined because employers realized that in order to comply with the law, they would have to pay quite a bit of overtime.

Without a doubt, collective bargaining has contributed to the increase in wages and registration in the BPS, results that were mentioned earlier in this chapter. The government, the Liga, and the SUTD are firmly committed to formalization of domestic work; this was included in the first collective agreement. The government has made it easier for employers to make their various social insurance payments. The Liga educates employers about their obligations regarding BPS and BSE payments, and the SUTD disseminates information about social protection to workers. The minimum wage for domestic workers has more than tripled since collective bargaining began in 2008, and the average real wage for workers rose almost by 100 percent between 2006 and 2012. The gap between domestic workers' earnings and those of other women workers also has narrowed during this period.[71]

Finally, the collective bargaining process has reaffirmed domestic workers' status as workers and made evident that the problems they face are shared by other workers and therefore require collective solutions. Furthermore, their participation in negotiations has bolstered the SUTD as the authority that legitimately represents the more than 100,000 domestic workers in Uruguay. Membership has increased substantially during the past few years, which suggests that more domestic workers are convinced that union membership is a means to safeguard their rights. Still, these form a small minority; less than 4 percent of domestic workers belong to the union. The union recognizes that despite their work and campaigns by the government, the majority of domestic workers still are unaware of their rights, are wary of union participation, or are afraid of employer reprisals. At the same time, Mabel Lorenzo de Sánchez has found that employers still show little interest in joining the Liga, whose membership has not grown. The reasons employers do not organize are unclear, but probably at least one obstacle is their lack of identity as employers derived from the often fuzzy boundaries between labor and family-like relationships in domestic employment.[72]

Collective bargaining for domestic workers remains exceptional globally and there is considerable variation as to its scope, content, and participants.[73] In the absence of other organizations that were willing to represent employers on the wage council in Group 21, the Liga accepted this responsibility not because it identified per se with employers of domestic workers or was aware of their rights and obligations, but because it believed in the importance of domestic work and a more just society. Liga participation on the wage council granted more visibility of housewives' contribution to society and their demand for a pension, but there has been no advancement in this regard. On the other hand, participation on the council forced the Liga to analyze what are the interests, rights, and obligations of employers, how to reconcile these with those set forth by the SUTD, and how to educate employers about their rights and obligations.

The collaboration between the SUTD, the Liga, and different sectors, as well as the emphasis on education, dialogue, respect, and, one might add, imagination, have been hallmarks of the politics of paid domestic work in Uruguay during the past decade. They have been effective. This experience also illustrates how the Uruguayan case can serve as a model to other countries.

Appendix 4

LIST OF INTERVIEW SUBJECTS

	NAME	ROLE	TYPE AND DATE
1.	Gladys Arévalo	Member of SUTD 2007–2011. Former sales worker and present domestic worker. Current member of the Association María Goretti.	Personal interview November 21, 2012
2.	Karina Batthyány Dighiero	Researcher about domestic work, Departamento de Sociología, Facultad de Ciencias Sociales—Universidad de la República.	Personal interview November 22, 2012
3.	Dolly Mariela Burlón	Member of SUTD 2005–2010. Participated as substitute delegate for the SUTD in the negotiation in 2008–2010. Has always been a domestic worker. Now a member of Las Jazmines, an NGO.	Phone interview November 26, 2012
4.	Mariselda Cancela	Pro bono lawyer for the SUTD 2005–2010. Participated in negotiation in 2008–2010.	Personal interview November 25, 2012
5.	Matilde Castillo	Member SUTD 2005–2011. Propaganda commission. Delegate to collective bargaining, 2008–2010. Former garment worker and present domestic worker. Current member of the Association María Goretti.	Personal interview November 21, 2012 Phone interview January 26, 2013
6.	Juan Carlos Cerreta	Lawyer, legal aid clinic for domestic workers, SUTD (agreement between Banco de Previsión Social and Universidad de la República).	Personal interview November 26, 2012 Phone interview January 26, 2013

	NAME	ROLE	TYPE AND DATE
7.	Valeria España	Coordinator of program for domestic workers (including blog trabajadorasdomesticasmercosur), Cotidiano Mujer (feminist NGO).	Personal interview November 25, 2012
8.	Graciela Espinosa	Member of SUTD since 2007. Current chief delegate of Organization Commission. Participated in negotiation 2008–2010 (more of an observer in 2008). Former meat packing worker; now employed as domestic worker.	Personal interview November 23, 2012
9.	Beatriz Fajián	Secretary of gender, equality and diversity, PIT-CNT. Health worker.	Personal interview November 23, 2012
10.	Mabel Lozano de Sánchez	President of the Liga de Amas de Casa, Consumidores y Usuarios de la República Oriental del Uruguay. Delegate to negotiation of first and second agreements and tripartite commission about union leave, categories, and written contract.	Personal interviews November 20 and 22, 2012 Telephone interview May 18, 2015
11.	Nelson Loustaunau	Vice minister of labor and social security, president of Group 21 (domestic service) of wage council. Author of various articles about legal aspects of domestic work.	Personal interview November 22, 2012
12.	Cristina Otero	Primary leader of SUTD in 2005–2009. Organization commission. Participated in negotiation 2008–2009.	Personal interview November 21, 2012 Phone interview January 26, 2013
13.	Nora Pacheco	Member SUTD 2006–2011. Organization commission. Delegate to collective bargaining, 2008–2010. Former garment worker and present domestic worker. Current member of the Association María Goretti.	Personal interview November 21, 2012 Phone interview January 26, 2013
14.	Jimena Ruy López	Ministry of labor and social security, delegate to Group 21 (domestic service) of wage council	Personal interview November 23, 2012
15.	Gonzalo Uriarte	Director of legal aid clinic, Facultad de Derecho Universidad de la República Uruguay	Personal interview November 26, 2102
16.	Various members of SUTD Commissions	Commissions of SUTD	Group interview November 21, 2012
17.	Various members ofAsociación María Goretti	Former members of SUTD. Members of Asociación María Goretti	Group interview November 23, 2012

BEER PROMOTERS IN CAMBODIA

Formal Status and Coverage under
the Labor Code

Mary Evans

Cambodia is a poor country, with most of its citizens still living in the rural countryside. Since the end of the Khmer Rouge, it has gone through a period of economic recovery, but working conditions remain poor and wages or earnings are too low for the average Cambodian worker to subsist on. Additionally, a large share of the country's workforce is engaged in informal employment. The Cambodian Labor Code covers workers who work for an employer according to an employment contract and under the direction of the employer; while in principle this does not necessarily exclude informal waged workers, in practice many forms of employment are treated as outside the purview of the law.[1]

This makes it difficult for unions to organize informal workers. Informal workers can join associations,[2] which, although beneficial, do not allow them to engage in traditional collective bargaining with employers.[3] One group of informal workers who have received a great deal of attention internationally and locally are women hired by beer companies to promote their brands. This chapter focuses on the struggle of Cambodian beer promoters to improve their working conditions. The case involves two components, the first a successful campaign to provide formal status for beer promoters[4] working for the Cambodian brewer Cambrew Ltd. and the second an ongoing struggle by the Cambodian Food and Service-Workers Federation (CFSWF) to engage in collective bargaining on behalf of the beer promoters. Each of the components of this case involves a wide array of actors, both international and local. These include Cambrew and its majority owner, the Danish company Carlsberg. They also include

Danish unions, the US-based Solidarity Center, and various nongovernmental organizations (NGOs). Locally, both the CFSWF and a government-affiliated (yellow) union contend for the representation of these workers and collective bargaining rights.

This case points to the role of several factors in improving the status and condition of informal workers. Particularly key has been the attention and efforts of international NGOs. Global labor solidarity has also been essential, with labor organizations based in Denmark, Australia, and the United States all playing a role. While the employers in the industry have created a code of conduct that led to some improvement for the beer promoters, they have been more resistant to collective bargaining with independent unions. This is also a story about a traditional union organizing a new constituency and the interunion conflict that has resulted. At the same time, the beer promoters themselves have acted on their own behalf, particularly through engaging in a strike against one of Cambrew's brands in 2011.

Cambodia's Economy and Labor Force

Cambodia, a small country consisting of 14.1 million people, has experienced rapid growth and development since its initial emergence as a market economy in the late 1990s.[5] The development of the nation created the conditions for growth in manufacturing, construction, and tourism. With the influx of new capital and foreign, direct investments, Cambodia's gross domestic product (GDP) has been on the rise. In the period from 2004 to 2007, the GDP grew an average of 11.1 percent.[6] Approximately 60 percent of the GDP can be attributed to the informal economy.

Despite robust economic growth in the past two decades, wages remain low in comparison to other countries. The average formal worker, working at least six days a week, earns an average wage equivalent to US $50 per month.[7] While the standard of living has gradually increased for some workers, many workers in the formal economy are paid a set salary that is too low to pay for their daily consumption, forcing many of them to also engage in informal work in order to supplement their fixed income.[8] Workers in formal employment include most government workers, administrators and office workers, some garment and industrial workers, and some tourism workers.

In 2013 in Cambodia, 82.8 percent of all people between the ages of fifteen and sixty-four were employed: 77.6 percent of all women and 88.5 percent of all men.[9] Almost 60 percent of all workers were still employed in the agricultural sector, producing rice as the chief export, which accounted for 36 percent of the GDP.

Extent of Informal Work

As in most countries, the exact scope and size of the informal economy is not fully known. It is estimated that the informal economy makes up approximately 80 to 90 percent of Cambodia's workforce, with over half of it women.[10] Studies performed in the past differ on the exact definition and extent of informal employment in the country.[11] According to 2013 data, 60.1 percent of women and 49.6 percent of men are "own-account/self-employed" workers, a category typically closely aligned with informality.[12] Informal work in Cambodia is not a temporary phenomenon. In fact, it is growing steadily.[13]

Informal workers have no social protections or benefits and are generally seen as excluded from the coverage of collective bargaining agreements. Informal employment is characterized by high risks and low earnings and a frequent lack of work or employment security. Workers are further marginalized due to fierce competition in a labor market saturated with unskilled workers. Due to rapid urbanization and the ensuing loss of land caused by development, an increasing number of workers flooded into urban areas in search of employment. Very few poor, internal migrants from rural areas qualify for formal jobs; they rely instead on low earnings from informal employment to survive.

Formal workers are normally covered by the country's social security system for health and insurance benefits. In an established employer and employee relationship, two types of employment contract can cover workers:[14] either a fixed duration contract (FDC)[15] or an undetermined duration contract (UDC).[16] Workers with an FDC can be hired for a period of up to two years.[17] These contracts can be continually renewed at the discretion of the employer. After two years, an FDC must become a UDC or a permanent contract.[18] Workers are typically considered as informal when they are not covered by any contract, are employed casually, or are employed or self-employed in a small, unregistered business.

Informal employment is sometimes a result of the employer's choice—either a formal firm, an informal unit, or a household—to not register the business with the Ministry of Labor in order to procure licensing. The process of registering is associated with high costs and confusing paperwork that can be time consuming. Registering also means that employers must then provide their employees with contracts, establish a set salary, provide benefits, and abide by the labor codes, which opens up the possibility of workers organizing into unions.[19]

Gender Norms and "Women's Work"

Even though one-quarter of households are headed by women, Cambodia is still a very traditional country in terms of gender equality.[20] In general, women are still viewed as unequal to men. Cambodian culture and customs dictate what is expected from women in terms of behavior. Women remain tied to the home, where they are primarily expected to fulfill their roles as housewives and mothers while men are expected to provide for the family and act as protectors. If a woman is employed, her work is not usually valued as highly as a man's and her responsibility is still primarily to her family.

Women's behavior is dictated by societal notions of what is decent or indecent. Customarily, women are expected to remain home at night. If they are employed, there are strong views as to what constitutes a respectable and decent job. Women who work in any employment that generally operates at night, including beer gardens, karaoke bars, coffee shops, night clubs, and other nighttime jobs are looked down upon and are often assumed to be engaging in prostitution.[21] They are labeled as "indecent, unrespectable, loose and promiscuous."[22] They are often viewed as amoral, even if they do not sell sex. Men are not held to this same standard. At the same time, in the service sector generally and in tourism in particular, appearance plays an important role in whether women will be hired. Employers will typically hire young and attractive women in order to entice their male clientele.

The sex industry in Cambodia is extensive. Aside from sex workers in brothels, there are a great number of women working as beer promoters and in other service or entertainment sectors who are selling sex to their customers to supplement their low income from their regular employment.[23] In the 1990s and up until the early 2000s, Cambodia had one of the highest rates of HIV in Asia. One out of five beer promoters is HIV/AIDS positive, according to a government survey.[24]

There have been efforts in the past few years to change the way women are viewed in Cambodian society. The Cambodian government has made an effort to encourage Cambodian society to respect and value women through a program called "Neary Rattanak" or "Women are precious gems," but the change is gradual in a society that still holds traditional beliefs.

Labor Movement Size, Scope, and Role in the Economy

After the Paris agreement in 1991, the Constitution of the Kingdom of Cambodia was established in 1993, designating the country a constitutional monarchy. Formally, it was based on the principles of liberal democracy and pluralism.[25] Over the past fifteen years, there has been political stability, with the country adopting a parliamentary system and evolving into a quasi-democratic system. The Constitution of 1993 included provisions for the formation of unions for peaceful demonstrations.[26]

The current independent labor movement in Cambodia is still in its fledgling stages at less than two decades old.[27] In 1997, following some years of nominal democratization, Cambodia established a new and more liberal Labor Code that allowed workers the right to form independent unions.[28] Like many countries, Cambodia has three levels of unions within its national borders: enterprise, federation, and confederation. There are a total of ten major confederations that are a part of Cambodia's labor movement, with many individual union federations and associations under each confederation.[29] Nuon and Serrano noted that the difference between associations and unions are that unions were legally created under the labor law framework, which includes only formal workers, while associations were created to represent informal and other workers who were not covered by the labor law.[30] Associations cannot legally engage in traditional collective bargaining with an employer.

Each of the confederations has its own ideology and agenda. It is not uncommon to have many different unions within the same factory based on different political party alliances, personalities, and opportunism.[31] This creates a confusing environment for both workers and management as each union's demands and philosophy can differ drastically from one another. Multiple unions in a shared workplace have a tendency to compete against one another for the recruitment of new members. Union membership retention can be problematic as workers go from one union to another.[32]

There are two main confederations, the Cambodian Confederation of Trade Unions (CCTU) and the National Union Alliance Chamber of Cambodia (NACC)[33] that are affiliated with the ruling government's party or the Cambodian People's Party (CPP).[34] Government-affiliated unions are often much more reluctant to engage in strikes because management and union leadership frequently work together. It is not unheard of for the union leadership positions to be held by company managers or government officials.[35]

The opposition to the CPP-affiliated unions is known as the Cambodian Confederation of Unions (CCU), which is affiliated with the SRP, or Sam Rainsy's Party (the Cambodian National Rescue Party, after its merger with the Human Rights Party). Initially they were the first to organize strikes within the garment factories. The CPP and the SRP unions tend to have frequent conflicts and confrontations with one another.[36] The Cambodian National Confederation (CNC) was originally affiliated with the Cambodian's People's Party, but after the September 2010 garment strike for higher wages, it became an independent union confederation.

The main independent labor movement exists within the Cambodian Labor Confederation (CLC), an independent confederation not affiliated with any political party. It claims 83,614 members from various federations in different sectors. There are nine associations and union federations within the CLC confederation, each based in a particular sector. One of these is the Cambodian Food and Service-Workers Federation (CFSWF).[37] Each of these federations is made up of local unions.[38]

The Cambodian labor movement claims more than 646,104 union members, or a little more than 8 percent of the working population.[39] The majority of union members work in the garment industry. Even though more men are employed in the formal economy, the majority of union members—approximately 84 percent—are women.[40] Conversely, men hold more than 80 percent of all major union leadership roles.[41]

Labor and Employment Laws and the Industrial Relations Framework

In 1993, a new Cambodian Constitution was created and implemented. The Constitution is by far the most important piece of legislation in the country, with all other laws and regulations lower in priority. It established a constitutional monarchy;[42] made provisions for the establishment of a Council of Ministers, a National Assembly, and a Senate;[43] recognized the United Nations Charter and the Universal Declaration of Human Rights;[44] recognized the right to form and be part of a union;[45] made provisions for the right to strike and hold demonstrations;[46] made provisions for a liberal, multiparty democratic government;[47] and had articles that dealt with discrimination, equal pay for equal work, and women's exploitation in employment.[48]

The Labor Code of 1997 is the next most important piece of legislation governing the workplace. The Labor Code sets the framework for labor and employment relationships by defining the rights and responsibilities of workers, unions, and employers. The Labor Code requires all unions and associations to register with the Ministry of Labor, and it makes provisions against discrimination for union activities and union member unfair dismissals.[49] It also details regulations for the use of strikes and collective bargaining and creates a mechanism for dispute resolution.[50] Importantly, the current Labor Code covers only workers with contracts, verbal or written, and requires employers to collectively bargain only with unions that have achieved "Most Representative Status" (MRS), or a majority of the workforce as members within one company.

Workplace disputes between unions or between employees and employers are typically first referred to the Ministry of Labor. When the Ministry of Labor cannot resolve the dispute it is referred to the Arbitration Council. The Arbitration Council has a tripartite structure and began resolving labor disputes in 2003.[51]

In the spring of 2011, the government of Cambodia released a draft of a new trade union law that could have provided real benefit to informal workers. That draft contained specific language that gave all workers the ability to form a union and not just an association, regardless of formal status. The associations for workers excluded from the current labor law would have been able to act as unions under the proposed trade union law. Unfortunately, this law was not enacted. Rather, following the garment workers strike in late 2013, a much more repressive trade union law was drafted by the government. Despite the extremely negative reaction from the ILO, the Solidarity Center, and other international labor groups, as of this writing the government is still threatening to sign it into law.

Social Protection under the Labor Code

The Cambodian Labor Code offers many protections for covered workers. It provides for regular time off, public holidays off, sick leave, and some basic maternity leave. It provides for premiums for overtime and for night shift work. The code also requires the employer to provide certain necessary medical assistance, treatments, medicine, hospital costs, and the worker's regular salary for the days not worked in cases involving temporary disability that is work-related. The National Social Security Fund, established in 2008, provides compensation for work-related accidents and illnesses.

Research Methods

Research for this chapter consisted of secondary literature reviews, twelve days of field research in Phnom Penh, focus group interviews, individual interviews, phone and Skype interviews, as well as e-mail correspondence with individuals, including key actors involved. Interviews were based on guided questions, which were translated into Khmer and read aloud.[52]

Interviews were conducted with representatives of the local independent unions CFSWF and the Independent Democracy of Informal Economy Association (IDEA); beer sellers, mainly from Cambrew and Cambodia Brewery Limited (CBL); tuk-tuk (three-wheeled taxi) and motorcycle drivers; vendors; business owners; the Ministry of Labor; Solidarity Center in Cambodia; LO/FTF (the Danish Confederation of Trade Unions Council for International Development) Denmark; the International Trade Union Confederation (ITUC), reporters, and various researchers who have covered informal employment and labor relations in Cambodia. Communication between the field research and those interviewed was established afterwards via e-mail communications, online Skype interviews, and follow-ups. Multiple focus groups were held with beer promotional workers from different brands.

The Beer Industry and the Beer Promoters

The beer industry in Cambodia has been growing rapidly for the past two decades. Due to globalization, there has been a rise in the consumption of alcohol, specifically foreign-owned beer brands in Cambodia. A small number of breweries exist within the country. The two major breweries are owned by Cambrew Ltd., located in Sihanoukville, and Cambodia beer in Phnom Penh. The other major beer companies that distribute products in Cambodia are Asia Pacific, CBL, Carlsberg, Guinness, and Heineken International.

Cambrew Ltd. has the largest market share in Cambodia. Carlsberg, a major Danish beer producer, owns the majority of the company. It produces Angkor Beer, Black Panther, Bayon Beer, Sting, and Klang beer, and it has licenses to various soft drink and bottled water brands in Cambodia. One of the Cambrew beer brands, Angkor Beer, currently holds the number one spot in the Cambodian beer market.[53] It employs approximately six hundred beer promoters and has been organized by two different unions. It currently operates a brewing plant in Sihanoukville. Since Cambrew is a privately owned company in Cambodia, information about the company's operation and profits is difficult to find. The company is a key member of the Beer Selling Industry Cambodia (BSIC).

Cambrew and other beer companies that operate in Cambodia employ beer promoter women to sell their brand to customers. Beer promoters are important to the profit of their brands, as they increase the total amount of product sold. Overall there are an estimated six thousand beer promoters working in Cambodia.[54] Beer promoter women are hired based on personal appearance and youth, important traits to their male clients. They normally wear the company colors, consisting of a top with the brand's logo and either black or matching bottoms. Their job is to pour and sell as much of the beer brand as possible. They typically work in bars, restaurants, and beer gardens late in the evenings, against the rules of what society deems as decent hours or decent workplaces, especially for women.

For more than a decade, the beer promoters in Cambodia have been of interest to the international community due to their precarious position and vulnerabilities within the workplace. Issues such as respectability, low wages, toxic workplaces that promote alcohol abuse, and sexual harassment by customers are characteristic of their daily work environment.[55] Approximately 80 percent of the beer promoters have dealt with unwanted sexual contact, while another 40 percent have been subjected to forced sex.[56]

Beer promoters often have little control over their workplace, experience frequent harassment by customers, and are forced to perform other serving duties by the local business owner. Most beer promoters try to avoid complaints by the restaurant or bar owners reported to their supervisor, since this will cause them to be transferred to a less busy location where they will earn less.[57]

Customers often associate them with sex workers and view them as prostitutes, often inappropriately touching, insulting, physically attacking, and verbally abusing them. Beer promoters often receive proposals from men while working to have sex with them in exchange for gifts or money. A few beer promoters have been threatened with guns by customers who abducted them and raped them afterwards.[58] Others have reported that they have been told by management and restaurant owners that "their job requires them to sell as much beer as possible and that they must do everything they can to appease the customers, including sometimes having sex with them."[59] Some beer promoters have said that complaints to management about a customer usually get ignored, or they are told that they are "beer girls, what did they expect?"[60] Many of them become drunk during work in an effort to get customers to drink more of their beer and then suffer from alcohol dependency.

All the beer promoters are female, and the company drivers are male. Most of these females have migrated from the rural countryside to Phnom Penh to look for work. They usually have attended school for a short time, and they are responsible for providing for their families back home in the village. Many women from the garment industry, due to the recent economic crisis that left so many workers unemployed, decided to become beer promoters. These women normally have a low level of education, if any at all. This makes it hard for them to find decent work that pays well outside of working in the garment sector or selling beer.[61]

Historically, beer promoters were paid by commission based on the amount of boxes or cases of beer that they were able to sell. Beer promotion workers who are signed to a contract with an employer are formal workers, while those who do not have a contract are informal.[62] While at one time all beer promoters were informal, in the past few years there has been an increase in the number of individual contracts that have been signed with the employers. The contracts are normally done on an individual basis and could last from six months to a year or longer. Commission-based workers are still considered informal, while salary-based workers are considered formal. Given the exclusion of informal workers from the Labor Code, there are substantial advantages to beer promoters if they can be formalized.

Labor Organizations

Cambodian Food and Service-Workers Federation (CFSWF)

Registered as a union federation in 2007 with the Ministry of Labor, CFSWF represents employees within the food and service sectors, specifically gas stations, the beer industry, garbage collection, wholesalers, and bakeries. Currently there are nine local unions within the federation. CFSWF is led by the union's president, Mora Sar. CFSWF claims a total of 2,165 union members, roughly one-third of whom work in gas stations.[63]

According to Sar, CFSWF began working with the beer promoter women in Cambrew and CBL in 2006. It did so because beer promoters were already receiving quite a bit of international attention from health organizations, researchers, and advocacy groups; IDEA, which often works together with CFSWF, was already involved with the promoters; and BSIC had opened the door for many beer promoters to receive contracts. This enabled them to be formally recognized as workers.

CFSWF receives support from the Australian Council of Trade Unions (ACTU) through APHEDA (Australian People for Health, Education and Development Abroad, "the overseas humanitarian aid agency of ACTU"), as well as the ILO Workers Education Programme, the US-based Solidarity Center, ITUC, and the sectoral global union federation, the International Union of Food, Farm, Hotel workers (IUF).

According to CFSWF, it is "working to empower beer promoters to protect their rights through organizing and raising awareness through activities." Its activities include organizing workers through outreach, holding union meetings, providing education and training, aiding in the formation of new unions, providing workers with protection in the workplace through dispute resolution, providing legal assistance and training, providing occupational safety and health training including awareness of HIV/AIDS, educating workers about alcohol abuse and where to seek help, educating workers about work violations and how to deal with sexual harassment. It also provides advocacy and support in instances where there are strikes, through campaigns, and through networking with other like-minded unions and social movements. It has been instrumental in trying to get the beer companies to recognize all their beer promoters and to get them to follow regulations regarding what workers are entitled to by law. The local CFSWF unions' right to represent the beer promoters in Cambrew and other beer companies in contract negotiations is based on gaining the majority of union memberships within a single workplace.[64]

CFSWF is the only trade union organization that organizes workers in more than one brewery within the BSIC membership group. In 2014, CFSWF had a total of 692 members in the beer industry. The CFSWF has 373 members at Cambrew, more than half of whom are women. CFSWF is a member of the CLC and recently affiliated with IUF.[65]

Independent Democracy of Informal Economy Association (IDEA)

CFSWF works closely with the Independent Democracy of Informal Economy Association (IDEA) to help the beer promoters. The organizations are affiliates of the same union confederation. IDEA is a 4,519-member association that organizes and works with informal workers. IDEA mainly organizes tuk-tuk and motorcycle drivers, street vendors, pull cart workers, and restaurant employees. Many beer promoters are affiliated with IDEA and have been aided by that organization regarding issues such as wage theft, grievances, and workplace abuses. IDEA was created in 2005; it originally had applied to register as a union with the Ministry of Labor but had been rejected due to the informal status of its members. Instead, it is now registered with the Ministry of Interior as an association.

IDEA's work includes educating members on their legal rights, constitutional rights, and land rights. They provide education on work and traffic laws and negotiate with local authorities on behalf of their members. They often negotiate for lower fees for street vendors. They also prepare complaints and seek compensation for damages when violations against their members are committed by often wealthy people. Approximately 30 percent of IDEA's members are women. IDEA has worked with the beer promoters since 2005.

Trade Union Workers' Federation of Progress and Democracy (TUWFPD)

The Trade Union Personnel Workers' Progressive of Angkor Beer (TUPWPAB) is a member of the Trade Union Workers Federation of Progress and Democracy (TUW-FPD) in the Cambodian Confederation for Workers Rights (CCWR), which is an affiliated member of the National Union Alliance Chamber of Cambodia (NACC). The union is the most representative trade union organization at Cambrew, representing 90 percent of the workers. It is also a member of the global union federation IndustriALL. TUWFPD is a government-affiliated union federation. It has organized the majority of Cambrew Ltd. beer promoters, with more than 430 members. The management of Cambrew Ltd. is also head of the TUWFPD union. TUWFPD is alleged to be a "yellow" union, a union that is set up and controlled by the employer.

Cambrew currently has a memorandum of understanding (MOU) with TUPWPAB and not with CFSWF. The company is also extremely secretive about what is contained in their MOU agreement with TUPWPAB.

The Campaign

International Attention

Initially beer promoters began receiving international attention due to their risk for HIV/AIDS. In the late 1990s, NGOs and public health advocates had taken an interest in sex workers and their risk for HIV/AIDS, but little was known about the beer promoters. Prostitutes and brothel workers were the main focus until the early 2000s, when various researchers began writing about the beer promoters, their working conditions, their low wages, and their high vulnerability to HIV/AIDS.[66] Ian Lubek, in collaboration with students and members of an NGO called SIRECHI (Siem Reap Citizens for Health Education and Social Issues) and then CARE International, a major NGO focused on the rights of women, girls, and marginalized ethnic minorities, found that the risk of HIV infection among beer promoters was 20–21 percent, a high risk. Both studies identified intoxication at work as a contributing factor. The CARE study found that beer promoters were engaging in unprotected sex based on a false assumption that they were safer because they were in control of selecting their customers.[67]

CARE contacted Heineken about its findings and with concerns regarding the high level of sexual harassment that beer promoters faced and the need for access to retroviral drugs through the company. They stressed the need for clear company policies to change the situation of the beer promoters. Heineken responded shortly thereafter and developed a Promotion Girls Policy in 2004 in conjunction with the "Selling Beer Safely" training and education program provided by CARE.[68] In 2005, CARE, in collaboration with Heineken International, Attwood Imports-Exports and Cambodia Breweries Limited, conducted a separate study on issues that affect the safety and protection of beer promoters in Cambodia. The study confirmed the sexual harassment and toxic work environment that beer promoters were subjected to.[69] CARE also listed recommendations to be taken by multiple stakeholders,[70] including the development of an international code of conduct for companies employing beer promoter women, recognizing and clarifying beer promoter women's employment status, and the development of a union or federation for beer promotion women that should be led by the women themselves.[71]

In the meantime, Lubek also published a paper on the consequences of the low wages paid by beer companies and the incentives low pay created to drive beer promoters to do whatever it took to sell more beer and keep the customers happy.[72] The media began to focus on the exploitation of the beer promoters, which attracted the attention of the most powerful Australian union.

In the spring of 2006, the Australian Council of Trade Unions (ACTU) launched a campaign to lift wages of beer promoters in Cambodia through its humanitarian arm APHEDA.[73] It began partnering with CFSWF to organize the Cambodian beer promoters. APHEDA had already made efforts to organize garment and hotel workers in Cambodia and also began an effort to get mandatory work contracts for "beer girls." It still continues to provide support to CFSWF.[74]

Beer Selling Industry Cambodia (BSIC)

Late in 2006, prodded by CARE, major beer producers in Cambodia came together to form the Beer Selling Industry Cambodia (BSIC). The membership of BSIC is made up of Asia Pacific Breweries, Cambodia Brewery Limited (CBL), Cambrew Ltd./Carlsberg, Guinness, and Heineken International. BSIC developed a code of conduct for its member companies, which sets voluntary industry standards.

In 2007, faced with international pressure and negative media associated with their brands from the exploitation of beer promoters,[75] BSIC began the implementation of its voluntary labor standards through its various members.[76] These standards included employment contracts according to Cambodian labor law; fixed basic salaries; clear supervision structures and grievance procedures; decent, branded uniforms; transportation and driver policies; "Selling Beer Safely" and life skills training; zero tolerance harassment approach and policies, no alcohol during working hours, including training on why and how to avoid it; and annual monitoring of compliance and impact by an independent party.[77]

BSIC brands account for more than 80 percent of the Cambodian beer market. BSIC relies mostly on CARE to provide training and workplace education on health and sexual harassment. In comparison to beer companies that are not a part of BSIC, BSIC members have a lower incidence of drinking in the workplace and fewer incidents of beer promoters selling sex.[78] CARE also helped to establish SABC (Solidarity Association of Beer Promoters in Cambodia), which provides peer-led training and education on sexual and reproductive health and acts as a sounding board for beer promoters and a place to share their experiences regardless of which brand they work for. SABC continues to work with beer promoters, with support from CARE, to offer training and education.

After much interest and campaigning from NGOs and international labor unions, such as ACTU and the local union, CFSWF,[79] many beer promoters gained contracts, formal status, and coverage under the Labor Code.[80] This created the possibility that a union could organize them. BSIC members also implemented a minimum wage of US $50 per month for all beer promoters promoting their brands, regardless of whether they met their sales targets. Many workers also moved from a commission-based pay system to a fixed base salary, with incentives that could be added to the basic salary. Others (around one-half) chose to remain on a commission basis.

Union Organizing

In 2006, CFSWF began trying to organize beer promoters. Since the union did not have contact information for the beer promoters, CFSWF had to approach workers directly at their restaurant and bar garden workplaces. Mora Sar, CFSWF's president, and a few other union members approached beer promoters at their workplaces, beer company offices, or on the street where beer promoters were known to get transportation back home.[81]

Since most workers had never heard of CFSWF or other independent unions, the first course of action was to build trust. The easiest way to build trust was to give them an outlet to vent their frustration and to listen to them talk about their problems.[82]

Beer promoters were afraid to talk to the union at first because they assumed that all unions were government affiliated and promoted only the government's own interest. One beer promoter indicated that she initially assumed that all unions were "bad and not interested in workers' rights, but were a way for the government to control the workers."[83] The beer promoters would eventually trust the union enough to give them their contact information, which enabled the union to maintain contact after they left the bars and restaurants.

Workers would eventually be invited to the CFSWF office to attend free vocationally related classes or meetings. To convince them to come, the union offered to cover their transportation costs (approximately US $2), which was more than what they made in one day. Free English classes were particularly good at generating interest from the beer promoters, many of whom wanted to learn English to make it easier for them to sell to foreigners.[84]

Once the beer promoters were more informed about their rights through workshops and training sessions, they gained confidence. They began to organize with the intention of forming a union and eventually branched out to organize others within their workplace, despite the restaurant owners' disapproval and Cambrew's displeasure.[85] As the number of beer promoters who were interested in joining the union grew, CFSWF established enough local unions with members from various companies in food service to file with the Ministry of Labor as an independent union federation in 2006.[86]

The Ministry of Labor gave CFSWF approval for the formation of a federation of food service workers in early 2007. After they received the approval letter, the union approached Cambrew to inform them that they were a union and that they wished to engage in collective bargaining on behalf of their members. Cambrew repeatedly refused to recognize CFSWF due to the presence of another union that had MRS status, TUPWPAB (Trade Union of Progressive Workers of Angkor Beer), the local union of the "yellow" TUWFPD.[87]

Many beer promoters did not realize they were part of the TUPWPAB. It was a government-affiliated union, with members automatically enrolled in the union and dues collected from their paychecks without their being aware of it. Some beer promoters in TUPWPAB claim that they were forced to join the government-affiliated union without their knowledge, while others claim that they didn't even know that they were part of the union until they saw that the union dues were taken out of their wages.[88]

With Cambrew consistently refusing to meet with CFSWF for years, CFSWF attempted to increase pressure. From 2007 until 2010, CFSWF tried sending letters to Cambrew to demand that they pay the Angkor beer promoters the overtime pay for all the extra days and hours they worked. Cambrew would order the staff to refuse to accept delivery of CFSWF letters and would ignore any attempts by CFSWF to engage them. According to Section IV and article 139 of the Labor Law, workers were entitled to at least one day off per week and were entitled to double pay on any holidays they worked. Many of the beer promoters who had been with the company before 2006 also claimed they were never paid overtime for any of the Sundays they had worked throughout their entire employment. Under the labor law, the company was only obligated to pay formally recognized workers the overtime. This included all the beer promoters who received a written contract from Cambrew since BSIC implemented their industry-wide standard for the beer industry in 2007.

As reports circulated about the success of the Cambrew brands in the beer market, the beer promoters fought for the company to pay them US $2 extra for overtime. Finally frustration mounted as Cambrew continued to slight the independent union. CFSWF beer promoters and TUPWPAB/TUWFPD beer promoters in Cambrew also clashed at the workplace.[89] The atmosphere was tense and words were exchanged between the two unions.[90] With the help of C.CAWDU and CFSWF, both affiliates of the same union confederation, the local union of beer promoters working at Angkor Beer took Cambrew to the Arbitration Council on June 15, 2011, over the unpaid wages. On July 7, the verdict from the Arbitration Council ruled in favor of CFSWF and the beer promoters.

By July 2011, Angkor beer promoters were getting ready to strike. CFSWF called for a national strike and boycott of Angkor Beer, with support from international press and support from the International Union of Food Workers (IUF). The management at Cambrew threatened to fire any beer promoter who participated in the strike. Many of the beer promoters were forced by management to thumb print (an alternative to a signature for illiterate workers) a document that stated "they would not participate in the strike and would be fired if they did." Management told workers that the document was necessary for work.[91]

In a case of "good timing," it was announced that a report by CARE Cambodia and the Solidarity Association of Beer Promoters in Cambodia about the exploitation of beer promoters was going to be released, which would bring added attention to the beer promoters who were about to go on strike.[92] Local media joined the cause by providing coverage of the women.

On July 25, 2011, approximately thirty of the beer promoters went on strike in front of Angkor Beer's distribution center in Phnom Penh. Originally, two hundred or more people had planned to show up, but due to fear of what the police might do, many were absent.[93] The leader of the local CFSWF union of Angkor Beer promoters was offered a management position and an increase in pay by Cambrew if she abandoned the strike.[94] She refused and the strike continued.

By August 1, 2011, Cambrew had threatened to fire the beer promoters for joining a union and for striking, while Carlsberg, the parent company of Cambrew Ltd., investigated the situation. By August 5, the Phnom Penh deputy governor asked the Angkor Beer promoters to suspend their strike for one week as a resolution was sought between the workers and Cambrew.[95]

On August 30, Cambrew finally agreed to pay the overtime wages that were owed to not only the beer promoters who went on strike, but also to all six hundred beer promoters at Cambrew.[96] The amount ranged from US $200 to US $300 for each beer promoter who was affected, depending on the worker's seniority.[97]

After the Strike

The beer promoters in CFSWF were successful due to the help and support they received from the local unions, the media, the international labor community, and NGOs. Their strike led to Carlsberg's taking interest and notice of the CFSWF union and the beer promoters. It also led to the government's being forced to intervene to stop the strike and demand that Cambrew and CFSWF resolve the issue of overtime wages quickly. CFSWF has been unsuccessful, however, in gaining negotiation rights at Cambrew given TUWFPD's Most Representative Status. TUWFPD does have an agreement with Cambrew, but the exact terms are not known, as they have refused to share the information with other trade unions or interested parties, claiming that there is "competitive" information included in the documents.[98]

Pressure from international organizations may have caused Carlsberg, as the parent company of Cambrew, to re-evaluate how they deal with unions in Cambodia. In the fall of 2011, the ITUC had asked the Danish union federation, LO, to contact Carlsberg about the issues in Cambodia. The ITUC had recently partnered with the LO to help increase dialogue between CFSWF and Cambrew and to focus on issues that affect beer promoters in Cambodia. Carlsberg and LO signed an MOU in 2012 that outlined steps to create collaboration between management and employees, including the establishment of effective social dialogue at Cambrew between management and trade union representatives. It also discussed steps to be taken to improve working conditions, including health and safety in general for beer promoters in Cambodia, and to address the negative view of beer promoters and the stigma attached to them. It committed the company to respect the freedom of association, the right of collective bargaining, the

BSIC's Code of Conduct, OECD guidelines for multinational corporations; and the UN Global Compact.

LO has been working with Carlsberg to help CFSWF get negotiation rights from Cambrew and has been encouraging CFSWF and TUWFPD to work together. CFSWF has expressed wariness about the LO's efforts to open up dialogue since they do not consider TUWFPD to be a legitimate workers' representative: "working with TUWFPD would not be possible, since as a yellow union, it would only be used as a tool for Carlsberg and Cambrew to weaken real workers unions [like CFSWF]."[99]

In the meantime, Cambrew still continues its attempts to discipline the members of CFSWF union. After the strike, CFSWF reported that twenty-one of the beer promoters who participated in the strike were transferred to different locations where they suffered a decrease in income due to the lack of business.[100] A few of the beer promoters were left with no choice but to accept the company's money and leave Cambrew. On the other hand, BSIC has accommodated the beer promoters' wage demands in the context of the successful campaign in 2013 by garment workers to increase the legal minimum in that industry. Although the government has established the country's minimum wage for all workers at $128 at the beginning of 2015, the beer promoters demanded $160 from the members of BSIC and, after a campaign including a job walk-off, were granted approximately that much, which increased their salaries to living wages.[101]

At the time of this writing (spring 2015) CFSWF has been able to organize two hundred of the Cambrew beer promoters, most of them in Phnom Penh and a smaller number in Siem Reap. Of the two hundred Cambrew beer promoters, eighty of them are employed under the Angkor Beer brand. The remaining 90 percent of beer promoters in Cambrew are organized by TUPWPAB. CFSWF has met with the production workers, drivers, and beer promoters in the other beer companies. Its strategy was to organize other workers starting in 2013. CFSWF claims that its strategy is supported by its federation leaders, with the international unions providing technical and financial support.[102]

CFSWF's campaign to organize beer promoters employed by Cambrew followed a series of events leading to the workers' formalization, beginning with increasing international pressure and attention with the assistance of international labor organizations and NGOs. Prior to 2006, NGOs, health activist groups, and international unions aided the beer promoters' broad campaign. International unions have been interested in the beer promoters because they work for well-recognized, profitable beer brands that come from countries known for their progressive views on social equality where the terms and conditions these women work under would never be tolerated. Under international pressure, the members of BSIC concluded that the beer promotion women should be considered direct employees, stipulating that they must have written contracts and receive benefits covered under the Labor Code. Once the beer promoters were able to obtain contracts, the beer promoters became clearly covered by the Labor Code, which granted them the right to overtime pay for work done normally on their weekly day of leave. This change in status also allowed them to form or join a traditional union instead of an association and to begin receiving benefits to which all formal workers are entitled. It enabled CFSWF to organize them as a union and the Arbitration Council to hear their case.

CFSWF has since been key to beer promoters' ability to gain decent work conditions and protections. Since 2006, CFSWF has worked steadily to advance the agenda of the beer promoters and has been instrumental in continuing to bring their exploitation in the workplace to the attention of the international unions and NGOs, who have more political leverage. At the same time, the beer promoters have also been caught in the middle of the conflict between the independent CFSWF and the allegedly "yellow" TUPWPAB. TUPWPAB has been able to take much of the credit for the gains achieved by CFSWF.

As a result of these campaigns, beer promoters have seen an increase in their wages. They have also seen a noticeable change in the way they are viewed and treated. Incidences of sexual harassment have dramatically decreased, in part due to their new image (crafted by CARE) and in part due to media attention and the help of unions and associations.[103]

Interestingly, although the situation of beer promoters has vastly improved, the burden and exploitation has shifted to a more vulnerable group of women, the hostesses. Hostesses are women who work within the same establishments as beer promoters, sitting and catering to the wishes of patrons. Working within the restaurants or local establishments and not hired by brands or companies, they operate without contracts and are dependent solely on tips for their earnings. They have no social protections from their workplace. They also are currently not unionized and have no collective bargaining rights. The burden of sexual harassment and forced drinking has, in essence, been passed on to the hostesses.[104]

This case clearly demonstrates what can be achieved when NGOs, unions, companies, and the international labor community combine to support workers' freedom of association rights to form or join independent unions. Informal employment in Cambodia is complex and not well understood. Workers themselves can often be employed in both the informal and the formal sectors. The many rights provided by the Labor Code are typically not accessible for informal workers, either waged or self-employed. Hopes for a more inclusive trade union law are currently on hold. Even with improvements in legal status, gaining respect for women working in informal employment also requires overcoming cultural gender-associated roles. This case makes clear that under the right circumstances, improvements in working conditions for informal workers are possible.

METHODOLOGICAL APPENDIX

Each person interviewed within the focus groups was given a copy of a consent statement and the guided questions. A group interview was held with CFSWF union elected officials, which consisted of two men and one woman. Another focus group was held with CFSWF-organized beer promoters from Cambrew. A group interview was held with the president and vice president of IDEA, while all other field interviews were conducted individually. Once the interviewer was back in the United States, the rest of the interviews were conducted via Skype in accordance with Cambodia's time zone and work hours, while other contacts were made via e-mail.

Interview Subjects

Local Unions and Associations

- Mr. Mora Sar—president of CFSWF
- Mr. Kri Suntha—secretary general of CFSWF
- Ms. Kinh Sopheap—deputy secretary general of CFSWF
- One female CFSWF beer promoter representative (Angkor/Cambrew)
- Three female CFSWF activists for beer promoters (Angkor/Cambrew)
- One female shop steward for CFSWF beer promoters (CBL beer/Tiger beer)
- One male union representative for CFSWF gas station attendant worker (Caltex)

- Mr. Vorn Pao—president of IDEA
- Vice president of IDEA
- IDEA tuk-tuk drivers and motorcycle drivers (ten males)
- IDEA vendor and sellers (three females and one male)

International Unions and Associations

- Mr. David John Welsh, country director in Cambodia's Solidarity Center
- Mr. Jeff Vogt, ITUC
- Miss Yon Sineat, LO/ FTF Council and former employee of Solidarity Center in Cambodia
- Mr. Jens Erik Ohrt of LO Denmark

Cambodian Government Official

- Ministry of Labor

Researchers and Reporters

- Mr. Shane Worrell, reporter covering labor issues for *Phnom Penh Post*
- Mr. Sam Grumiau, researcher and field investigator on the beer girls and beer companies, SOMO report "Promoting Decency?" 2012
- Ms. Melisa Serrano, coauthor of *Building Unions in Cambodia.*
- Mr. Veasna Nuon, coauthor of *Building Unions in Cambodia.*

Focus Groups

There were three focus groups held at different times with the beer promoters. The first focus group had all eight promoters present, while the second only had the union activists and leader. The third and last focus group held a combination. All eight beer promoters who were interviewed were female and represented various beer companies. They were commissioned and salaried workers. In order to maintain confidentiality, any information that might be linked to them or that could identify them has been removed or altered. They are known as beer promoter number 1 through 10, or BP1 to BP8.

- BP1, commissioned beer promoter (Angkor Beer/Cambrew Ltd.)
- BP2, commissioned beer promoter (Angkor Beer/Cambrew Ltd.)
- BP3, commissioned beer promoter (Angkor Beer/Cambrew Ltd.)
- BP4, commissioned beer promoter and former yellow union member (Angkor Beer), salary beer promoter (Angkor Beer/Cambrew Ltd.)
- BP5, salaried beer promoter (Tiger Beer/CBL)

- BP6, commissioned (Heineken)
- BP7, commissioned (San Miguel)
- BP8, commissioned (Tiger Beer/CBL)

Others

- Business owners of small and micro businesses in Phnom Penh
- Beer garden owners (interviewed while field researcher posed as customer)
- Police officers
- Restaurant and beer garden customers
- Restaurant wait staff
- Hotel owners

Documents and Secondary Literature

At present, Cambodia has a limited amount of economic statistical resources available. Most data before 1969 were destroyed, while data afterwards are limited. There is not much research or empirical data available on the unionization of the informal economy or informal employment in Cambodia. Most research on Cambodian workers focuses on the garment industry. Nuon's and Serrano's overview of the labor movement in Cambodia was an important source for understanding the past and present history of unions in this study. Other research by NGOs and academics on the informal economy and informal workers gave invaluable insight in understanding the need for unions and change in the workplace. Newspapers such as the *Phnom Penh Post* and the *Cambodian Daily* were used to provide background to the study.

INFORMALIZED GOVERNMENT WORKERS IN TUNISIA

Reinstatement as Formal Workers with Collective Bargaining Rights

Stephen Juan King

Subcontracting labor to avoid unionization and to deny workers their basic rights pertaining to social protections, job security, adherence to minimum wage laws, and respect for deadlines for the payment of wages has been a part of the Tunisian private-sector landscape since movements toward economic liberalization began in the 1970s. In some industries such as textiles, construction, and the hotel trade, a large majority of the workforce is temporary and recruited by subcontracting agencies. During the process of economic reforms in Tunisia in the 1990s, especially after International Monetary Fund (IMF)– and World Bank–sponsored reforms and the free trade agreement Tunisia struck with the European Union in 1994, the practice became widespread in the public sector.[1] This chapter analyzes the successful campaign waged by Tunisia's national labor federation, the Union Général Tunisienne du Travail (UGTT), and its affiliates to transform subcontracted labor (back) into standard employment in the public sector, and the UGTT's relative lack of success, so far, in accomplishing the same goal in the private sector.[2]

Subcontracting labor in the public sector pushed public-sector workers, mainly security guards and those employed in cleaning services, into informal employment. The UGTT's successful campaign has returned these workers to standard employment; subcontracting has been banned in the public sector. The research described in this chapter is based on secondary literature and documents from the International Labor Organization (ILO) and the Tunisian Bureau of National Statistics. In addition, the chapter is based on three focus group interviews: one with five leaders of the UGTT, including the current secretary-general, a second with six male subcontracted workers, and a third with six female subcontracted workers.

The chapter concludes that the Tunisian government capitulated to the UGTT's demand to end subcontracting in the public sector for several reasons: continuous pressure from the UGTT, which began before the fall of Ben Ali's regime in 2011; mounting public pressure from strikes and sit-ins that were publicized by a press freed from authoritarian strictures; the extraordinary opportunity presented by the regime breakdown, which made transitional governments in Tunisia desperate to lessen social conflicts by showing that they were bringing justice to workers and ending exploitation; and the fact that the union had allies within Tunisia's transitional governments who favored standard employment over subcontract labor and would have sought to end it without external pressure.[3]

The UGTT has also made some, though less, progress in eliminating the negative aspects of subcontracting labor in the private sector. Public and worker pressure to end subcontracting has led private-sector employers to increasingly utilize direct short-term contracts between employers and workers in the place of subcontracting agencies. For the private sector, in a sense, subcontracting has mutated into short-term contracts that yield the same material conditions and lack of labor rights. The UGTT is currently attempting, with limited success, to eliminate both serially renewed short-term contracts and subcontracting practices in the private sector.

Background on Tunisia

Prior to 2011, Tunisia could be described as a single-party regime that had been transformed from a populist Arab socialist orientation to a crony capitalist form of authoritarian rule in the decades that followed independence in 1956. Intensive civil resistance led to the swift, dramatic, and unexpected collapse of Zine El Abidine Ben Ali's authoritarian regime and launched the Arab Spring. Protests began December 18, 2010, and by January 14, 2011, Ben Ali had fled the country for Saudi Arabia. Ben Ali was only the second president of independent Tunisia and had come into power in 1987.

Subcontracting labor became a prevalent practice in the private sector in Tunisia in the early 1970s as the country launched an economic liberalization program and took steps to expand foreign investment. Economic liberalization policies were expanded in Tunisia in the late 1980s. In the public sector in Tunisia, subcontracting labor meant the end of standard employment for approximately sixty thousand workers, thrusting them into informal employment arrangements. As a whole, informal work represents a large part of the Tunisian economy. In a country of approximately 10.5 million people, it involves 35 to 42 percent of the labor force, around 50 percent of 800,000 unemployed individuals, and it represents 50 percent of the Tunisian gross domestic product (GDP).[4]

There are eight main types of informal work in the country: (1) microenterprises, often those who set up shop on streets or other public spaces, which can be fined by the authorities; (2) domestic service employment, those who do housework and clean offices; (3) economic activities such as embroidery and baking that take place in homes; (4) security services such as guards working at apartment buildings, in hotels, and in offices; (5) agricultural activities undertaken by seasonal or temporary workers; (6) smuggling goods across borders; (7) towing or repair services of any kind wherein the relationship with customers is through telecommunication; and (8) activities related to the weekly flea markets held throughout the country.[5] Tunisia also suffers from high unemployment; in 2014 the IMF reported an unemployment rate of 31.4 percent, 40.8 percent for women.[6]

In a country so dependent on informal employment, successful efforts to formalize informal waged employment by subjecting its activities to state control and regulation would offer enormous benefits to the population. It could improve labor market security (adequate employment opportunities through high levels of employment ensured by macroeconomic policies); employment security (protection against arbitrary dismissal, regulation on hiring and firing, employment stability compatible with economic dynamism); job security (the opportunity to develop a sense of occupation through enhancing competencies); work security (protection against accidents and illness at work, through safety and health regulations, and limits on working time); skill production security (widespread opportunities to gain and retain skills through innovative means as well as apprenticeships and employment training); income security (provision of adequate incomes); and representation security (protection of collective voice in the labor market through independent trade unions, employers' organizations, and social dialogue institutions).[7]

The UGTT and the Campaign to Reduce Subcontracting

The story of the success of trade union efforts to return public sector workers to standard employment in Tunisia begins within the context of the breakdown of an authoritarian regime in 2011, which opened up opportunities for collective action waged by Tunisia's national trade union federation. The next section discusses the history of the UGTT prior to the recent political opening, which increased its power and autonomy. This will be followed by a description of subcontracting practices, then an analysis of the UGTT's successful campaign to end subcontracting in the public sector and an evaluation of the progress made in the private sector to date.

The UGTT: Autonomy and Dependence

The UGTT is the primary trade union confederation in Tunisia. Currently, it claims 800,000 members, half of whom are women. It has regional structures and separate departments for public service and the private sector. As a confederation, it brings together numerous sectoral union federations, including those in public services such as transport, utilities, and health care. In Tunisian history, from the struggle for independence from French colonialism to the present day, the UGTT has had a varied relationship with the Tunisian government, with some periods of independence and other times of state control. Breaking from the French trade union organizations in the colonial era (1881–1956), the UGTT was the first independent trade union federation in Africa. The UGTT played an important role in the nationalist struggle and participated in the first independence government.

The secretary-general of the UGTT sat on the political bureau of the ruling party, and the UGTT automatically had a bloc of deputies in the National Assembly. Neo-Destour party leader and first president, Habib Bourguiba, named the head of the UGTT, Ahmed Ben Salah, economic czar in 1961. During his decade in power, Ben Salah was the architect of Tunisian Arab socialism.

The UGTT became a part of a corporatist regime of national unity that sought to organize and mobilize interest groups within the economy—labor, agriculture, business, students, professionals, etc.—under the ultimate control of the party-state. The UGTT's power was put to the test in the 1970s when the government shifted its policy from Arab socialism to gradual economic liberalization. Neoliberal economic policies led to painful material losses for Tunisian workers and peasants, especially in the late 1970s. Despite bureaucratic ties to the state apparatus and state co-optation efforts, in the 1970s and early 1980s the UGTT maintained an independent streak at times and often fought to defend the important gains made by workers and peasants during Tunisia's Arab socialist phase. Abdellatif Hamrouni, current secretary-general of Tunisia's federation of public works employees, describes this period of UGTT history in this way: "The question of the relationship between the UGTT and the regime is a complicated one. The federation's independence has indeed been relative. It has ebbed and flowed; there have been periods of estrangement from power and periods of strategic alliance."[8]

In the mid-1980s, during a period of public unrest, the head of the UGTT, Habib Achouar, and more than one hundred UGTT unionists were arrested, accused of mishandling union funds and lack of patriotism, and jailed.[9] Security forces and state party members took control over provincial offices of the UGTT and its headquarters in Tunis. The control of the UGTT was handed over to state party loyalists.[10] By 1987, an Islamist movement, later to become al-Nahda, the current dominant party in power in Tunisia, had replaced the UGTT as Tunisia's primary opposition social force. President Bourguiba's effort to neutralize the Islamists and the threat of civil war in retaliation led to the bloodless coup by Ben Ali in 1987. Once in power, Ben Ali sought to rehabilitate the UGTT but at a high cost to its independence.[11] UGTT members were freed from prison and free to rejoin a much more tightly controlled organization. Any strikes at any level had to be approved by the general secretary of the UGTT. No strikes were allowed at places of work. The regime had to be notified ten days in advance of the intention to strike. A closer collaboration between state authorities and the UGTT was instituted. The UGTT leadership for all intents and purposes had to be chosen by the regime. Dissident unionists were harassed by the security police.[12]

The co-opted leadership of the UGTT signed on to Ben Ali's economic policies, which were oriented toward the acceleration of economic liberalization including the full privatization of the economy. By 1992, the UGTT general secretary offered full support for the regime's structural adjustment policies that, at least in the short term, entailed severe pain for workers and peasants:

> Our union . . . has chosen in principle to adapt to international transformations by adopting new methods of work and intervention . . . in order to expand social justice and prosperity. Today, the union is trying to adapt to changes in the international economic system, the structural adjustment program, the new world order and the market economy. The task of meeting these challenges is the union's preoccupation.[13]

The Emergence of Subcontracting in the Public Sector

Within the context of a structural adjustment program supported by the World Bank, the International Monetary Fund, and the European Union, Ben Ali's government decided to outsource public services such as cleaning services and security guards. These activities were subcontracted out to the same agencies that supplied workers for private-sector enterprises.

The Tunisian government nominally selected subcontracting agencies because they had an existing process for ensuring that subcontracted workers were paying the correct social taxes from their wages and because the companies operated according to the Tunisian labor code.[14] According to both leaders of the UGTT and the laborers themselves, however, proper procedures were seldom applied. In practice, the switch to subcontracting meant that the Tunisian government would pay the subcontracting companies—typically small, local companies—the same amount that the government had previously paid the workers directly. The third-party subcontractors would pocket part of this payment for themselves and pay the workers the remaining portion, which obviously reduced their salaries.[15]

By the time of the Tunisian revolution, subcontracted work fell into a gray zone in the Tunisian labor code. Subcontracting in the Code de Travail (the primary legislation regulating labor in Tunisia) falls under the general provisions for the formation of contracts between employer and employee, and few specific provisions for subcontracting are found in the Tunisian law code as a whole.[16] The Code de Travail at the time of the UGTT campaign against subcontracting did provide the following guarantees to workers employed by businesses that subcontract labor:

> Article 28 stipulated that any business that subcontracts labor through a third party has the responsibility to pay for all salary, vacation, reparation for job-related accidents, and charges related to the national social security system due to workers in the case of insolvency of the third party.
>
> Article 29 stated that the business engaging in subcontracting is responsible, with the third party, to observe all the legally prescribed standards relating to work conditions, hygiene, safety, child labor, weekends, working at night, etc.
>
> Article 30 stated that the subcontracting business must, in the case that the employees under subcontract are working at a location other than its own offices, stores or factories, clearly post a sign indicating its full contact information.

Despite these provisions, subcontractors often failed to provide the social protections legally required in Tunisia for both standard employment and subcontracted labor, and they kept the length of contracts short to further immiserate this population and increase its vulnerability. Some elderly workers found out only at the moment of retirement that they in fact did not have any social security income at all. In addition, some cleaning services' workers in the public sector and security guards reported that they were asked to sign a contract to work and a letter of resignation at the same time. If the workers asked for benefits required by Tunisian labor laws, the subcontractor would simply implement the letters of resignation and fire the workers.[17]

The informalization of labor in Tunisia's public sector worsened the lives of workers in myriad ways. In many cases, there were no contracts at all, which enabled the subcontractors to avoid paying taxes and providing benefits. When asked about signing a contract a worker replied:

> No. He gave us money in the street. Someone would come to us carrying a folder. He would gather women together and ask us if we knew others that would like to have a job. When we met him in the street again he would take us to the places to clean. At the end of the month, we would meet the same way and he would pay us in the street. The amount of money was very little, forty to sixty Tunisian dinars (one Tunisian dinar equals approximately sixty cents). This was in 1998.

Workers in the public sector complained about losing health insurance and retirement benefits when they became employees of subcontractors.[18] Their pay was sharply cut. Some claimed that subcontractors kept two-thirds of their former pay and paid them one-third:

> Life was much cheaper [in 1998] but that [forty to sixty dinars a month] wasn't enough at all. You can't do anything with so little money, but I had to do it. Women that are working in cleaning are usually forced to do it. We have children. We are widows. Some can't read. We have to pay rent. You have to have any job to survive with your kids.

Another said:

> Working for the subcontractors my family could not afford to eat meat for two years. We ate bread and harissa (Tunisian spicy paste).

Public-sector security guard salaries at the end of the 1990s ranged from 45 TD to 170 TD a month. By then, for the most part, they had become informalized workers paid in cash and without benefits. Even a guard receiving pay on the higher end of the range claimed that after paying his bills he would be left with 10 TD for expenses for the rest of the month.

In addition to sharp pay cuts and the frequent loss of health care insurance and retirement benefits, informalization and subcontracting produced work schedules that strained family life. The jobs were fully segregated by sex. (Women worked for the cleaning services, usually in split shifts, and men worked as security guards.) The women who worked for the cleaning services subcontractors often worked for a few hours in the mornings and then returned home at night. Due to the distance from their homes, most spent the time in between daily shifts loitering in public areas, usually public parks. Security guards worked twelve-hour shifts five days a week. Due to the low pay many had to work all seven days for twelve hours each day in order to earn a livable wage through overtime pay. They complained of having to stand outside for long hours in the cold in cheap uniforms, conditions that made them sick.

For women the move from standard employment to subcontracting dramatically increased sexual harassment. Their split schedules forced them to walk home, usually several miles away, at night, and they confronted aggressive harassment in the streets. The people working in the public offices lost respect for them and some sexually harassed them with impunity. As one woman who has since regained her standard job put it:

> To this day I remember the suffering from working for subcontractors. I used to be miserable and hungry. We got back home late. We faced sexual harassment in the office and in the street. In the office they touch you and if you don't let them do that they will get you in trouble and create a problem for you. Added to that when you go out at night at 8 and you live far from work like me, thirteen kilometers away, you are walking in the streets at 11 pm at night when you finish work. Men harassing you everywhere.

Both the women working for the cleaning services and the men working as security guards in the public sector claimed that moving from standard employment to subcontracting engendered humiliating treatment:

> They treated the women who are cleaning very badly. They treated us much worse than they treated slaves. They had no respect for us. They didn't care about our dignity. They didn't even consider us as human beings. They shouted at us all the time. If you made any mistake or forgot to do anything even if it was not important you were treated worse. If the boss told the subcontractor about poor performance, you would have to work two or three days without pay. People were fired for no reason, beaten, bitten, hit, slammed around. Workers in the offices sometimes took things from each other, but the women cleaning and the people guarding the buildings were always the ones accused of stealing.

A security guard complained that a colleague was fired and put in jail for eight months after being accused of stealing a box of chocolates:

> What was the value of that box of chocolate? He has a family to take care of. They saw him on camera picking the box up from the floor. It was part of his job to check everywhere in the building. I have cleaning women working with me and I saw how badly they got treated. They look at them and us in the same way, with no respect. I said hello to someone in the office once and she answered, "is that the door talking to me?" I said, "no the person watching the door is talking to you." They considered us as nothing, like we didn't exist. They didn't consider us as human beings doing this work.

Even the co-opted UGTT of the 1990s could not ignore the effect of the spreading practice of subcontracted labor in both the public and private sector. The UGTT fought the practice from its inception.[19] There were also spontaneous protests from the workers themselves when the phenomenon appeared in the public sector.[20] But the pressure generated by the UGTT and public sector workers was not enough to end the practice. The practice remained in force from the 1990s until the breakdown of Ben Ali's authoritarian regime, which facilitated successful collective action by the UGTT to end subcontracting in the public sector.

The UGTT Campaign to End Subcontracting

During the Ben Ali era, there was a concerted attempt by the UGTT to organize and bring standard employment to government workers in Tunisia. In 1999, eliminating the practice of subcontracting labor in the private sector became a formal part of the agendas of the National Congress of the UGTT and of regional unions in Tunisia. There were heated debates about the issue at all levels of the UGTT—economic commissions, national congresses, regional and sectoral unions—running into the 2000s. The overall message from the UGTT was that subcontracting labor amounted to inhuman exploitation of labor.[21]

The UGTT deployed a number of tactics during the Ben Ali regime to end labor subcontracting in the public sector. At one point, the head of the UGTT's Federation Generale des Professions et des Services (FGPS), Mongi Abderrahim, conducted a hunger strike in support of these exploited workers. The AFL-CIO and other international unions signaled their support for Abderrahim. The British Parliament voiced their solidarity with the UGTT leader. In response to the hunger strike, UGTT pressure, and the internationalization of the issue, the head of the Ministry of Social Affairs in Tunisia negotiated an end to Abderrahim's hunger strike. The negotiations included a promise by the government in 2002 that it would open a dialogue with the UGTT to eradicate labor subcontracting.

In addition to Mongi Abderrahim's hunger strike, the UGTT organized sit-ins at the working places of these laborers. Sectoral heads of the various federations of trade also took a leadership role to end labor subcontracting. This occurred throughout the country in Tunis, Sfax, Ben Arous, Manouba, Ariana, Sousse, and elsewhere. It was a long struggle that was prominent for the UGTT from 2002 to 2011. The leaders of the UGTT's sectoral affiliates organized strikes and awareness seminars for the workers they organized. They waged a perpetual media campaign during these years to highlight the everyday exploitation of subcontracted labor in the public sector. Despite these various efforts, however, the practice remained throughout Ben Ali's time in power.

The Tunisian Revolution

Corruption involving close members of the president's family, high unemployment rates, regional disparities, fatigue from an oppressive security apparatus, and the lack of political freedom fueled the popular uprising that brought down Ben Ali on January 14, 2011. The spontaneous popular uprising began in the poorer interior part of the country. The UGTT, sensing the end of the regime and government control, helped to maintain the momentum and to spread it to the country's urban centers and wealthier coastal regions.[22] Pressure from its base and the spontaneous protests, strikes, and demonstrations ignited in Tunisia's poorer interior regions in December of 2010 and fueled the UGTT leadership's new confrontational stance toward Ben Ali's regime.

Successive interim governments were formed after the regime's collapse. These interim governments faced enormous challenges as they tried to steady the country until the election in October 2011 of the Constituent Assembly charged with writing Tunisia's new constitution and making a formal transition to democracy. The interim governments of the transition faced extremely volatile social conflicts. The economic problems that fueled the uprising were exacerbated by the regime's breakdown. Strikes and demonstrations, spontaneous and organized, paralyzed economic productivity. The tourism industry collapsed. New political freedoms of voice and association made it impossible for transition leaders to ignore rising expectations for economic improvements from various groups in society. A free press publicized the demands for social change.

Immediately after the fall of the Ben Ali regime, the UGTT trade union federations capitalized on the weakness of the central government and the spontaneous mobilization of subcontracted laborers—street protests, strikes, sit-ins—to put great public pressure on the transition government to abolish all precarious work in Tunisia, especially subcontracting in the public sector.[23] While leading the way in organizing protests against subcontracting, the UGTT and its affiliate, the Federation Generale des Professions et des Services (FGPS), were aided by spontaneous worker protests and efforts at self-organization. Sometimes organizational forces from above and below met in the middle. After the revolution, strikes and protests became common. People working for subcontractors began to talk among themselves about how to improve their deplorable working conditions. A small group of cleaning services workers at the Tunisian National Social Insurance Office, SNSS, decided to go to the UGTT for help. The UGTT sent them to the office of the FGPS. At that point, the FGPS coordinated their efforts to protest subcontracting and recommended specific tactics.

Strikes were conducted throughout the public sector, including in transport, water distribution, communications, utilities, health care, and education. There were daily sit-ins in some workplaces and regular street demonstrations in sup-port of dignity for workers and the right to decent work. In one case, workers brought in journalists to film their strikes and sit-ins. They made a documentary film of their protests called "The Whistle" (Le Sifflet).[24] Mongi Abderrahim once again played a pivotal role in organizing UGTT efforts in this domain, and for his efforts he was honored with an award from the global union federation UNI, for whom he later went to work.[25]

It should also be noted that the National Women's Committee of the UGTT was particularly active in the post–Ben Ali attempts to end subcontracting. They supported the claims of the women in the cleaning industry, framing their con-cerns in a politically viable way, by organizing and mobilizing workers who had not participated in the protests and by staging events to encourage these workers to defend their rights and reasonable demands for equal pay.[26] Women workers actually sat on train tracks shouting, "No to outsourcing! Either we work or we die." Other women conducted a hunger strike.[27]

Once workers in the public sector began organizing and advocating for their rights, their bosses tried to fire the "trouble makers." Colleagues initially hesitated to join strike leaders, but after a time they united to protest the firing of labor activists. That show of collective power convinced the subcontractors to rehire the leaders.

Seeking stability and social control, interim president Foued Mebazaa promised national-level negotiations to arrive at a new social bargain that would mollify the various social groups in Tunisian society. Transitional prime minister Mohamed Ghannouchi warned that the country could "collapse" if the mass walkouts and protests, sometimes interspersed with violence, continued. Sensing an opening, UGTT leaders made the case for a rapid increase in stability by transforming deeply unpopular subcontract work into standard employment: "There is an immediate response that the government can provide, namely tenure for hundreds of thou-sands of [Tunisians working for subcontractors] in order for them to be integrated into [standard employment] said [UGTT leader] Mr. Briki."[28]

The UGTT's campaign against subcontracting in the public sector was aided by UNI, which has provided UGTT's affiliate FGPS support for more than a decade. That support has included training, workshops, meeting, and exchanges along with campaign material (brochures, banners, T-shirts, and even whistles) to be used in direct actions.[29]

Ultimately, the UGTT campaign against subcontracting in the public sector has been a great success, although it is still ongoing in some sectors. On April 22, 2011, an agreement was signed outlawing subcontracting. Table 6.1 lists spe-cific examples of affiliates of the UGTT and workers reintegrated into direct and therefore formal employment.

TABLE 6.1 Changes in Worker Status by Sector ("Sous-Traitance Tunisie") (document prepared by Solidarity Center staff based on information from the UGTT, April 29, 2015)

FEDERATION	SECTOR	# OF INTEGRATED OUT-SOURCED SINCE 2011	TYPE OF WORKER	PENDING
Fédération Generale des Professions et des Services	Transport Caisses Nationales de Sécurité Sociale (CNSS)	6,000	Housekeepers Guards Gardeners	
Fédération Générale d'Electricité et de Gas	Electricity and gas	1,300	Technicians Laborers	1,800 are supposed to receive benefits but have not
Syndicat Générale des Caisses Sociales	Caisses Nationales de Sécurité Sociale (CNSS)	1,000	Housekeepers Guards Laborers Office workers	
Fédération Générale de Pétrochimie	Gasoline and Chemicals	1,000	Laborers Cadres Others	
Fédération Générale de la Santé	Health	5,500	Housekeepers Guards Gardeners Cooks	500—Negotiations are in progress
Fédération Générale des Transports	Rail Sea Earth Air	1,100 (400 women) 2,000		
Fédération Générale de l'Agro-alimentaire, Tourisme, et Commerce.	Tourism Food production Trade Grain milling Restaurants Bakeries	Thousands 1,480 1,000 1,200 500 500	Maintenance Workers Workers Workers Workers Workers	

The return to standard employment has doubled or nearly tripled the salaries of the affected workers. For instance, the typical pay for security guards and cleaning services' workers in the public sector has increased to around 400 TD per month. They have secure health insurance and retirement benefits again, although, unfortunately for older workers, the return to standard employment has come too late for them to accumulate much in their social security retirement accounts. Their work lives are being regulated according to the Tunisian labor code. They are paid in offices not in the streets. They can go to an office and discuss small and large issues concerning their jobs.

Some public institutions, for example the Société Tunisienne de Banque, Banque de l'Habitat, and the Banque Nationale de l'Agriculture, have not yet delivered on the promise to rehire workers directly. The UGTT continues its struggle to insource additional public workers, particularly through staging various direct actions.

There were some negatives in the successful campaign to end subcontracting in the public sector. For example, women working in the cleaning services complained that some men in the UGTT (workers at the airport were named) did not like the idea of women working in cleaning services joining their organization.[30] The reason seemed to be linked to both gender and the status of jobs in the cleaning industry. UGTT leaders, however, doubt that the sentiment is widespread, and one of the most effective UGTT/FGPS leaders of the campaign to end subcontracting is female.

The Private Sector

After the revolution, when the UGTT revitalized its campaign to end subcontracted labor in the public sector, it sought to do the same in the private sector. The success in the public sector did not fully spill over into the private sector, although the UGTT media campaign and organized pressure, along with a fresh rejection of subcontracting by workers in both sectors, contributed to a sharp decline in the use of subcontracting agencies throughout Tunisia. Some of these agencies folded because they lost contracts with the government.

The success at ending subcontracting in the public sector made the practice deeply unpopular. Many employers chose to initiate direct short-term contracts to replace subcontracting agencies, which led to the mutation of subcontracting in the private sector into direct short-term contracts between employers and employed. This mutation has improved the ability of private-sector workers on short-term contracts to unionize more easily and has also improved their negotiating position vis-à-vis their employers. Most private sector employers, however, have attempted to renew short-term contracts with lower pay and fewer benefits for years at a time rather than increase standard employment in their enterprises.

The UGTT has continued an active campaign to increase the use of standard employment in the private sector. Currently, the FGPS continues to press for an end to subcontracting in private banks, textiles, metallurgy, graphics, petrochemicals, and electronics. The unions are also protesting the mutation from subcontracting to short-term contracts in the private sector. They are negotiating with the national business association (UTICA) and individual business owners to improve the working conditions of hundreds of thousands of Tunisian workers in the private sector still seeking standard employment. In this regard, UGTT leaders lament that their leverage against private-sector employers and UTICA is weaker than their leverage against the Tunisian government. With the help of UNI, the UGTT continues to work with subcontracted workers, educating them on their rights and how to organize and generally trying to raise awareness of the issues.

From the point of view of private-sector workers affected by these issues, working for a subcontracting agency and working directly for an employer under a short-term contract is often indistinguishable. They see the UGTT's success in the public sector and understandably seek the same for themselves:

> I want to understand, since we are all living in Tunisia why was subcontracting eliminated for the public sector but not for the private sector. [The legal end of subcontracting agencies obviously did not improve her working conditions as this discussion occurred after the implementation of the law.] We are all cleaning why are we treated differently? Are they better than us? The others are getting paid 400 TD and they get loans to take care of their kids and to improve the conditions of their houses. My daughter was crying today because I told her that we are not buying a sheep for El Aid (holiday). I make 140 TD a month and I can't pay the rent with that, food, and everything else.[31]

The UGTT is currently seeking to eliminate all third-party subcontracting agencies (including those in the private sector). They are also addressing the use of indefinite short-term contracts that last for years, another method used by employers to avoid paying decent wages and providing benefits and labor rights. Currently, according to Tunisian law, any employee who is employed continuously for three years has the right to a standard full-time contract, since the establishment clearly needs the worker. It has proven difficult, however, to demonstrate three years of consecutive employment, so the UGTT is currently in negotiations with the government and with UTICA to find a solution to the problem of indefinite short-term contracts. As of this writing, the UGTT is in agreement with the government (but not yet with UTICA) on the form that a subcontracted employment contract should take. The UGTT is also working to update the Tunisian Labor Code to bring it in line with international ILO Convention norms, with the aim of addressing problems with subcontracting, short-term contracts, and seasonal work.[32] In addition to improvements in the law itself, it seems clear there is a need for better enforcement of existing law.

Subcontracting labor, which reduced workers' pay and deprived them of benefits and labor rights, was a festering wound in the fabric of Tunisian society before the January 14, 2011, revolution. The UGTT had spent years prior to the revolution unsuccessfully trying to end the practice. Sustained efforts led by the UGTT's FGPS, including Mongi Abderrahim's hunger strike, opened up a dialogue in 2002 between the central government and the UGTT to negotiate an end to labor subcontracting in the public sphere. The strikes, protests, organizing of workers, awareness campaigns, and media engagement by the UGTT from 2002 to 2011 put the end of labor subcontracting on the Tunisian government's agenda, but it did not end the practice.

Regime breakdown made transitional governments in Tunisia desperate to lessen volatile social conflicts by demonstrating that they were bringing justice to workers and ending exploitation. Subcontracting in the public sector was ended for a number of reasons. Tunisia's interim governments had some sympathizers to the cause of ending subcontracted labor. The general director of the public sector seemed sympathetic at the start of negotiations with the UGTT, even though some ministers fought against it, claiming that the change would put more pressure on their budgets. It should be noted that this is a dubious claim since under the policy, subcontracting agency operators were supposedly paid the same amount that would ordinarily have been paid directly to the workers.

In addition, the interim prime ministers and presidents (interim governments were formed and disbanded rapidly shortly after the revolution due to public pressure to eliminate those who sympathized with the prior regime) needed to demonstrate that the revolution could produce social justice and end exploitation. The strikes and protests organized from above and below were so widespread after the regime breakdown that government leaders were anxious to take steps to gain social control and stability. The newly free press and media kept labor conflicts in the public eye during the sensitive regime transition phase. Finally, ending subcontracting labor was a long-standing UGTT goal, which began early in the Ben Ali era, so success was partly due to continuous pressure.

Many of the subcontracted workers are female, and the UGTT's National Women's Committee played an important role in the organization of their attempts to defend their rights and make strides to equalize pay. According to the

UGTT, women make up half of the union's overall membership. While women have struggled to enter into leadership roles in the union, they were active in the struggle for regime change and during the transition period. In addition to collective action led by the UGTT, female workers in the public sector mobilized spontaneously on occasion and were creative in their efforts, producing a film documenting their plight.

The efforts to end subcontracting during the delicate time of regime transition in Tunisia ended with almost complete success on one front: an agreement that subcontracting agencies would be banned in the public sector and subcontracted workers in that sector, roughly sixty thousand of them, were able to move (back) into standard employment. More recently, at least one source claims that the UGTT has successfully won permanent contracts for 350,000 temporary workers from both the public and private sectors.[33]

Hundreds of thousands of workers, however, remain subcontracted in the private sector. The campaign against subcontracting in the public sector led to a drop in but not elimination of subcontracting in the private sector. In the private sector the practice mutated from subcontracting to a series of short-term contracts with the same low pay and lack of full benefits. UTICA and individual employers have proven to be much more intransigent than the Tunisian government when pressured to use standard employment contracts. The UGTT simply has weaker leverage in negotiations with these actors. The UGTT is seeking to end employer abuse of subcontracting and temporary short-term employment by seeking better labor laws and better enforcement of these laws. The elimination of subcontracting in the public sector has increased the leverage of the UGTT as they try to eliminate the practice and its mutation in the private sector. The successful campaign in the public sector and the way it has inspired similar workers in the private sector has increased the number of union members, who are now using their union membership to negotiate for better protection. It also has pushed forward the negotiations on improving the labor code. The UGTT hopes that the agreement to end labor subcontracting in the public sector will act as a lever to better defend unionized workers in the private sector seeking permanent employment. The negotiations on this front between UTICA and the UGTT have already begun.

Part II

SECURING RECOGNITION AND RIGHTS FOR THE SELF-EMPLOYED

MINIBUS DRIVERS IN GEORGIA

Secure Jobs and Worker Rights

Elza Jgerenaia and Gocha Aleksandria

After years of stagnation and political cataclysms following the collapse of the Soviet Union, the republic of Georgia tried to turn itself around by launching a radical economic and political reform program starting in 2004. After the "Rose Revolution" of 2003, the Georgian government made an unequivocal choice to liberalize the economy with fundamental changes made to existing social policies. These developments inevitably affected workers in Georgia. The new ultraliberal labor code adopted in 2006 greatly contributed to informalization of work and put Georgian labor legislation into conflict with ILO (International Labor Organization) fundamental standards.

At the same time, various cities within the country began to reform the public transport systems, with particular attention to the minibus sector. The minibus sector was largely informal and featured numerous intermediaries eating up revenues and leaving little for either employed drivers or owner-drivers. As cities began to formalize the sector, the interests of drivers were threatened, and for the first time they began to join the Transport and Road Building Workers Trade Union of Georgia in large numbers.

This chapter focuses on three recent cases of organizing and collective bargaining in the public transport sector of the three largest municipalities in the country. The Tbilisi case is the main focus while the Rustavi and Batumi cases illustrate how labor activism in one city may ignite similar actions in other places. All three case studies present a description of collective negotiations between the minibus drivers (who account for a major part of public transport in all three cities), the route operators (now mostly formal enterprises that encompass both self-employment and informal wage employment labor), and the municipal governments. The labor and economic relationships in this triangle have been and largely remain informal.

The three cases have similarities, but they differ in terms of the policies adopted and implemented by the city governments. While the Tbilisi and Rustavi cases are clearly about privatization and reprivatization of the minibus sector of public transport, the Batumi case is primarily about the attempt of the municipal government to nationalize (or municipalize) the municipal transport sector by replacing the minibuses with buses of normal size, thereby cutting jobs. The union has been largely successful in protecting the employment and, at least in Tbilisi, improving working conditions of minibus drivers through the willingness to engage in direct actions, including protests and strikes and through alliances with particular political forces at the local level.

Georgia's Population, Economy, and Politics

Georgia covers an area of 97,000 square kilometers (a little smaller than Belgium and the Netherlands together) and has a population of 3,700,000. It was previously part of the Soviet Union, which collapsed in 1991. Of all the former Soviet republics, Georgia suffered most severely from this collapse. Several political revolutions and a tough geopolitical situation prolonged the economic crisis, and by 2003 the country had sunk to its lowest level—political, economic, and social—in modern times.

Its largest city is Tbilisi, the capital (1.2 million residents), followed by Kutaisi (235,000), Rustavi (159,000), and Batumi (136,000). According to the national statistics bureau, Georgia's total gross domestic product in 2012 was US$37.27 billion.[1] The real annual GDP growth rate was 8.2 percent (like the rest of the world, the growth rate in Georgia dropped precipitously after the worldwide recession but has rebounded substantially). The transport sector, which is the focus of this chapter, makes up 11.5 percent of GDP.

After years of stagnation and political cataclysms, Georgia tried to turn itself around by launching a radical economic and political reform program starting in 2004. After the "Rose Revolution" of 2003, the Georgian government made an unequivocal choice to liberalize the economy with fundamental changes made to existing social policies. While the Georgian economy developed positively following 2003, the economic situation of Georgian citizens remained (and remains) difficult. Even according to official data, 20 percent of the Georgian population lives below the poverty line and 60 percent lives below the average consumption level.

The challenges for the poor are increased by the fact that Georgia is a country with a small and open economy and is largely dependent on imports. Foodstuffs and fuel are especially sensitive for the Georgian economy, since all consumers, including those below the poverty line, need foodstuffs, and the expenses incurred on them represent a significant proportion of consumer expenditure. In 2007–2009, for example, food accounted for 43 percent of consumer spending and in 2010–2011 it accounted for 38.8 percent. Increases in fuel prices affect virtually all sectors of the economy and also directly or indirectly affect the standard of living of the population. The fuel price is of particular importance to the transport industry.

The Labor Market

According to statistical data for 2011, the economically active population (workforce) numbered 1,959,300 or a little under half the population. Of the workforce, currently employed persons amount to 795,300, of whom 52.9 percent are self-employed. Unemployment in Georgia is at a record high when compared to other CIS (Commonwealth of Independent States) countries: 15.1–13.1 percent for females and 16.7 percent for males.[2] The majority of jobs in the private sector and especially those in services are precarious, unstable, short-term, and often informal. This is especially the case in relation to street trade, hotel, casino chains, transport, and construction in the capital city of Tbilisi and major regional principal cities. The informal sector accounts for more than 60 percent of employment in Georgia according to independent experts. Informality is widespread not only in agriculture, but also in transport, services, and construction. Transport has been particularly vulnerable to self-employment, tax evasion, and informality of labor relations over the past two decades.

Politics

Shortly after regaining its independence, which marked an end to seventy years of a one-party political system, Georgia saw a surge of political activism in the country. More than 150 political parties formally registered, none of them seriously committed to advocating for workers' rights. Although all six parliaments before the parliamentary elections of October 2012 were formally multiparty, Georgia has never experienced genuine separation of powers. The country has always been run in an autocratic way by a strong president who simultaneously runs the ruling party, enjoys an absolute/constitutional majority in the parliament, and decisively influences the judiciary.

The cases described in the present study largely took place in the period of total domination of the United National Movement (UNM) over the federal government, parliament, and judiciary. At this time, the UNM was also in charge of all (without exception) local governments and controlled all the governors of the regions. The Christian-Democratic Party, however, did enjoy representation in most local governments, including in all three cities discussed in this chapter.

More recently, the situation has significantly changed. The 2012 elections brought in an opposition coalition, the "Georgian Dream," consisting of five parties (none of which had been represented in the previous parliament) to a majority in parliament. In October 2013, the Georgian Dream candidate was elected president (the head of state). These elections marked a new beginning for Georgia's democracy. Further, with victories in the 2014 June municipal elections, all the mayors are from the new ruling coalition, which also holds the majority in all the city councils across the country.

The Labor Movement

The Georgian Trade Union Confederation (GTUC) is the only trade union federation in the country. Its transition to a democratic and independent trade union confederation started in 2005 with the election of a new team of union leaders. This was followed by the massive educational programs to identify, train, and promote young and promising union activists to replace the old "leaders" who carry the legacy of the Soviet past. Union militancy has been strengthened and a strong youth structure has been created. The confederation has developed a communication strategy and created strong legal and analytical units. The confederation has nineteen affiliated sectoral unions and, at the end of 2012, the total number of members affiliated was 176,547, representing about 9 percent of the economically active population.[3] The GTUC is affiliated with the International Trade Union Confederation and encourages its sectoral affiliates to join the relevant Global Union Federations. GTUC's affiliates include the Self-Employed Workers' Trade Union, the Transport and Road Building Workers Trade Union of Georgia, and three regional trade union federations. The Self-Employed Workers' Trade Union is the "youngest" affiliate of the GTUC with a membership of slightly more than five hundred workers in the commerce and services sectors, of whom one-half are women. It has successfully organized market vendors in Tbilisi and the municipality of Gori.

The Transport and Road Building Workers Trade Union (TRBWTUG) covers the transport sector. In addition to covering formal sector workers, the union bargains for and organizes workers who are self-employed as well as those who have informal jobs within formal enterprises. The transport union has 7,148 members, approximately 10 percent of whom are women employed in the informal sector.

Labor Legislation and Regulations

The documents that provide the legal basis for labor relations in Georgia include the Constitution of Georgia, ratified ILO conventions, the Labor Code, the Law on Trade Unions, and the Law on Gatherings and Manifestations. Article 30(4) of the Constitution safeguards labor rights and provides for fair remuneration, safe and healthy conditions of work, and appropriate employment conditions of minors and women. Georgia has ratified the several ILO conventions, and the ILO has several times provided recommendations to the government of Georgia in respect to modifications to the Labor Code and other legislation in order to bring them in line with Conventions 87 (freedom of association and the right to organize)[4] and 98 (right to organize and collective bargaining).[5] In addition, in 2005, Georgia ratified and partially adopted the European Social Charter,[6] a Council of Europe treaty that guarantees social and economic human rights.

The Law on Trade Unions[7] has not been substantially modified since its passage in 1997, while the Law on Collective Bargaining Agreements and the Law on the Rule of Regulating Collective Labor Disputes that were passed together with the Law on Trade Unions were abolished in 2006, leaving gaps in legislation. For instance, employers now have no legal obligation to engage in collective bargaining and there is no mechanism for mediation of disputes. The Law of Trade Unions declares the freedom to form and join trade unions. Trade unions are allowed in public as well as private institutions with the exception of certain categories relating to law enforcement bodies. Article 12(2) states that an employer is obliged to bargain with trade unions with the purpose of reaching collective bargaining agreements.

The Law on Trade Unions stipulates that both individual persons working for a specific company or organization with a labor contract as well as an individual entrepreneur can form or join a trade union of their choice. But the Labor Code mentions only the organization of the employees who work under "labor contracts" as counterparts for collective bargaining. Despite this ambiguity, and anticipating the discussion below, the Law on Trade Unions gave the TRBWTUG a free hand to organize minibus drivers, some of whom are independent entrepreneurs (own their own cars, employ drivers, mostly with a verbal contract, or drive those cars themselves), while others are disguised employees (who rent the cars from others and are made to pay for gas and maintenance of the cars).

The Labor Code was adopted in May 2006. The code is especially important for this chapter as it covers employees working under informal arrangements, giving them the same protection, rights, and freedoms as the workers who have a formalized labor relationship with their employers. Unfortunately, neither the Labor Code nor any other piece of legislation provides definitions for the formal and informal sector or employment. While the code recognizes the right to collective bargaining, it does not make it mandatory for the employer to engage in collective bargaining. Also, the Labor Code does not recognize the right of unorganized workers to bargain collectively. The code defines a collective bargaining agreement as an agreement between an employer and any group of employees that comprises more than two members. An employer is not obliged to bargain collectively even when this is demanded by a trade union. The role of trade unions in collective bargaining is not defined and the bargaining may be done by any worker representative. This is contrary to Article 4 of ILO Convention 98.[8]

Article 49 of the Labor Code recognizes the right of workers to strike, but Article 51 imposes a number of limitations. For example, an employee may not strike in a case where the employer downsizes staff, provided the employee had been warned in advance about possible dismissal. A strike must be preceded by a warning, which requires the parties to attempt to reach agreement through negotiations for fourteen days. The law does not explicitly determine the procedures for these negotiations. If, as a result of exchange of written notices, agreement is not reached, one party is authorized to apply to court for arbitration. This then restricts the right to strike. Further, the duration of a strike is limited to ninety days, and strikes are not allowed where they can cause harm to the public.

Certain aspects of Georgian labor legislation are both in conflict with ILO fundamental standards and have promoted precariousness of employment. These include the employer's right of arbitrary dismissal with the only condition being to compensate the employee with one month severance pay, the optionality of collective bargaining for the employer (discussed above), the establishment of normal working time at twelve hours per day and at seventy-two hours per week with no mandatory overtime pay etc., the rights of an employer to conclude unlimited verbal contracts with the workers, the lack of essential terms of employment contracts established by the law, the lack of restrictions over the application of fixed-term contracts, and the erosion of collective bargaining rights by marginalizing unions and substituting employment relations by individual civil contracts.[9]

In addition to purely legal aspects, practical deregulation of management by the state has also resulted in the failure to protect labor rights. The abolition of labor inspection has created a gap in terms of controlling employment conditions. No specialized courts or mediation institutions are in place for the consideration of labor disputes. In addition to legislation directly related to employment relations, the success of social dialogue depends on the quality of the protection of overall civil rights and freedoms in the country. This has been deteriorating over time through an increase in legal and practical restrictions of political and civil rights.

The Case Studies: Collective Bargaining in the Minibus Sector

Methodology

Both desk-based and fieldwork methods were used for the case studies. In terms of desk-based methods, the relevant legislative regulations were identified. In addition, materials from various public and nongovernmental organizations and various Internet sources were analyzed. For the fieldwork component, a list of relevant individuals was developed. Interviews with these individuals provided a further source of information. The list of persons interviewed, their positions, and organizations and institutions is included as an appendix to this chapter.

The Minibus Sector

The Ministry of Economy and Sustainable Development of Georgia develops and implements state policy relating to transport. There are also several legal provisions that regulate transport in the country. These include the Law on the Management and Regulation of Transport, which sets out the legal and organizational basis for the management and regulation of transport throughout Georgia. Local government is also responsible for regulating passenger transport in the respective municipality; the Organic Law on Local Self-Government permits charging the service provider associated fees in relation to regular transport of passengers. All local governments across the country are governed on the basis of this law except for in Tbilisi, where the mayor is elected directly by residents of the city. The mayors in other cities are elected by the City Councils. Tbilisi's local government is run on the basis of a separate law, the Law on Capital City, which determines the amount of the service fee paid by providers to the municipality and the payment process, done on the basis of tender announcements and related procedures.

Reforms in recent years have aimed to formalize the transport sector. The reforms include stricter tax administration, renovation of parking spaces for buses (including minibuses), and regulation of the contractual system. Despite these reforms, though, the situation has not changed substantially, especially in Batumi and Rustavi, where management of minibuses has not been brought under the municipality and transport remains privately owned and managed.

For twenty years, minibuses have been the main form of transport within the cities of Tbilisi, Batumi, and Rustavi. The economic collapse that began in the early 1990s, ethnic conflicts promoted by Russia, and armed civilian standoffs (including civil war in the capital city) resulted in a deep and all-encompassing crisis of public administration all over the country. Public services became ineffective as many public officers became deeply involved in corruption, which caused an absolute collapse of municipal services, including municipal transport. The gap in transport services was filled by an unorganized self-employed sector. Due to the weak buying power of the population and the lack of demand for quality services, it was mostly second-hand minibuses from Turkey and Germany that became the key means of transportation. In addition, dilapidated, Soviet-produced minibuses from the 1980s were still in use.

In this situation, city transport traffic routes were established spontaneously and in an unorganized way. Initially, private individuals transported passengers in minibuses they owned, either driving themselves or using hired drivers. In the late 1990s, when there was relative stability in the country, federal and municipal governments managed to introduce some order in passenger transport through the measures described above. Due to widespread corruption and oligarchic capitalism, however, transport operated largely as part of the shadow economy (for example, without paying taxes). Up until at least 2010, labor relations were based on informal self-employment. The so-called minibus passenger transport system that developed posed effective competition to municipal transport services such as the subway/Metro and large buses.

Against this backdrop, the change of the government in 2003 (following the so-called Rose Revolution) and the successful government policy of fighting corruption and instituting order gradually reached municipal transport. Given the increase in local budgets with moves to self-government, cities started to introduce new regulation mechanisms, spending more on improving city infrastructure and renewal of the transport fleet (buses of various seating capacity). In Tbilisi and other large cities, these became major reforms. But local (and federal) government attempts to bring more transparency and accountability to the cities' transport systems confronted a "vicious scheme" that had been taking root for almost two decades. This approach was found in almost every large city of Georgia, including in Kutaisi, Rustavi, and Batumi.

The scheme can be described as follows. The transport system within the cities is divided into several minibus routes. After winning formal tenders announced by the municipal government(s), separate legal entities known as "route operators" manage one or more routes for a specified period of time, usually one to two years. In Tbilisi, the route operators claim that in the 1990s, they unofficially paid for the permanent right to manage the routes, making them de facto owners of the respective routes. For this reason, and also to differentiate the various actors, it is better to refer to them as "route owners." Despite these legal arrangements, the real "route operators" are the individual persons who actually manage minibus traffic under unofficial lease agreements with the route owners.

The route operators select minibuses and their owners to work on the various routes. They also informally collect monthly fees from the minibus owners and pay part of that money to the route owners. In many instances the minibus owners are also drivers, while in other cases they employ drivers to drive their vehicles. In many instances, the route operators actually use their own minibuses on the routes they manage.

The only formal relations in this scheme are those between route owners and minibus owners (and owner-drivers), though even there the contracts between these entities are not enforced. No services (such as safety inspection, car repairing, spare parts, etc.) are provided to the minibus drivers by the other actors. Moreover, at some point in recent years drivers were asked by either route owners or minibus owners to do their own bookkeeping, which usually meant that they needed to contract and pay an accountant. This measure partly formalized the business and labor relationships in this sector, but it increased the financial and administrative burden of drivers. All the personnel, apart from a few employees in the route operation offices, are men.

It is clear that the driver is the most vulnerable actor in this system, "feeding" all others above him: the minibus owner (when that is someone other than the driver), route operator, and route owner. This is an upside-down pyramid-like scheme with the driver at the base exploited through semilegal methods. At times, drivers publicly expressed discontent with their labor conditions, but their protests would have no result. Because of the informal nature of the relationship and despite strong attempts by the transport workers' union, it was difficult to unionize the drivers. The main problem was the lack of a concrete employer who could serve as a common target for collective actions. Local authorities did not have a direct relationship with drivers although indirectly they influenced the employment conditions of the drivers.

Reforms implemented in Tbilisi eliminated route operators and minibus owners from the system and substituted companies that have won a tender obliging them to bring in new minibuses, select and employ the drivers, provide insurance (car accident, health care), operate and manage the routes, and provide safety inspections for a period of twenty years. The only legacy from the previous approach is that the drivers remain largely self-employed and responsible for taking care of the vehicle themselves in terms of repairs, spare parts, and other running expenses. But they are now formally registered as individual entrepreneurs and are paying taxes according to this status.

Removal of the other two groups of actors—route owners and route operators—caused a lot of tension and many protests against the municipal government. Furthermore, the Tbilisi city council was accused of encouraging monopolization of city transport, as there were rumors that all four tender-winning companies had the same owners registered in an offshore area. At the time of this writing, Batumi and Rustavi have not yet brought about similar changes, but there are plans for this to happen in the near future.

The reforms occurred against a background of developing social dialogue in the sector at the national level. The first memorandum of cooperation was concluded on July 27, 2009, between the Unified Transport Administration of the Ministry of Regional Development and Infrastructure, the TRBWTUG, and the League of Passenger Transport Operators. The League of Passenger Transport Operators represents the route owner companies and is seen as being close to the authorities in all cities.

The focus of cooperation was safe, timely, and quality transport of passengers to meet the demands of consumers. The three bodies formed a permanent council, which serves as a platform for exchanging opinions and information on ways of addressing the problems and challenges. Further, under the memorandum, agreement was reached about the refinement of the technical regulations governing motor vehicle passenger carriage and the creation of mechanisms to implement the laws and regulations.

A significant aspect of the agreement was the creation of a permanent joint consultative board. The main task of this board was to develop recommendations to identify and resolve problematic issues in the sector. The heads of the agency and the league along with the president of the TRBWTUG constitute the board. The board meets twice a year unless there is need for an urgent meeting. It can come up with recommendations regarding important issues such as labor disputes.

The memorandum paid special attention to regulations safeguarding the employment and health of employees (primarily drivers), skills development, professional training and in-service development, minimum conditions for work and rest hours, establishment of legal, stable, socially oriented relationships between employees and employers, ensuring social dialogue, conclusion and enforcement of collective agreements, and smooth functioning of auto stations.

Tbilisi

By 2010, between eighteen and twenty thousand people were employed in Tbilisi in the transport sector, approximately five thousand of whom were employed in the minibus subsector. In September 2010, the Tbilisi municipality issued a tender aimed at transport reform. Information about the tender triggered the initiation of collective bargaining and the formation of a trade union of minibus drivers under the umbrella of TRBWTUG. This was possible because the TRBWTUG constitution and structure are flexible enough to allow for membership of any employee irrespective of the degree of the formality of his or her labor relations with the employer. There was some initial resistance from formal workers who thought all informal workers were self-employed persons seeking to avoid taxes and regulations. But now most of the affiliates of the GTUC and their members have come to understand that informal employment is how the poor survive and is a global phenomenon. Furthermore, the policy of the GTUC (to which TRB-WTUG is affiliated) is to encourage its member sectoral unions to make it easy for informal workers, including the self-employed, to join the unions and enjoy representation and protection equal to those who have formal labor relations with their respective employers.

Fearful of losing their jobs, the drivers—who had for a long time avoided unionization—quickly approached the TRBWTUG for help. The TRBWTUG immediately responded and launched a campaign against the municipal government demanding greater transparency and respect for the drivers' job security. The union activists from the municipal bus company played a key role in organizing the minibus drivers, with the belief that organizing and being united with minibus drivers would increase their bargaining power with city governments. Finally, within a period of one week, the Primary Union of Tbilisi Minibus Drivers was set up and the TRBWTUG was given the mandate to represent the drivers in the negotiations with the municipal government.

To focus public attention on the problems of the drivers, the TRBWTUG decided to act in alliance with the Christian-Democratic faction of the Tbilisi City Council. Meetings held in the council, joint press conferences, and participation in TV talk shows strengthened the alliance and forced the municipal government to include the TRBWTUG representatives in the Tender Commission. This moment marked the final split between the interests of the drivers on the one hand and the route owners and route operators on the other. The latter, recognizing the possible loss of their places (and privileges) in the existing scheme, tried to use the drivers to avert or at least postpone the reform. They tried to provoke the drivers to go on strike and paralyze transport in the city. The drivers, who had been exploited by the "vicious scheme" for many years, were smart enough to identify the real intentions of their former "employers" and did not strike. Their memories were still fresh enough to remember the attempt of the "employers" to prevent them forming a union. Backed by some radical political forces, the route owners and route operators tried to rally against the government, but without the participation of drivers their protest was not successful.

Besides the motives noted above, the drivers—led by the union—understood that the reform could bring more decent work and greater employment security. They needed to fight to save their jobs and wages and to try to improve working conditions. It was clear that they could achieve this only by acting together as a union.[10]

Most political parties focused mainly on preventing monopolization of the sector, due to the rumors mentioned above that all four tender-winning companies had the same owner. The tender was for long-term outsourcing of municipal minibus transport, which required that participant companies invest heavily and completely change the fleet of vehicles within one year (bringing in 1,250 new minibuses in 2011), urgently address safety conditions, and so on. In this process, former route owners and route operators (who are small entrepreneurs and thus unable to engage in major investment) claimed, not without reason, that they had been deliberately sidelined.

The trade union shared the concern over the possible monopolization of the sector, but retention of 100 percent of the jobs for those already working as drivers was its main objective. In order to influence the city authorities (who enjoyed strong backing from the federal government) to have the relevant clause on job retention included among the conditions of the tender, the TRBWTUG requested that the GTUC intervene. The GTUC support, coupled with assistance from the Christian-Democratic party, played an important role. Nevertheless, the TRBW-TUG had to organize a protest rally in front of the mayor's office in Tbilisi to secure the drivers' rights and interests. After the rally, the municipal government invited TRBWTUG's leader and the ad hoc committee of the drivers to negotiations. After a series of negotiations, all the demands of the drivers were accommodated, including retention of jobs, medical insurance, working hours, paid annual leave, and safety conditions. It was also agreed that no matter which companies won the tender, they would conclude a collective agreement with the TRBWTUG as the workers' representative organization. This agreement was memorialized in written minutes of the meeting and widely publicized in the media.

Seven companies expressed an interest in the tender, and four were announced as winners. The four winners were widely seen as belonging to a big business grouping close to the then ruling party. Tbil Line won two lots, while Tbil Car, Capital Group, and Public Car each won one lot.

Despite relatively successful negotiations with the four companies, at a certain stage drivers had to threaten to strike. This was necessary because of disagreements over wages and over the responsibility of companies for routine maintenance and repair of minibuses. Fortunately, through intensive mediation that involved the GTUC and some senior government representatives, consensus was reached and industrial action was averted.

The cooperation of the trade union with the Christian-Democratic Party proved to be successful, as demonstrated by the united front for safeguarding the jobs of drivers. Drivers were also offered assistance by various nongovernmental organizations (NGOs), such as the Georgian Young Lawyers Association and the Human Rights Center, mainly legal advice. Nevertheless, the trade union was the most important form and means for collective advocacy for and representation of workers' rights and interests even though the drivers' employment was mainly informal and in some cases not fully in line with the law.

Ultimately, the trade union concluded the memoranda of cooperation with the four companies that later resulted in the signing of collective agreements. With its flexible structure and constitution that allowed drivers with any type of employment to affiliate, TRBWTUG succeeded in recruiting approximately five hundred members (out of a total of a thousand drivers) who currently pay union dues and actively participate in union activities. The majority of the drivers are registered as individual entrepreneurs and have commercial contracts (rather than employment contracts) with the employer.

Memoranda and Collective Agreements

On April 8, 2011, the four winning transport operator companies concluded a cooperation memorandum with the Trade Union of Transport and Motorway Workers. The main objective of the memorandum was the retention of drivers of minibuses. In addition to the need to remain employed, the drivers needed trade union assistance in another important issue: the threat that all drivers would be required to pay the same fee, GEL 20 a day, while daily income from lines differs significantly. Because of this variation, the drivers' demand was for differentiated fees, and this demand was included in the agreement.

On December 24, 2011, a further agreement was signed between the Tbilisi Transport Company, Ltd. and the TRBWTUG. Key items of the agreement were as follows:

- safeguarding the employment and health of employees;
- skills development and professional and in-service training;
- creating norms of work and rest hours;
- establishing just, law-based relations between employees and employers; and
- ensuring social dialogue and conclusion and implementation of collective agreements.

The parties also agreed to discuss the issue of re-employment of three hundred drivers who were laid off as a result of previous waves of reorganization.

On January 9, 2012, a collective agreement was signed between Sakavtotransporti Branch, Ltd. and the TRBWTUG. Under this contract, the employer agreed to enter into a labor contract with each driver and agreed that these contracts would disallow forced labor or discrimination. The antidiscrimination provision was important because discrimination based on union affiliation as well as on political preferences is widespread in Georgia. The agreement also stated that labor contracts with employees would not be terminated without approval of the transport trade union. The parties further agreed that members of the trade union employed at the company would pay a monthly membership fee to the union, equal to 1 percent of their salary.

On February 1, 2011, a cooperation agreement was signed between TRBW-TUG and Capital Group, Ltd. The agreement obliged the company to give priority to those working at the time of the announcement of tender when employing drivers, as well as to consider professional development of drivers and driving experience. Under the same agreement, the employer was obliged to move away from verbal employment contracts and conclude written contracts with employees that clearly reflected the work schedule of drivers and their rights and obligations. The parties also agreed to design activities to refine the social partnership system and to conclude a collective agreement between Capital Group and TRB-WTUG. On the same day, a mutual agreement memorandum was concluded between Tbil Car, Ltd. and the TRBWTUG, and a joint collective agreement was concluded between Tbil Line, Ltd. and Public Car, Ltd. and the TRBWTUG.

Batumi

In early spring 2012, the Batumi municipal government decided to follow the example of the Tbilisi municipality and reform its city transport service. This was not a copy-and-paste exercise, as Batumi is the capital of the Ajara Autonomous Republic and enjoys some independence in deciding on policies and institution building. The Batumi government came up with a plan to significantly reduce the number of minibuses in the city and substitute them with large buses. The reform also aimed to reorganize existing minibus routes to adapt them to the new circumstances. It further aimed to oblige the route owners to renew the vehicle fleet by either bringing in totally new minibuses or repairing the existing ones. The city government made it clear from the beginning that it would not take care of the drivers who would lose their jobs.

As in Tbilisi, the TRBWTUG became actively involved in the process through its branch affiliated in Ajara, which is part of the Ajara Trade Union Federation (ATUF). As a regional structure of the GTUC, the ATUF leadership as well as the TRBWTUG's branch union were given extensive information about the experience of the Tbilisi case and also given advice on relevant action.

There had been several unsuccessful attempts in the previous two years to get Batumi informal transport workers to join the union. This time, with the minibus drivers facing an imminent threat to their jobs and income, it was much easier for the TRBWTUG to organize them. The unwillingness of the municipal authorities to engage in dialogue with the drivers increased the TRBWTUG and ATUF's role in mobilizing drivers to form a united front and focusing public attention on the issue. Within a few days, an absolute majority of the drivers (almost three hundred) signed union cards and developed a list of demands. In parallel, a process of voting for engaging in industrial action was launched. The strike took place on April 5, 2012, and substantially paralyzed transport in Batumi. Only the municipal buses did not join the strike, as at that time the drivers of municipal buses in the city were not organized. The union demanded that the mayor of Batumi extend the deadline for repairing or bringing in new vehicles; retain the jobs of route operators, owners, and drivers for at least three years; ease of the grading system to prove fitness of a vehicle, continue the use of a lottery for reorganizing and reallocating routes and minibuses, restore three routes abolished unilaterally by the municipal government, and maintain of the current number of vehicles per line.

It is interesting to note that in the case of Batumi, the interests of the drivers and route operators/owners were closely interconnected. If the latter lost, the drivers also would be under the threat of unemployment. Further, Batumi is a small city with fewer minibuses operating. Almost all the drivers own their vehicles and are similar to route operators in the other cities. Therefore, an absolute majority of the drivers are self-employed (individual entrepreneurs) and take care of the vehicles themselves.

The strike came to an end within five hours following strong public statements of the Tbilisi minibus drivers about a possible sympathy strike. The sensitivity of the Batumi municipal government toward what might happen in Tbilisi reflected the fact that both these cities (as well as all other municipalities across the country) were under the control of the United National Movement (UNM), the ruling party at the federal level. So the decision to soften the stance vis-à-vis the drivers' union was made in the UNM's head office in Tbilisi by the federal government.

This was an extremely important moment. Solidarity forced the Batumi government to retreat and to not only satisfy the demands of the drivers, but also to invite two representatives of the drivers' union to participate in the work of the commission as observers, with the right to speak and express opinions. Over the next four weeks, agreement was reached on many of the union's demands, including the date for the tender; the dates, process, and the grading system for assessments of vehicles; and the restoration of routes.

With these amended rules, all 670 vehicles qualified and met the new conditions set out by the commission. Despite the fruitful cooperation, the relationship between the municipal government and the union remained tense. The parties could not agree on a number of important issues, including defining the types of new vehicles and use of a lottery to redistribute the drivers on different lines. It was obvious that for a small town like Batumi, the reform was poorly prepared and planned and was subsequently unpopular. Therefore, in mid-June 2012, the Batumi City Council voted to postpone the rest of the reform without identifying a new date. It is clear that this decision again came from the UNM's head office because as of May, the parliamentary election campaign had entered its decisive phase, with polls suggesting that the opposition was gaining the lead over the ruling party. By postponing the reform, the ruling party tried to avoid further loss of its popularity. Nevertheless, without the TRBWTUG-ATUF-GTUC, concerted action, and strong union solidarity, the lives of 670 drivers and their families would have been negatively affected.

Rustavi

In February 2012, the Rustavi municipality announced a tender to recheck the fitness of the minibuses to carry passengers. The process was much better prepared and organized than it was in Batumi. The TRBWTUG's main concerns were the lack of transparency and doubts that the assessment would be done objectively. To ensure sufficient publicity and exclude subjectivity in the local government's approach, the TRBWTUG put forward demands that its representatives be included in the work of the government's commission.

Unlike in Batumi, the TRBWTUG had established a local union branch back in 2010. This made it easier to convince the local authorities, who were distrustful of and hostile to unions that were created during a reform process, of the usefulness of cooperation with the union. The government accepted the demand, and two union representatives (both drivers) became members of the commission. The same commission was also responsible for evaluation of the vehicles. In response to a demand of the TRBWTUG, the local government also invited a professor from the Automobile Transport Department of the Tbilisi State Technical University to observe the process. As a result, the tender went smoothly. All existing route operating companies had their fitness to the new conditions confirmed and qualified successfully. All eight hundred drivers retained their jobs.

Collective agreements with all operator companies were the added value of the process. Even those who had been refusing to negotiate and engage in dialogue with the drivers now decided to adopt a more constructive approach. This change resulted from the union's effective work, demonstrated by its capacity to mobilize if necessary, and its professionalism in dealing with complex issues.

A collective agreement covering the period February 25, 2012, to February 25, 2017, was signed between Sovrak, Ltd. and the TRBWTUG. Sovrak, Ltd.

undertook to submit to the trade union one calendar month in advance a letter on any reorganization planned by the company. The company also undertook to provide full information about the protection of labor, safety, and other issues. Further, a paragraph on membership fees prescribed how deductions would be made and money transferred on a monthly basis to the trade union account. The parties also agreed that they would not allow any form of forced labor and discrimination against the employees (mainly drivers) working on minibuses.

In February 2012, a collective bargaining agreement was signed between Rustavi Municipal Motor Transport Enterprise, Ltd. and the TRBWTUG covering the period from February 25, 2012, to February 25, 2017. Another agreement, covering the same period, was signed between Transit 2009, Ltd. and the Trade Union of Motor Transport and Motorway Workers of Georgia. Currently six hundred drivers out of eight hundred in Rustavi are members of the union.

The example of all three cities demonstrates the importance of union representation for informal transport sector workers in Georgia. The openness of the TRBWTUG to organizing and representing informal workers is part of a general openness to informal workers in the Georgia Trade Union Confederation. The cases show that the union movement in Georgia was mature and knowledgeable enough to properly represent and protect informal workers. While there was initially some skepticism from the formal workers who constitute the membership base of TRBWTUG, those workers have chosen to act in solidarity with informal workers in their sector. Based on the example of the TRBWTUG, it is safe to say that there is potential for other unions to grow and unite informal workers from other sectors under the union umbrella. Solidarity and mobilization of informal workers can be as effective as with formal workers. Targeted and well-planned actions are possible only when workers are organized. Skepticism over whether unions can effectively organize informal workers seems exaggerated, as the cases above clearly demonstrate that success depends only on the union's ability to be proactive and willing to disregard skepticism.

In Tbilisi drivers could not previously be united due to the lack of a common employer and because the municipal government avoided taking responsibility for drivers' working conditions. The minibus sector reform was largely successful in addressing these gaps, and the investors, in the form of the winning companies, became the genuine and responsible employers while the municipal government was shown to be the body directly responsible for the process of monitoring transport traffic with the capacity to intervene on either side to promote compliance with policies and labor standards. The unions have been actively involved in all the processes from the beginning to the end and have provided information to every driver about the tender criteria and the challenges and problems they would face.

Tbilisi and Rustavi are clearly successful examples of collective bargaining. The jobs of drivers have been protected and reform of the sector has moved forward. While drivers remain largely self-employed, their interests in employment security and improved working conditions are now protected by collective agreements with both the city and with the bus route operators. In Batumi, municipal authorities reached some agreements with the union, but disagreement over other issues stalled the reform of the sector. The challenges experienced in Batumi provide a clear indication of the then government's anti-union tactics. There has been political change since then at the federal level. In the June 2014 elections, the Georgian Dream coalition won the elections in every municipality. This means that the UNM is now the main opposition party in the national parliament and in city halls. The Georgian Dream party is considerably less hostile toward labor unions than is the UNM. Although it has become relatively easier to exercise labor and union rights, there are still cases of ongoing persecution of the union leaders and activists both in the private and public sector. The successes in each city have been primarily a result of the use or threats of direct actions including protests and strikes coupled with alliances with particular local political parties and a more or less willing party on the other side of the table.

The study has highlighted the importance of collective contracts for the improvement of labor rights and standards of employees in Georgia. The lessons learned from the cases described above will assist transport workers in municipalities that have not yet opted for reforms. By replicating the successful steps and activities of the unions in Tbilisi and Rustavi, the drivers in other towns can effectively oppose ill-designed reforms and claim their rights.

PERSONS INTERVIEWED[11]

- Akhvlediani, Giorgi. Political leader and Member of Parliament for the Christian-Democrat party.
- Alania, Lavrenti. President of Transport and Road Building Workers Trade Union of Georgia.
- Ananidze, Djemal. Deputy mayor of Batumi City Hall.
- Japaridze, Davit. Deputy mayor of self-governing city of Rustavi.
- Jokhadze, Akaki. Head of the Department of Transport Service in Tbilisi Municipality.
- Jebashvili, Gigla. Head of "Tbilisi Minibus Ltd."
- Nikuradze, Kakha. Head of Transport Agency, Ministry of Economy and Sustainable Development of Georgia.
- Petriashvili, Irakli. President of Georgian Trade Union Confederation (GTUC).
- Saluqvadze, Ketevan. Head of Transport Policy Department, Ministry of Economy and Sustainable Development Department of Georgia.
- Samushia, Jaba. Vice chairman of Tbilisi City Assembly.

WASTE PICKERS IN BRAZIL

Recognition and Annual Bonus

Sonia Maria Dias and Vera Alice Cardoso Silva

Informal waste picking is a significant source of jobs for millions of people world-wide who make a living by collecting, sorting, recycling, and selling thrown-away materials. In some places waste pickers may supply the only form of solid waste collection. In spite of their contribution to public health and to lowering the costs of solid waste management borne by municipalities, they are often treated as a nuisance and their contributions as environmental agents and economic actors are often ignored.

The past two decades have seen Brazil gradually replacing repressive policies on waste picking with new inclusive policies that give legal backing to redistributive measures and social recognition of informal waste picker organizations. As a result, Brazil has been in the forefront of inclusive policies regarding waste pickers.[1] Advances at the national level include the creation of funding lines for cooperatives, national capacity-building programs for waste pickers' organizations, and a legal framework backing formal recognition and integration of waste pickers. In 2010, the National Solid Waste Policy was approved, which recognized waste pickers' cooperatives as service providers and, as a result, instituted a number of mechanisms to support cooperatives and municipalities that integrated informal workers into solid waste systems.[2]

The state of Minas Gerais and its capital city, Belo Horizonte, have been at the center of social activism and progressive policy since the early 1990s, with many of its experiences, projects, and programs serving as models for the rest of the country. This chapter focuses on collective bargaining over the "recycling bonus law" in Minas Gerais during which the waste pickers sought compensation for providing environmental services. These environmental services include collection of recyclables and scrap, which benefits the environment (extension of the life span of sanitary landfills through the diversion of recyclables, contribution to the city's cleanliness, reduction of pollution, etc.).

The claim that *catadores* provide an environmental service has been one of the main strategies adopted by the Movimento Nacional de Catadores de Recicláveis (MNCR or in English, National Movement of Waste Pickers) in Brazil. The state of Minas Gerais was the first state in the country to propose and implement payment for environmental services for waste pickers' cooperatives. This chapter traces the genesis of the bargaining process that led to the approval of the first payment for environmental service in Brazil: the recycling bonus law. It describes its main features, how informal recyclers perceive the law, and its main impacts and challenges. First, background on the waste pickers and on the integration scenario in Brazil is given to contextualize the bargaining process that led to the recycling bonus law and to situate the law within a wider context of strategies applied by the MNCR and the enabling policy environment for integration in the country.

Important lessons emerge from this case. The successes of the waste pickers in Brazil in general and Minas Gerais in particular have been won in stages and over a long period of time. These stages include recognition from the state, formalization of the relationship between waste picker organizations in some cities and states, the passage of the bonus law in Minas Gerais, and negotiation over details of implementation. The support of nongovernmental organizations (NGOs) has played an important role, especially in the early stages. Many of the gains are a result of the interplay of the waste pickers movement and sympathetic policy makers.

Background

Brazil is the fifth largest country in the world in terms of geographical area and is also the fifth most populous country. In the past two decades it has experienced both economic growth and a drop in poverty and inequality levels. During this economic boom, formal employment in Brazil increased by 43.5 percent from 2001 to 2009,[3] while informal jobs grew at a much slower pace, on the order of 9 percent during the same period, and yet informal employment accounts for about thirty-one million workers. The diversity of informal work in Brazil is huge, spread across various occupations and activities. The informal workforce in solid waste management (SWM) in Brazil, according to data available on the national system of information on the sanitation sector—SNIS—is largely involved in the collection of recyclables rather than on refuse collection generally, since the latter is done by formal workers hired or outsourced by municipalities.

Brazil is the only country that systematically captures and reports official statistical data on informal waste pickers.[4] Efforts to organize waste pickers and improve their livelihood have been ongoing for more than two decades and have led to the official recognition of waste picking in the Brazilian Classification of Occupations (CBO). Since its adoption in 2002, the category "*catador de material reciclável*" (picker of recyclable materials) has been used in all relevant data collection efforts in the country to include those who pick, select, and sell recyclable material such as paper, cardboard and glass, as well as ferrous and nonferrous metals and other reusable materials (though not those who collect other types of solid household waste).

The recycling industry, especially that of aluminium and paper, has always relied on the work carried out by informal collectors of recyclables in Brazil, called "*catadores*." The sector is also characterized by middlemen—some legalized and some not—who have functioned as the link between the waste pickers and the recycling industry. Working most of the time in an autonomous and isolated way[5] in a market where the recycling industry has extraordinary market power to determine prices, waste pickers are often prone to various forms of exploitation, including low prices for the materials they sell, fraud and tampering of scales by middlemen, and poor working conditions.[6] Until the late 1980s work had traditionally taken place in two ways: (i) street waste picking activities carried out from the trash bags found on the curb or taken from offices and shops, and (ii) waste picking at open dumps.[7] *Catadores* suffered from negligence and were stigmatized as vagrants; they were not recognized socially and professionally, resulting in low self-esteem.[8] Due to the lack of places for storing their material or the lack of money to go home after a working day, street waste pickers were forced to live in improvised cardboard shacks since they could not leave their material unguarded, which created problems from the perspective of the urban environment.[9]

Table 8.1 provides some data on the size and demographics of the current waste picker workforce. These numbers likely underestimate the total number of waste pickers in Brazil.[10] The National Movement of Waste Pickers—MNCR claims that there are 800,000 to 1 million pickers in the country.

TABLE 8.1[i]

	PNAD 2006[ii]	RAIS[iii]	2010 CENSUS
Total number of waste pickers	229,568		387,910
Number with a formal contract	10,272	11,781	
Percent women	33%	20%	31%
Schooling	12% have attended school	80% with a contract have levels of education beyond 4th grade and over 60% have an 8th grade or higher education	25% have primary school
Waste pickers in Minas Gerais	14,029		

    i. Helena M. T. Crivellari, Sonia M. Dias, and A. de S. Pena, "Informação e trabalho: uma leitura sobre os catadores de material reciclável a partir das bases públicas de dados," in *Catadores na cena urbana: construção de políticas socioambientais*, by Valéria H. Kemp and Helena M. T. Crivellari (Belo Horizonte: Autêntica Editora, 2008).

    ii. PNAD (National Household Sample Survey) is carried out by the Brazilian Institute of Geography and Statistics—IBGE—on an annual basis between the censuses. It provides information on work, population, education, etc. The fact that it is household-based permits identification of the population that works informally and even those who have a contract but work in households, such as maids. The PNAD enables, therefore, a view of the waste picker collected in his or her own home and according to his or her own statement. Note that PNAD provides estimates, not absolute numbers of workers.

    iii. RAIS (Annual Listing of Social Information) is a national administrative register of the Ministry of Labour and Employment. Employers are obliged to declare the individual status of each employee with whom they maintain continued employment. With the inclusion of waste picking as a profession, waste pickers can be formally employed by commercial establishments. Therefore, RAIS captures data for individuals hired by contracts under the profession of waste picker.

Organizing Waste Pickers

By the late 1980s, NGOs from the Catholic Church had begun to organize waste pickers in the capital cities of the states of São Paulo, Minas Gerais, and Rio Grande do Sul.[11] The NGOs noticed that within the street dwellers they were working with, there was a group of people who lived in the streets but collected recyclables for a living; they thought this subgroup had the potential to get organized around labor issues.

With the first administration of the Workers Party in the cities of São Paulo, Porto Alegre, and Belo Horizonte[12] in the late 1980s and early 1990s, the first experiences of integration of waste pickers as service providers in formal recycling schemes began to take shape. Later on this inspired other municipalities and helped boost the cooperative movement in the sector.[13] This interest in the organization and integration of waste pickers derived from the willingness of the first municipalities run by the Workers Party to incorporate waste pickers' demands. In turn, this willingness was due to this party's high responsiveness to claims coming from Brazilian social movements in general.[14] The process of democratic empowerment of local government through decentralization in the 1980s, which conferred more autonomy and financial resources to municipalities to address their issues, made it possible for these governments to pursue a social agenda on their own.[15]

Thus the early years of the 1990s saw an increase in the number of organized waste pickers into cooperatives and also an increase in support these organizations received from NGOs and then from public-sector agencies. As the literature shows, individual waste pickers have no tradition of cooperation with one another, and thus NGOs were decisive and still are in facilitating the organizing process; they help in the creation of trust and trustworthiness among waste pickers.[16] The National Waste and Citizenship Forum (FNLC),[17] a multistakeholder platform, was launched in 1998 as a result of the United Nations Children's Fund's (UNICEF) work on child waste pickers. The forum was made up of nineteen entities[18] whose objectives were to eradicate child labor at open dumps, replace open dumps with sanitary landfills, and promote partnerships between municipalities and waste pickers. Waste and citizenship forums were later created at state and local levels with the same objectives.

The FNLC helped to give more visibility to the social and environmental importance of the work carried out by the waste pickers, and it also brought the existing cooperatives/associations into the spotlight. This visibility had an impact nationwide as it inspired other groups of waste pickers to get organized, creating the basis for social activism that led later on to the creation of their national movement.[19]

In June 2001, the "First National Congress of Brazilian Waste Pickers" was held in Brasília with the support of organizations such as the Catholic NGO Pastoral de Rua, the FNLC, UNICEF, Belo Horizonte's municipal administration, the University of Brasília, and the Ministry of the Environment, among others. It was at this event that the MNCR was created.

The state of Minas Gerais had been in the forefront in organizing waste pickers and in the interaction between government agencies and waste pickers' organizations. Since 2002, a festival called Waste and Citizenship, backed by the FNLC, was organized by Asmare (then the only existing waste picker organization in Belo Horizonte, the capital city of the state) with the support of NGOs, the municipality, and other actors. The festival was a three- to four-day event with workshops, public talks, art performances, and internal meetings of the nascent MNCR. It was a meeting place for waste pickers from all over Brazil, as well as NGOs, public officers, and sympathizers of the waste pickers' movement.

Notwithstanding all the challenges waste pickers still face in the country, it is undisputed that there is a strong network of multiple stakeholders linked together with the purpose of strengthening these workers as political and economic actors in solid waste systems. This has enabled the formation of partnerships between many waste pickers' organizations and local governments in municipal recycling schemes. Also, the national government has a strong commitment to public policies geared to this sector, indicating that waste pickers' organizations have managed to achieve a semipublic status[20] in the country, with support coming from various levels of government and from various institutions such as development agencies and the private sector.[21]

In 2003 the federal government established the Inter-ministerial Committee for Social Inclusion of the waste pickers to propose and develop policies for the waste pickers. Among other things, this committee has made financial resources available for studies and research, for training and capacity building, for the purchase of vehicles and other equipment, and for setting up facilities. Brazil's National Solid Waste Policy, which ensures the rights of informal recyclers as preferential service providers in municipal recycling programs, was established in 2010.

Cooperatives

According to the National Solid Waste Diagnostic,[22] there are 1,200 organizations of waste pickers in the whole country; this must be a "guesstimate" obtained from the MNCR since the national movement has not yet managed to have a reliable database on their affiliates. The National Sanitation Survey[23] identified 994 municipalities (18 percent of the total number of municipalities in Brazil) with selective waste collection, of which 653 (66 percent) have partnerships with waste pickers' cooperatives. In the remaining 279 municipalities existing cooperatives rely only on selling recyclables for their income. Broadly speaking, waste pickers may develop the following work specialization in a cooperative:[24]

- *Street waste pickers:* Reclaim recyclables from mixed wastes disposed in garbage bags placed on the streets or dumpsters. Some pickers may have arrangements with commercial and office buildings and be able to access previously segregated material. Street pickers can carry up to 800 kg with their pushcarts. It is the most strenuous work performed by waste pickers.
- *Motorized pickers:* Collect recyclables as part of door-to-door selective waste collection scheme run by municipalities in partnership with waste picker cooperatives. Some cooperatives may enter into direct agreements with commercial and office buildings to collect large quantities of recyclables by truck or other vehicles.
- *Sorter:* Work picking and sorting by type recyclables disposed either on a conveyor belt or other sorting area or device.

- *Operational:* Coop members who process sorted recyclables, weighting, baling, shredding, storing, and other operations.
- *Workshop:* Some coops run special workshops such as carpentry and crafts and therefore have members allocated to these special activities.[25]

There are various revenue models for waste picker cooperatives. In cities where official recycling schemes include waste pickers, there may be formal agreements (covenants) whereby the city recognizes the contribution a given cooperative makes to the city's waste management system by providing it with monthly subsidies. These subsidies are not directly linked to service delivery and are sometimes financed out of the social welfare budget. In other cities, cooperatives are hired under a contract with terms similar to that of formal solid waste contractors.[26] These two arrangements with municipalities are a result of the activism of the waste pickers' movement. Cooperatives without either formal agreements or contracts have to generate income exclusively from the sale of recyclables. Cooperatives may also enter agreements with private companies for collection of recyclables generated at their premises. For instance, waste pickers' cooperatives were hired to provide collection of recyclables at the stadiums of the 2014 World Cup.

Usually, waste picker cooperatives supported by municipalities have a recycling warehouse,[27] a place where they can sort materials, store, and process them for sales. These places may be improvised sorting sheds or proper warehouses with individual or collective boxes for sorting and proper places for all the other processes. In these spaces, recyclables are sorted, weighed, shredded, baled, and stored for further commercialization by the cooperatives. Revenues are split among members according to internal rules established by each cooperative. Though there have been significant improvements in infrastructure at waste pickers' recycling warehouses, levels of internal efficiency and working conditions leave much room for improvement. Compared to other countries that do not support waste pickers,[28] working conditions might appear satisfactory. Working hours for waste pickers are usually long (eight to ten hours) but can even be longer for those cooperatives with no municipal support and for autonomous waste pickers.

Working in a cooperative can be daunting for some waste pickers, especially those who are "freedom lovers," that is, those who have difficulty working under collective regulations (such as opening and closing hours that limit the freedom of waste pickers compared to those outside the cooperative environment). But for some it can be a liberating escape from the difficulties of family life. This is especially so for women pickers since time flexibility, equity in earnings, and facilities for child care are among the reasons given why women find the cooperative model more advantageous. In fact, fieldwork carried out in Minas Gerais found that women pickers identified cooperatives as a safe haven where they can escape domestic violence.[29]

Waste pickers in Brazil also form second-level cooperatives (networks of many cooperatives), which function as a network for bulk selling of recyclables and for semi-processing of materials in order to aggregate value to them. There are a few networks in Minas Gerais, such as the Redesol, Cataunidos, and in other states such as the Catabahia (Bahia state), Catasampa (in Sao Paulo) and others.

Waste Pickers in Minas Gerais

The state of Minas Gerais is located in the southeast of Brazil and has a population of 19,597,330.[30] Its capital city, Belo Horizonte, has a developed industrial sector, being traditionally a center of the Brazilian steel and metallurgical industries. The industrial recycling park in Minas Gerais is not strong, so recyclables are usually taken elsewhere for processing, generally to São Paulo state. This represents a difficulty for waste pickers' cooperatives in terms of moving up in the recycling chain. It makes them more dependent on middlemen who have huge storehouses, which makes it easier for them to meet the required minimum quantity for commercialization demanded by recycling industries.

The FNLC encouraged the creation of state and municipal forums. The first state forum created in Brazil was the Waste and Citizenship Forum of Minas Gerais (FELC-MG) in 1999, under the leadership of the State Secretariat for the Environment and the local waste picker association Asmare. The FELC-MG convened societal and governmental agencies, private and public universities, the state legislative chamber, and others.

The FELC-MG supported the organizing of cooperatives in the capital city and elsewhere. It also played a major role in building the capacity of municipalities toward inclusive solid waste management, and it was a space where important demands from the Minas Gerais Chapter of the MNCR were discussed and alliances with key actors formed. One such alliance, forged within the FELC-MG, was with the Committee of Popular Participation of the State Parliament, sympathetic state members of parliament who were crucial in supporting many advances demanded by waste pickers in the state.

Two organizations joined the FELC-MG in the 2000s, which became very important in furthering the agenda of social inclusion in the state of Minas Gerais. One was from the civil society, the NGO Instituto Nenuca de Desenvolvimento Sustentável (INSEA), and the other one was a governmental body, the Reference Centre for Recycling of the state of Minas Gerais (CMRR). INSEA was created in 2001 with the purpose of integrating professionals from different backgrounds, such as engineers and social scientists, who could give advice to municipalities on integrated solid waste management and also to help the MNCR in their efforts to organize waste pickers. CMRR was created in 2008 by the government of Minas Gerais. Its mission was to offer administrative and organizational support to waste pickers in Minas Gerais and to act as linkage between their organizations and the state government.[31]

The capital city of Minas Gerais, Belo Horizonte, formed its Municipal Waste and Citizenship Forum (FMLC-BH) later in the year 2000.[32] This forum came out of necessity since the number of cooperatives in Belo Horizonte grew at one point from one to ten. New groups were formed, inspired by the success story of Asmare's involvement in a partnership with the city and due to rising unemployment. A public space was needed to discuss rules for engagement with and support from the municipality. While Asmare, the oldest group, had around three hundred members in the year 2000, membership in these new cooperatives varies from ten to twenty-six members. Growth of cooperatives in the capital city inspired organizing in the rest of the state. Recent figures indicate there are two hundred cooperatives in the whole state.[33]

Since the creation of the FNLC the federal government started to focus on national capacity-building programs for waste pickers' organizations and for waste experts, on issues concerning integrated solid waste management in general, and on specific themes concerning recycling in particular, including management of cooperatives (democratic governance, business, etc.). In Minas Gerais, the FELC-MG, in partnership with the State Secretariat for the Environment and other state and nongovernmental agencies, also started to focus on capacity building of cooperatives and technical staff from municipalities as a way to spread the concept of an inclusive approach to solid waste management. Over time these capacity-building programs started to rely increasingly on participatory methodologies, and thus the knowledge from waste picker leaders who had on-the-ground expertise on recycling and on organizing became fundamental.

Social Movements and Political Actors

The MNCR, founded in 2001, is a social movement committed to organizing waste pickers and advancing their main collective demands. Its affiliates are cooperatives and associations that abide by their guiding principles: worker control of the organization, that is, by waste pickers; direct action; autonomy from political parties, governments, and the private sector; class solidarity; direct democracy; and collective decision making.[34]

MNCR's governance structures include the National Committee, a major decision-making body, a National Articulation Committee (with representatives from the regional committees), regional commissions, and state committees. Cooperatives elect their coordinators on a regular basis and these coordinators elect representatives for the regional commissions, which in turn elect representatives for the state commissions and so forth up the power hierarchy.

As the waste pickers' movement developed, it moved from reliance on NGO staff or the Waste and Citizenship forums to represent their interests to representing their interests themselves. Waste picker leaders take on organizing and mobilizing work and play a role in governance. Thus the waste pickers' cooperatives developed a system whereby leaders are paid for time taken away from work to perform leadership roles to make up for their loss of income due to less time spent in routine duties; the income they receive may sometimes come out of the budget of capacity-building programs or sometimes from the cooperative budget. Some elected leaders, no matter how busy their agendas as representatives are, strive to keep a certain routine and continue to work as waste pickers.

MNCR's class analysis of society sees waste pickers as workers, as part of a broader class of the oppressed, and thus as a movement MNCR has fought for the collective rights of waste pickers and for their recognition of service providers in solid waste systems. MNCR's demands have been directed both to governments and to the industry as they realize that they are both part of an urban system and part of a value chain.

One of its early strategies was to create a collective identity of pickers as workers and to struggle for public policy. One of the characteristics of the MNCR since its creation has been

> its ability to act both as a social movement (with its distinctive features: engagement in protests, social marches and other activities associated to social activism) as well as an strategic actor (its willingness to participate in committees, working groups and forums—meeting places with other actors from governments and the private sector).[35] *This is one of the distinctive features of the whole scenario of social activism in this area in Brazil.* This could be identified in the performance of earlier organizations of waste pickers like Coopamare (São Paulo) and ASMARE (Belo Horizonte).[36] (. . .) As put by one of Asmare's advisor, we have always been good at occupying spaces at strategic moments. (. . .) We tried to occupy space where the State was changing its mode of governance. . . . We had the cleverness of seeing that public policy has a fundamental role in social changes.[37]

The existence of a social movement is important for the advancement in integration of waste pickers in the country, but another factor contributing to the push for progressive policies and legislation in SWM was and still is to some extent "the role played by people in key position at governments (first at local and later at sub-national and national level) that were sensitive to their cause and had had in the past opportunity to work with them either as consultants and/or as social agents."[38]

In the words of one of the key advisors of Asmare:

> We have leaders (. . .) that have a fundamental role in making the State overcome bureaucracy and centralism (. . .) occupying strategic positions in government: municipal, state and national level (. . .) this is the *distinctive feature in Brazil* to have committed leaderships, for example, in many ministries, at the Banco do Brazil Foundation, Petrobras (. . .) So this has provoked important achievements.[39]

These alliances have enabled strategic openings that helped waste pickers and their supporting NGOs pursue their goals of social inclusion in SWM, initially on left-oriented local governments but in following years on many other levels and with administrations from different political affiliations. Within the political system waste pickers managed to have strategic alliances not only with the executive but also with the judicial and legislative branches. The Ministério Público (Public Office for the Defense of Individual and Collective Rights) at the national and subnational levels was a relevant actor in many success stories of waste pickers' struggles.[40]

Lastly but not least, another key factor in furthering a progressive agenda has been social communication and social mobilization by the MNCR and their supporting organizations to change the social identity of waste pickers from vagrants to environmental agents. The symbolic construction of an identity of waste pickers as environmental professionals has contributed to their visibility and recognition.[41]

Payment for Environmental Services: The Recycling Bonus

In the past, waste pickers relied only on the selling of recyclables for their income.[42] Over time, the pickers have been successful in their struggle to be formal partners in municipal recycling systems. In some cases they were able to win proper *contracts* regulating their relationship with the cities, arguing they should be paid in the same terms formal contractors are for collection of domestic waste. At the same time, the MNCR continued to fight for a legal framework at the national level, and eventually the MNCR was successful in having the 2010 National Solid Waste Policy state that cooperatives should be preferred service providers in recycling schemes. The national government instituted the legal framework that enabled municipalities to hire waste pickers with contracts instead of social accords as in the past.

While having laws in place is an important achievement, it is no guarantee that cities will in fact hire their cooperatives rather than formal contractors. MNCR found that it lacked bargaining power to fight the industry for fairer prices. Thus, in addition to fighting for contracts with the cities, they started fighting for *payment for environmental services*, a kind of compensation for the services they render by retrieving recyclables that would otherwise be dumped. In Minas Gerais, waste pickers went further and took advantage of strategic alliances they had with members of parliament (the Minas Gerais Chamber) and with public officers of the state government and pursued payment of environmental service in what came to be called "*bolsa reciclagem*," the recycling bonus.

Payment for environmental services had been the subject of discussions in the state and municipal Waste and Citizenship Forums, in many editions of the yearly Waste and Citizenship Festival, and other venues. The mobilization for the recycling bonus predates the process of discussion and approval of the law itself. With the support of the Reference Center for Recycling (CMRR), the idea of a state law for environmental payment gained momentum. The bargaining process began in 2010 when the governor asked his party[43] to present the proposal in the House of Representatives. The party accepted his proposal. This set in motion the bargaining over the specific provisions of the law. Debates and consultations took place in meetings called by the director of the CMRR during the first half of 2011. The participants were representatives of waste pickers, INSEA, governmental agencies in charge of environment regulations, and CMRR.

The main issue in the debate was the nature of the recognition to be awarded to waste pickers as providers of environmental services to the state. There were two contrasting positions. The waste pickers had started to demand that they be offered contracts for service provision. Further, they wanted the state government to require municipalities to hire cooperatives for selective waste collection systems instead of leaving it to a municipality's discretion. The state government argued, however, for a law that addressed the compensation for environmental services only. The state government accepted that the waste picker must be paid for the work he or she performs. But it argued that since the waste pickers are already paid in their commercial transactions in the recyclable market, any extra money transfers authorized by the State would be an incentive to waste pickers to continue to provide the service. This interpretation prevailed in the negotiations.

The law was approved on November 22, 2011, without opposition or any major debate in the House. The justification of the law reads as follows: "The institution of the recycling monetary incentive aims at promoting the reintroduction of recyclable materials in regular processes of production through the incentive to reduce the squandering of natural resources and energy, in the setting of a major priority, that is, the economic and social inclusion of waste pickers."[44]

The phrasing reveals the wider political meaning of the law. The social purpose (social inclusion of waste pickers) is stressed as the major priority, along with preventing the depletion of natural resources. The waste picker is presented as a worker who, by providing a service that public authorities must provide by force of law, deserves a bonus in addition to the payment obtained in commercial transactions not regulated by the state, that is, which are realized in the private realm.

The law establishes a monetary incentive to be paid by the state government to waste pickers who are members of a cooperative or workers' association. The payment was due at the end of a three-month period of work. It is the first law approved in the country that authorizes the use of public money for ongoing payments for environmental work done by waste pickers.

Payment for environmental services should not be mistaken for the payment for service collection of recyclables some cooperatives receive from agreements or contracts they may have with municipalities. While payment for service collection comes from municipal budgets, the recycling bonus comes from the state of Minas Gerais budget as a compensation for protecting the environment. It provides additional revenue for cooperatives.

The recipients of the payment are cooperatives and workers' associations, who receive the money after every three months of work undertaken. To receive the bonus, the cooperative or association is required to demonstrate that it is in good standing in every legal and administrative aspect of its organization. The allocation of the money for each recipient follows the general rule according to which 90 percent will be distributed to waste pickers based on their monthly commercialized production and 10 percent will be used to improve the organization and administration of the cooperative or association. The calculation of each worker's production is based on daily records of production and commercial transactions covering ninety days (three months). The funds for the payment come from the state treasury. The total amount per year reserved for financing the incentive is determined by the state government and may vary depending on its investment priorities and fiscal capacity.

It is worth pointing out that this bargaining did not arouse any great enthusiasm or mobilization among the organized waste pickers. According to some leaders who were interviewed, many waste pickers did not believe that the government would really "keep the promise" of reserving money every year for the incentive. But the majority was happy about the possibility of getting more money without the need for extra work.

Implementation of the Law

The recycling bonus law provided that the law should be implemented according to rules approved by a coordinating committee. The establishment of this committee and its responsibilities were defined in a governmental decree, signed by the state governor on June 4, 2012. In contrast to the law, the decree connected the monetary incentive with the state policy for the management of solid waste approved in 2009. The decree presented the incentive as a means of minimizing discarded waste, thus reducing "environmental pressure." The priority of promoting socioeconomic inclusion of waste pickers was not referred to in the decree.

The decree established the composition of the coordinating committee, which includes representatives of various government agencies and of waste pickers; one representative of the CMRR; three statewide representatives of the waste pickers; and one representative of the Ministério Público Estadual (Public Office for the Defense of Individual and Collective Rights of Minas Gerais, or MPE). This composition of members would place the waste pickers in the minority in any voting, but the MPE usually sides with the citizens and many times against the government.

The decree gives the committee the responsibility to define the rules for the implementation of the monetary incentive; validate the registration of every cooperative and association in the list of eligible recipients of the incentive; define procedures for monitoring the use of the incentive by each cooperative and association; and create incentives for a network for sharing information and experiences related to waste picking, which helps to bring together cooperatives and associations throughout Minas Gerais. This committee is also in charge of monitoring administration and managing procedures for each cooperative or association to register the production and the commercial transactions of the individual waste pickers who are the final recipients of the money.

The committee quickly reached agreement on the procedure for the identification of cooperatives and workers' associations eligible to receive the incentive. A public announcement about the incentive was made through mass media, which asked cooperatives and associations to request registration. In the first year (2012–2013), only cooperatives and associations within the metropolitan area of Belo Horizonte would be eligible (thirty-four municipalities). There was more conflict over whether or not a cooperative or association had to fully comply with the requirements to be in "good standing" in order to receive the bonus. While waste picker representatives wanted more flexibility, the government insisted that the organizations must be fully in good standing before they could receive bonus payments. The committee agreed, however, that the CMRR and the INSEA should provide assistance to cooperatives and associations in their efforts to overcome administrative problems and debts with fiscal authorities as quickly as possible.

For the definition of the unit of measurement and the criteria for the pricing of different kinds of recyclables, the committee established a task group of waste picker representatives and technical experts to draft pricing criteria for the recyclables to be included in the list of items eligible for the monetary incentive. The task force agreed on the use of the metric ton as reference unit for calculating the payment, but the pricing of different kinds of recyclables was an issue. Should the pricing simply follow market practices? Or should the pricing reflect the amount of work required for picking and preparing specific kinds of recyclables (a higher price than that provided by the market)? The issue centered on the expected influence of the monetary incentive on the waste picker's behavior. If the main justification for the bonus is to add social value to waste picking, to encourage waste pickers to remain on the job, and to encourage street dwellers and unemployed people to join waste pickers' cooperatives and associations, then the list of recyclables eligible for the benefit and the respective price should follow the logic of the market. That is, the idea of using the monetary incentive to compensate for lower prices paid for specific recyclables in the market should be rejected.

In the debate, the waste pickers' representatives argued that the monetary incentive must take into account the actual work of waste picking. Are materials abundant or rare? Are they regularly or irregularly found? Do they have high or low value in the market? It is worth noting that the separation of waste by kind is not a widespread practice among urban dwellers in Minas Gerais, which makes waste picking more work-intensive for the individual waste picker. In the end, the task group accepted the argument of the waste pickers, who thus decided the composition of the list of recyclables eligible for the benefit. The recyclables so defined were paper, plastic, glass, and scrap metal. Further, higher prices were set for the two items less valued in the recycling market: scrap metal and glass. These two items require greater effort from waste pickers in the routine work of collection. The monetary bonus then adds a real incentive for picking less valued and more work-intensive recyclables. The coordinating committee approved the rules recommended by the task group.

Finally, the committee discussed procedures for monitoring the routine functioning of the monetary incentive. Government representatives favored formal and bureaucratic procedures. The waste pickers' representatives were concerned with the uncertain amount of money reserved for the incentive and the danger implicit in the legal autonomy granted to municipal governments to enter into contracts with private concerns, which would allow them to plan the management of urban waste without the inclusion of recycling practices.

Outcomes of the Recycling Bonus

Challenges for Cooperatives

Representatives of the government stress the need to improve the organizational and management skills of the people in charge of accounting, administration, and supervision of the different functions in the "line of production" (waste picking, sorting recyclables, preparing recyclables for marketing, the commercial transactions proper). The waste pickers' representatives agree that some degree of professionalism is required to transform waste picking into a competitive and lucrative economic activity. But they also call attention to the strong desire for individual freedom that leads many pickers to choose waste picking as a source of income. This freedom is obviously curtailed whenever waste picking is organized as a "line of production." The waste pickers' representatives insist that each cooperative or association must define and promote its own organizational project and respect decisions made in assemblies of members. According to this view, any monitoring rule designed to establish external control over the functioning of the work process must first be debated by the assembly of members. The waste pickers' representatives are not free to accept proposals discussed in the committee without formal approval of the members.

The second challenge refers to the need to balance the social and the business function of cooperatives. This poses challenges to leaders and members alike. It is worth mentioning here that waste pickers' leaders recognize that the role they play is not easy or simple. They note that there are cooperative or association leaders who are too authoritarian, who keep relevant information for themselves, who lose legitimacy but continue to present themselves as representatives of base members. There are even some cases of leaders who have been dishonest in their financial dealings. Given their relationship with the leaders of cooperatives and associations, who are entitled to speak for the assembly of members, the waste pickers' representatives in the committee are careful when asked to discuss procedures that may interfere with the practices of each cooperative or association. These issues of internal governance and representation are intertwined with issues related to labor processes. They can be highly disruptive of services provided by cooperatives, as internal conflicts can drive away the energy necessary to perform effectively as a service provider.

Another challenge comes from legal requirements that each cooperative or association must comply with in order to receive the money. These requirements include daily registration of the volume of production of the individual waste picker, daily registration of commercial transactions of recyclables traceable to individual waste pickers, and daily registration of individual production by kind of recyclable.

These registrations are part of the routine administration of the cooperative or association and require professional capabilities that are not generally found among waste pickers. When the law requires these procedures, it requires not only new people in the work process, but also new costs that may diminish individual monetary gain, even if only temporarily. It should be pointed out, however, that capacity-building courses on administrative skills have been offered for a decade or so through different government agencies or NGOs. Given the level of formal education of most waste pickers, the education process can be slow. One leader argued that less-well-organized cooperatives need to be supported by the CMRR to overcome problems regarding compliance with the regulations. Cooperatives that have not enjoyed long-term assistance from NGOs, for instance, face more problems either in getting registered in the CMRR's database or in providing the necessary documents after payments are done.

Impact on Waste Pickers

As already mentioned, there are different opinions about the reach and meaning of this law. For some, the law is a success in improving waste pickers' working and living conditions; for others it's a setback in the struggle for full recognition of the waste picker as a provider of services to the state that must be acknowledged and regularly paid. For non-waste-picker supporters of the law, it both provides extra income and stimulates better working practices promoted by the workers themselves without intrusive outside interference.

Waste picker leaders who are positive about the law focus on the realities of the lives of waste pickers: It is hard work for very low pay. These leaders agree that the monetary incentive is a concrete gain in the individual income that does not have a negative influence on the waste picker's commitment to the movement's major cause. It is also a way out of frequent periods of financial instability. At the same time, they acknowledge the law's limitations and challenges. One leader argued, for instance, that "we need ... to make it a state policy in the sense of having financial resources included in the PPAG not as a parliamentary amendment."[45] Another waste picker leader seconded this by stating that "as a waste picker I have fought for this policy as an improvement to our lives (. . .) the bonus forced us to be more organized in managerial terms (. . .) but we need the payments to be more on time (. . .) we have to comply with the regulations and the government should pay us on time."[46] Delayed payments have continued to be a problem. In addition, waste picker *members* of different cooperatives in Belo Horizonte were positive about the recycling bonus.[47]

But others see the law as a setback and call attention to the wider political context of the debate concerning available models for organizing solid waste management in urban areas. These critics are concerned that political authorities will favor incineration without restrictions or another model of waste management that does not preserve a place for recycling. For this group, the recycling bonus law is a governmental strategy aimed at neutralizing waste pickers' opposition to the ongoing negotiations coordinated by the state government geared toward the formation of municipal consortiums for waste management.[48]

The state government is promoting municipal consortiums as an economic solution for the provision of efficient solid waste management in small and medium-sized towns. Some waste picker leaders fear that incineration might prevail as the model.[49] These leaders further fear that the monetary incentive—for them a mere palliative for the low income derived from waste picking—might demobilize the waste pickers at a time when political mobilization is crucial to preserve the long-term future of waste picking in Minas Gerais. As a waste picker leader[50] says, "we are afraid that granting of the recycling bonus is going to be used by the state government to neutralize our opposition to their proposal for a PPP."[51]

From 2012 to the first trimester of 2014 there had been ten payments.[52] The number of cooperatives participating has fluctuated from between forty-seven and sixty-six.[53] A parliamentary amendment for US $1.54 million[54] was approved by Parliament to cover 2015 payments. Because each cooperative decides how they split the money between members, it is hard to estimate the amount an average waste picker might have received. As one example, however, waste pickers from the cooperative Coopert received around 4,000 Brazilian reals each trimester in the first year of the scheme. Last year they were receiving only around 700 reals for each trimester because the number of participating coops in the scheme increased.

It will take a few years before we can fully assess the impacts of the recycling bonus on the sector. It will be important to assess the bonus in terms of its economic impact on the management of cooperatives in addition to its political effects. Whether the bonus will in fact contribute significantly to improve the status of cooperatives in the value chain and whether it will curtail social mobilization is still an open question. The MNCR's past history of acting both as a social actor and as a strategic actor seems to indicate it can resist co-optation, but only the future can provide an answer.

The mobilizing that led to bargaining over the details and implementation of the recycling bonus law took place in many different spaces and over many years. Victories came in stages. In 2010, after nearly two decades of struggle by activists, Brazil's National Solid Waste Policy, which ensures the rights of informal recyclers, was established. Waste picker organizations have been able to begin to formalize their relationship with some municipal governments and formalize their place in the solid waste management system. The recycling bonus law is seen by some—but not all—as another step in this process. The law has enabled waste pickers' organizations in the state of Minas Gerais to receive payment for the service they provide to the environment (reclaiming recyclables from the waste stream and selling them to the industry).

Key to these successes have been two moral claims by the waste pickers and their allies. The first claim is that they are workers deserving the protections that other workers in Brazil enjoy. The second is that they provide an important environmental service and should be rewarded by the state for that service. Organizing has proven beneficial to waste pickers in both tangible and intangible ways, raising social status and self-esteem along with incomes and quality of life through better working conditions. When asked if organizing brought better social and economic conditions to their lives, 81 percent of the organized waste pickers from Cataunidos network in Brazil responded yes, and most responses pointed out that the sense of solidarity found in a membership-based organization was one of the reasons for them to join.[55]

The progress toward more inclusion of waste pickers into solid waste systems in Brazil seems to be part of an all-out effort toward democracy building (understood here as going beyond the procedural terms). This includes fostering civic engagement, organizing informal workers, designing participatory platforms, and social mobilization for state responsiveness.[56] The national movement of waste pickers and their supporting NGOs managed to form strategic alliances within the political system (sympathetic public officers) that helped them to pursue changes in public policy. They also found allies in the private sector.

Despite the benefits of the recycling bonus, it has also provided some challenges for waste pickers and their organizations. These include pressures to improve organizational skills at cooperatives, pressure for productivity, and possible demobilizing effects for continued political struggles. We might end by adding a challenge common for all stakeholders. Elsewhere, Dias[57] had called for a more balanced view about waste picking activities. The author argued that failure to understand waste picking in a holistic way, that is, in its service provision dimension as a sociotechnical system (urban waste with its public health component), in its economical dimension as part of a value chain, and in its social dimension (income generation for less disadvantaged communities), can be detrimental to sustainability. A one-dimensional view of the occupation (whatever dimension it might be) conspires against coupling waste and citizenship in the long run.

There are costs to the kind of formalization waste pickers are undergoing. As they advocate to be recognized as service providers for public systems of solid wastes, demands for efficiency and efficacy are bound to increase. After all, municipalities that hire them need to be accountable to their citizens. Both waste pickers' organization and the sociogovernmental organizations that support them need to arrive at a multidimensional understanding of the occupation and agree on a common set of performance indicators, indicators that take into account that cooperatives have a social function (its livelihood dimension), perform a service in public health (by providing service for urban solid waste systems), and is an important economical actor in the recycling chain. Whether the recycling bonus can contribute to push all actors toward a transformative change will need further assessments in the future, though.

DOCUMENTS CONSULTED

- CMRR Reports: 2008, 2009, 2010 Waste and Citizenship Festivals.
- CMRR Relatório de Prestação de Contas do Bolsa Reciclagem, 2014 (internal document).
- Forum Estadual Lixo e Cidadania (State Waste and Citizenship Forum). 2011. *Manual para organização e negociação dos serviços—sistemas de coleta seletiva com a participação dos catadores.* Belo Horizonte: CMRR.
- Governo de Minas Gerais/Secretaria de Estado Extraordinária de Gestão Metropolitana (Government of Minas Gerais/Special Agency for Metropolitan Planning and Management). Prioridades de Gestão para as Regiões Metropolitanas de Belo Horizonte e do Vale do Aço (Management Priorities for the Metropolitan Areas of Belo Horizonte and of the Steel Valley).
- Governo de Belo Horizonte/Gabinete do Prefeito. 2011. Projeto de lei regulamentadora do serviço de limpeza urbana e de manejo de resíduos sólidos em Belo Horizonte. (Government of Belo Horizonte/From the Mayor's Office. Proposal of bill regulating the management of urban waste and of recyclables in Belo Horizonte).
- INSTITUTO NENUCA DE DESENVOLVIMENTO SUSTENTÁVEL. *Perfil sócio-econômico dos catadores da rede CATAUNIDOS—2007.* Belo Horizonte: INSEA/UFMG/FELC, 2007. 31 p. Relatório.
- Minas Gerais. Law no. 19.823, approved on November 22, 2011. It authorizes the state government to reserve public revenue for the payment of a monetary incentive to waste pickers: recycling bonus law.

- Minas Gerais. Governmental Decree no. 45.975, signed on June 4, 2012. It defines procedures for the payment of the monetary incentive authorized by the state Law no. 19.823; it establishes the composition and responsibilities of the coordinating committee in charge of the implementation and monitoring of the recycling bonus law.
- WIEGO—IEMS fieldwork notes and key interviews for Belo Horizonte City.

Acronyms

- Asmare—Association of Waste Pickers of Belo Horizonte
- Coopamare—Cooperative of Waste Pickers of São Paulo
- CMRR—Recycling Reference Center of Minas Gerais
- FEAM—Environmental Foundation of Minas Gerais
- FELC-MG—Waste and Citizenship Forum of Minas Gerais
- FIEMG-MG—Federation of Industries of Minas Gerais
- FNLC—National Waste and Citizenship Forum
- FMLC-BH—Municipal Waste and Citizenship of Belo Horizonte
- INSEA—Nenuka's Institute, an NGO
- MNCR—National Movement of Waste Pickers of Brazil
- MPE—Public Office for the Defense of Individual and Collective Rights of Minas Gerais
- SEMAD—Environmental Agency of Minas Gerais
- SLU—Superintendency of Public Cleansing of Belo Horizonte city
- SNIS—National Sanitation Information System
- SWM—Solid Waste Management

STREET VENDORS IN LIBERIA

A Written Agreement With Authorities and a Secure Workplace

Milton A. Weeks and Pewee Reed

Street vendors are an integral part of urban economies around the world, offering easy access to a wide range of goods and services in public spaces. They sell everything from fresh vegetables to prepared foods, from building materials to garments and crafts, from consumer electronics to auto repairs to haircuts. Street vendors are a large and visible workforce in cities, yet it is difficult to accurately estimate their numbers.[1] While government statistics are not available for Liberia, official statistics from other countries confirm that street trade accounts for a significant proportion of informal employment in African cities: 13 percent in Dakar, Senegal; 19 percent in Cotonou, Benin; and 24 percent in Lomé, Togo.[2]

Low barriers to entry, limited start-up costs, and flexible hours are some of the factors that draw street vendors to the occupation. Many people enter street vending because they cannot find a job in the formal economy. But earnings are low and risks are high for many vendors.[3] The lack of a secure place to vend is a key problem for street vendors, as is lack of a safe place to store their goods. Vendors are vulnerable to harassment, confiscations, and evictions by the police and local authorities. Even vendors with a license may face problems finding a secure vending location, and even those who comply with regulations may have their goods confiscated.[4] Further, competition among vendors for space in the streets and access to customers is strong in many cities. And vendors must be able to negotiate effectively with wholesalers and customers.[5]

Most street vendors are self-employed and must learn to negotiate effectively not only with wholesalers and customers but also with the police and local authorities. Membership-based organizations help street vendors navigate their relationship with the authorities, build solidarity, and solve problems with other vendors. Several have developed innovative ways to work with cities to keep the streets clean and safe while gaining a secure livelihood for vendors.

The situation of street vendors in Monrovia, Liberia, fits this general pattern. Before and during the protests and negotiations documented in this chapter, both the city police of Monrovia and the Liberian National Police conducted repeated raids and evictions of street vendors in Monrovia, arguing that the vendors were obstructing the free flow of vehicular and pedestrian traffic. This chapter focuses on collective negotiations between the National Petty Traders Union of Liberia (NAPETUL) and the city government in Monrovia and the events leading up to them. The term "collective negotiations" is used here since the mainly self-employed street vendors do not negotiate with an employer, as in standard "collective bargaining." Individual street vendors have to negotiate with multiple stakeholders: wholesalers and customers to off-street businesses to police and other local authorities. Organizations of street vendors, where they exist, typically engage in collective negotiations with the police and municipal governments. In these negotiations, as in collective bargaining, the organizations tend to represent the collective interests of their members. In addition, these organizations often have to also negotiate relationships with other street vendor organizations competing for favor with the authorities.

The success of NAPETUL in reaching a memorandum of understanding with city authorities is a result of numerous factors. These include consolidation of organizations, which makes it possible to speak for vendors with one voice, street marches and demonstrations, press attention, and support, especially training and skill building with the assistance of nongovernmental organizations (NGOs). But the vendors also needed willing partners on the other side of the negotiating table.

Background

The West African country of Liberia is bordered by Sierra Leone, Guinea, and Cote D'Ivoire. The country is made up of 111,369 square kilometers divided into fifteen subdivisions, which are referred to as counties. Liberia is one of Africa's oldest nations and declared its independence on July 26, 1847. The official language is English, and the country is rich in natural resources including iron ore, rubber, diamonds, timber, and gold. Eighty percent (2000 estimate) of its 3.9 million citizens, however, live below the poverty line.[6]

The country and its people experienced a bitter civil war between 1989 and 2003. This led to the deaths of an estimated 250,000 people, or about 7 percent of the population, and many thousands more fled the fighting. In 2003, an interim government was installed and took the country to free and fair elections in 2005. After the elections, Madame Ellen Johnson Sirleaf became Africa's first female head of state. Sirleaf was re-elected for a second six-year term in 2011.

Since the end of the civil war and the installation of the democratically elected government, Liberia has experienced relative but fragile peace and stability. Most of the infrastructure of the country was destroyed during the years of conflict. Economic and social progress has been slow but positive. The prolonged civil war left the country overrun with weapons and in economic ruin. Even now, nine years after the end of the conflict, the capital has limited electricity and running water. Corruption is rife in government and in the private sector. Unemployment and illiteracy are endemic. Protection of civil rights, however, has become a top-of-the-agenda issue, and numerous civil society groups have sprung up to advocate for people's rights. The rights of workers have improved, but a long debated Decent Work Bill, which focuses on the rights of employees, was only passed quite recently (May 2015).[7]

The informal economy in Liberia is very large. The majority of the Liberian workforce is engaged in the informal economy. According to Core Welfare Indicator Questionnaire (CWIQ) 2007, out of an estimated 1.1 million people in the workforce, just 170,000 (15 percent) are employed in the formal economy.

Monrovia is the capital of Liberia and as such is the cultural, political, and financial hub for the entire country. The population of Monrovia ballooned during the civil war and has further ballooned since the end of it. Many Liberians migrated to the capital city seeking refuge as the fighting around the country intensified. Most of these have not returned home, and a city that was built for a population of 300,000 inhabitants now has a population of more than one million, containing 29 percent of the total population of Liberia. This population explosion has put significant strain on the resources of the city, including in the areas of garbage collection, water and sanitation, traffic control and congestion, housing, and crime.

Monrovia is governed as a metropolitan city called the Greater Monrovia District. The Monrovia City Corporation (MCC), established in 1973, is the city's governing body and is responsible for running many of Monrovia's services. The MCC is headed by a mayor, who is appointed by the president of Liberia and supported by a city council, which is also appointed by the president. The MCC has stated that it is dedicated to the task of revitalizing Monrovia and taking it into the future as a clean, green, and progressive capital city. The city government has been actively involved in promoting the cleaning of the city, initiating "green" projects, constructing a new landfill for secondary waste collection, and decongesting the city center.

The mayor during the initial negotiations with the street vendors was Madame Mary Broh, known as a no-nonsense administrator. Prior to her appointment as mayor, she had previously successfully held a number of "tough" public assignments. At both the Liberia Passport Office in the Ministry of Foreign Affairs and again as deputy managing director for administration at the National Ports Authority (NPA), she was applauded for cleaning up corrupt and inefficient operations. When the president appointed her to head the Monrovia city government, it was with the express mandate to clean up what had become a dirty, unhygienic, and congested city and a generally poorly run city administration. By 2009, she had achieved significant success in cleaning up and giving a facelift to City Hall and had started developing a waste management system for the city and instituting various other innovative initiatives to improve the city's image.

Street Vendors and Their Union

The National Petty Traders Union of Liberia (NAPETUL) was established in November 2009 with the objective of "interceding and advocating for the social and economic emancipation and rights of all street sellers in Liberia and to inject into them the spirit of awareness, self-esteem and self-actualization."[8] Members of NAPETUL are engaged in the sale of dried goods (nonperishables) including shoes, handbags, slippers, cosmetics, clothing, and electronic goods. They hawk their wares on major streets. Most do not have permanent structures from which they operate. Some use wheelbarrows or set up a table on sidewalks and street corners. Perishable goods including foodstuff are sold in open-air markets by marketers grouped under a separate organization, the Liberia Marketing Association (LMA).

The membership of NAPETUL, estimated to be about three thousand, is made up of both Liberians and non-Liberians. NAPETUL strives for gender equality among its membership. This is evidenced in the leadership structure of the organization, in which the national chairperson, treasurer, and field coordinator are currently all women while the co-chairperson, secretary general, and assistant secretary general are men. Many of the members of NAPETUL are single young women, most of whom are also single mothers. NAPETUL estimates that roughly 60 percent of its total membership is female. A little more than 3 percent of members are migrants from other African countries, the largest group (five hundred) coming from Nigeria.

According to the NAPETUL database, more than 50 percent of NAPETUL's members are youths, many of whom lost their parents, sponsors, and guardians during the civil crisis. As a result, these youths have decided to engage in street vending, petty trading, and hawking as a means of ensuring economic survival.

As many were very young and had no sustainable source of income after they lost their parents or guardians, they were unable to pursue higher education or vocational training.

Many thousands of Liberian youths are also former combatants from the civil crisis. According to NAPETUL, of the more than forty thousand petty traders, only 1 percent are college graduates or college dropouts. A little over 50 percent have some level of high school education while about 45 percent are elementary or junior high school students or dropouts. This is not surprising as, according to the World Bank (World Development Indicators database), the average years of formal schooling of Liberians over the age of fifteen is only 2.5 years. According to NAPETUL's 2013–2014 registration record, 60 percent of its members are young women who have invested all of their savings in the few goods they were selling on the streets.

Starting in 2009, NAPETUL leadership engaged the Monrovia City Corporation in a collective negotiation to protect the rights of the NAPETUL membership. The initial negotiations involved the leadership of the two organizations that later joined to form NAPETUL. The Small Business Alliance (SBA), which was made up entirely of street vendors, formed in October 2008 through the assistance of Mr. Daniel Johnson, the former city mayor of Monrovia, and the Petty Traders Association (PTA) formed in 2009.

Street Vendors Engage in Collective Action

Events Leading Up to Collective Negotiations

The story of NAPETUL's collective negotiations with the Monrovia City Corporation began with repeated raids on street vendors by the city police and the Liberia National Police. The police said the raids were due to the petty traders selling on the sidewalks and roads of Monrovia, which was resulting in obstruction of the free flow of vehicular and pedestrian traffic. With the confiscation of these goods, many traders essentially lost all their savings and assets and were literally destitute.

The Petty Traders Association (PTA), numbering about a thousand men and women, decided to march to the Monrovia City Hall to protest the police actions. At City Hall, the petty traders presented a petition to the mayor suggesting that the parties should meet to see how the matter could be amicably resolved. The suggestion for collective negotiations was thus instituted at the initiative of the petty traders, who felt they were being unduly harassed and were incurring significant losses. In response to the concerns raised by the traders, the mayor

promised to work with them, and she immediately joined the traders in a solidarity march to central Monrovia to demonstrate unity of purpose. This was the
start of a complicated and ongoing period of negotiations between the traders
and the city government.

A competing organization of street vendors, the Small Business Alliance (SBA),
was headed by Seyon Tweh as its chairperson. The SBA, in an attempt to build
governance structures for street vendors, had been working with a local business
consultant who provided pro bono advice, the former mayor of Monrovia who
served as SBA's board chair, and the international NGO, Realizing Rights, represented in Liberia by Armah Gray.[9] Realizing Rights activities in Liberia focused
on promoting the Decent Work agenda and greater job opportunities for the
most disadvantaged.

The crux of the MCC position regarding the petty traders selling in the streets
was based on what was then an obscure old city ordinance from 1975 titled Monrovia Ordinance No. 1 (Revised), which "prohibits the selling of foodstuff on the
street, sidewalk or through government offices" and calls for a "fine of not less
than $200.00 for each offense." The law also sets hours of operation for vendors to
operate in city markets (6 a.m. to 6 p.m. Mondays through Saturdays) and levies
fines of $100 to $200 for each violation of this provision. The ordinance also gives
MCC the responsibility of keeping the city and its sidewalks and streets clean:

> The Monrovia City Corporation shall have the sole responsibilities for,
> and to ensure the proper collection and disposal of garbage within the
> limits of the city of Monrovia, so as to enhance not only the beautifica-
> tion and orderliness of the city, but also for conducive sanitation and
> health environment, food and water condition for its residents in accor-
> dance with municipal regulation on public health and environmental
> safety law. (Section 2(b))
>
> The City Government shall bear the responsibility of cleaning side-
> walks and streets ONLY. Any owner, lessee, or occupant found violating
> this provision shall be subject to fine of not less than $100.00 and not
> more than $250.00. (Section 4)

Although the ordinance appeared to focus on selling foodstuffs on the streets,
the MCC in its interpretation extended it to include any form of selling on the
streets. In addition, the MCC stated that the street sellers were depositing a lot of
trash on the streets and were contributing to the continuing decline in the cleanliness of the city. As MCC was responsible for cleaning the city streets, MCC's rea-
soning was that if the street hawkers were contributing to the filthy streets then
it could remove them to ensure cleaner streets. The traders countered that the
ordinance did not apply to selling nonfood items. The traders also said they were

prepared to oversee the cleaning of the streets at the end of a workday instead of having the MCC be responsible for the cleaning.

MCC also pointed to a 1979 city ordinance (Ordinance No. 3) titled "An Ordinance Making it a Misdemeanor for Hawkers or Peddlers and Petty Traders to do Business Within the City Limits of Monrovia Without Securing Business Permits from the Monrovia City Corporation." Section 2 of Ordinance No. 3 states:

(a) It shall be an unlawful business practice for hawkers or peddlers and petty traders to do business within the City limits of Monrovia without securing permits at $20.00 each from the Monrovia City Corporation.

(b) Any hawkers or peddlers and petty traders found engaging or attempting to engage in the offering of their goods or wares for sale to the public without permits shall be guilty of a misdemeanor.

(c) Any hawkers or peddlers and petty traders found liable of the offense shall be subject to a fine of not more than $50.00.

Section 3 of this ordinance also gave MCC the right "to approve or to deny the locations hawkers or Peddlers and petty traders" could sell in.

Collective Negotiations Begin

The PTA's march on City Hall led to an initial meeting between the street vendors and the mayor on the day of the march. The street vendors were led by Abel Jones, who served as chairperson of the association at that time. Other members of the team included Comfort Doryen, co-chairperson responsible for mobilization, Daoula Kamara, Christian Obi, and Cecelia Teah, the latter three being non-officeholders of the PTA. The membership of the PTA negotiating team was agreed at an informal meeting of the PTA after the march. The MCC team was led by Mayor Broh and included the then special advisor to the mayor, Abraham Ganeoh, Frank Krah, consultant to the mayor, and Fasiah V. Keivway, one of the MCC's directors. The PTA negotiating team's mandate was verbally agreed to during the informal meeting of approximately a thousand members after the march. The singular objective was to get the MCC to stop raiding the street vendors and seizing their goods, but the vendors did not approach the meeting with a formal defined objective or document.

At the meeting, the MCC informed the street vendors that it would introduce a vendor license system whereby each petty trader would pay a US $10 annual fee to the MCC and then be issued a license to operate on the street. The US $10 fee was below the $20 stipulated in MCC Ordinance No. 3. The street vendors were happy with this development and agreed to work with the MCC for its immediate implementation. There was no written document signed by the MCC and the vendors on the outcome of their meeting. The vendors were excited that they had made progress in their discussions with the MCC and did not further pursue any documentation of the decisions.

At the end of the meeting, Abel Jones met with a throng of reporters and confirmed that the vendors had agreed to work with the MCC and informed them of the decision reached on the vendor license system. The very next day, the vendors began to register. The mayor told the vendors that, in line with MCC Ordinance No. 3, the MCC city planning director would demarcate zones to facilitate the registration process as licenses were issued for specific areas. A total of five zones were identified for demarcation. The demarcations were quickly completed and registrations begun.

The MCC appointed Fasiah V. Keivway to serve as director of the vendor registration program. Ms. Keivway served as primary liaison with the traders and established teams from the city government that went out into the streets of Monrovia to register the street vendors. This registration process only applied to street vendors, as traders in the open-air markets were registered separately by the Liberia Marketing Association. Each vendor was issued an official receipt by the MCC, but no actual licenses were issued at this or any time. Soon more than 450 vendors had paid the registration fee. Despite these developments, after a short lull the Liberia National Police and the city police, for reasons that are not clear, once again started harassing the vendors on the streets and seizing their goods. The street vendors said they were surprised by the police action, especially since they had already started to pay the registration fees to the MCC.

The situation quickly deteriorated, and there was a loud outcry from the vendors. Subsequently, a meeting was arranged with the president of Liberia, Madame Sirleaf, to discuss the grievances of the vendors. The meeting was initiated by the president's office because of the huge publicity that accompanied the police action against the street vendors. At the end of the meeting, the president suggested that the vendors get together and formalize themselves into a legal entity to negotiate with the city government. She also made a personal donation of US $200 plus L$14,000 (approximately US $430 in total) to assist the vendors to formally incorporate and register as a union. As a result, the Petty Traders Association was formally registered. Abel Jones, a street vendor but also president of the Beauticians' Union, continued as chairperson. Comfort Doryen, also herself a vendor, served as vice chairperson.

Organizational Merger Creates NAPETUL

The SBA had heard of the PTA's efforts and had also attempted to advocate for petty traders at City Hall. The city leadership, however, said it could not be talking to two different groups at the same time. As a result, Armah Gray of Realizing Rights suggested to the Small Business Alliance that it consider merging with the PTA into a union in order to have a more effective voice in promoting the petty traders' cause. After numerous negotiation sessions between the SBA and the PTA, an agreement to merge into a union was reached. To this effect, a letter was written to the minister of foreign affairs on November 23, 2009, declaring that the Small Business Alliance was evolving into the National Petty Traders Union of Liberia. One of the ministry's functions is to oversee the incorporation of all organizations and institutions in the country (organizations must be incorporated before they can be registered). In November 2009, ten representatives from each institution participated in electing the first eight officials of the NAPETUL.[10] The newly established board included members of both the SBA and the PTA: Comfort T. Doryen (former vice chair of the PTA) as chairperson; Seyon L. Tweh (former chair of SBA) as vice chairperson; Charles W. Konnah (former vice chairperson of SBA) as secretary; and Helen Z. Walker of PTA as treasurer.

Throughout late 2009 and into early 2010, NAPETUL struggled to get the mayor's attention and specifically to reach a written memorandum of understanding (MOU) that would address all issues related to the street selling and resurrect the earlier vendor license scheme. At the same time, the mayor's office pushed the union to relocate vendors from the streets and sidewalks of the city, onto first one and then another plot of land in the central business district (CBD). NAPETUL attempted, unsuccessfully, to condition any such move on the signing of an MOU. Instead, the major's office coerced vendors to move by unleashing the police on them.

MCC next tried to move vendors out of the CBD altogether, telling NAPETUL that there was land in the city of Brewerville, a small town on the outskirts of Monrovia. An additional site identified was on the highway that led out of Monrovia to the Roberts International Airport. The vendors rejected these sites as being too far out of the city. The official response to NAPETUL by the MCC was that the government did not have land in the city to make available but would look around to see if some could be located. NAPETUL complained that the vendors were still being harassed by the police at the other site they had been moved to.

NAPETUL Escalates the Conflict to the Presidential Level

As a result, on July 21, 2010, NAPETUL took the extreme move of writing directly to the president of Liberia to request her intervention to stop the MCC from continuing the raids on its members and seizure of their goods. In the letter, NAPETUL reminded the president that she had financed the establishment of the group through her personal contribution and implored her to intervene "following several attempts to abide by the agreement reached with Madam Broh." A meeting with the president, the mayor, and NAPETUL eventually took place on August 28, 2010, in the president's office. The president listened to both sides and tried to explain to the NAPETUL leadership the challenges the mayor was facing to decongest and keep the city clean. She agreed that it was not necessary, however, to have broken the tables and used force. She asked the two groups to work together, as it was in everyone's interest to avoid conflict. By the end of the meeting, the president told the mayor to pay the vendors for the market tables that were broken during police actions and work out an amicable solution to stop the raids and seizure of the vendors' goods.

A few days after the meeting with the president, Mayor Broh invited the NAPETUL leadership to a meeting with the visiting mayor of Freetown, Sierra Leone. In the presence of the Monrovia mayor, NAPETUL's leadership sought to find out from Freetown's mayor how his city was handling the issue of street vendors. During the discussion, the Freetown mayor confirmed to NAPETUL and Mayor Broh that vendors in Freetown have rights that the city ensures are not trampled upon. NAPETUL used the Freetown mayor's comments as ammunition to press the Monrovia city government to stop the harassment of street vendors.

Following this meeting, the mayor invited NAPETUL to resume discussions on how to come up with an amicable solution to the street trading problem; in the ensuing meeting, the mayor and the city planning director presented an updated plan on where street vendors would be allowed in the city. Despite the good will on both sides, the negotiations did not result in an agreement, and the talks eventually broke down.

As 2010 drew to a close and the holiday season approached, the city government and the Liberia National Police, represented by the deputy director for operations, Col. Al Karley, again engaged NAPETUL. In a letter to NAPETUL, Col. Karley stated that the intent was to "arrange its street vendors orderly so as to create space for the free movement of pedestrians and vehicles within the city limits." In response, NAPETUL wrote a letter to Mayor Broh on December 20, 2010, in which it unconditionally agreed to cooperate and specifically proposed the areas where its members were concentrated that would be cleaned up. The letter did not, however, provide any specific details on how NAPETUL intended to comply with the MCC's insistence on the removal of street vendors from the city streets.

In response to the NAPETUL letter, a series of meetings was organized by the MCC between the MCC, the police, and NAPETUL. As a result, a temporary arrangement was worked out whereby the street vendors were given specific areas on identified streets to sell their goods. It was further agreed that immediately after the holidays, the parties would meet again to review the plan and come up with a more long-term and sustainable arrangement. The temporary arrangement significantly reduced the congestion and avoided further confrontation between the parties during the holiday season. Some suggested that the relatively soft approach adopted by the authorities was due to the upcoming presidential elections in 2011 because the president could not afford to antagonize the petty traders, as she needed their votes. This, of course, was just speculation.

On January 10, 2011, the street vendors met with Mayor Broh and her team to discuss the vendors' plan and the deadline given for them to move off the streets. Apparently, the mayor was not happy with the plan submitted by the street vendors or that some of the street vendors had apparently contacted the president's older sister and confidante and tried to get her to intervene on their behalf. In a newspaper article dated January 20, 2011, the mayor discussed the lack of understanding between the street vendors and the city corporation. The mayor was quoted in the article as saying, "I don't have time for those stupid people. They think by telling the president's sister and threatening not to vote will make me afraid of removing them from the street? That's a lie. I will make sure I remove them through the court process." According to the news article, the mayor was not happy with the "structural plan" the vendors submitted to the city.[11]

No evidence has been located to suggest that the mayor went ahead with her threat to sue the street vendors to get them off the streets. Instead, the temporary arrangement that had been put in place for the previous holiday season was maintained, and the Liberia National Police took the lead in negotiating with the NAPETUL. The inspector general of police subsequently, on a number of occasions, wrote to NAPETUL to invite its leadership to meet with the police to review the arrangement of street vendors on designated streets. There was no set schedule or agenda for the meetings, which were called by the police as and when they deemed it necessary and which were held at the National Police headquarters on Capitol Hill. In addition, no minutes were issued from any of these meetings, although NAPETUL officials confirmed a generally cordial relationship with the police in each meeting.

In 2012, the situation remained unresolved; the street vendors remained on the streets (not just the sidewalks) in certain concentrated areas of the city. Based on the agreement with the police, however, certain streets were designated specifically for use by the street vendors, and these streets were also being actively used by certain street vendors. The police still made intermittent raids on the vendors when they were found on streets not designated for street peddling. The MCC had not paid the vendors for the destroyed market tables as had been previously agreed. The vendor licensing scheme had not been reintroduced, so the traders had not been asked to pay any new fees. The city confirmed that the funds collected by the MCC from the petty traders were still held by the MCC in a special account and once negotiations resumed, the MCC and the traders would agree on how the funds would be used.[12]

Naturally, the parties held diverging views about the reasons for the stalemate. The mayor of Monrovia appeared to believe that the street vendors and NAPETUL were intransigent, standing in the way of her objective of making Monrovia a cleaner, less congested capital city. NAPETUL felt that the mayor lacked interest in the concerns of NAPETUL and its members and the fact that trading is the only source of income for most petty traders. There may also have been a personality clash between the mayor and the former chair of the Petty Traders Association, Seyon Tweh.[13] NAPETUL points to the better working relationship with the Liberia National Police in reaching compromise.

The Signed Agreement

In November 2013, President Johnson replaced Mayor Broh following a no-confidence vote in the Liberian Senate. Clara Doe Mvogo was appointed as mayor. NAPETUL leadership approached the new mayor along with the Ministry of Commerce and Industry through its MSME (Micro, Small, and Medium Enterprise Division) director to discuss the plight of street vendors and petty traders in the city of Monrovia and its environs. Mayor Mvogo agreed to enter into negotiations, and after several rounds, an MOU was signed on October 31, 2014, between NAPETUL, Monrovia City Corporation (MCC), and the Ministry of Commerce and Industry (MOCI).

The MOU, a two-year agreement, is interesting in many respects.[14] It recognizes NAPETUL as a "non-governmental organization vested with the legal right and opportunity to enter or engage in lawful act or activity." It confers moral and economic as well as legal legitimacy on the organization by declaring it:

> an informal or self-employed entity [that] plays an important role in the development of Liberia's economy through the positive impact it has on the indicators concerning... unemployment, the GDP and social stability of Liberia to the point of forming a new economic sector that is governed by principles and values of responsibility, entrepreneurship indicia [sic] of the development of democracy and economic citizenship of Liberia.

Substantively, it commits MCC to protect NAPETUL members and their goods in designated sites, including protection from unannounced raids. It also commits MCC to return confiscated goods of members for the first offense of operating outside those designated sites if the traders pay a fine. In exchange, NAPETUL members agree to operate on designated sidewalks while allowing enough space for pedestrians and motorists to move freely. The union also agrees to provide MCC with a database of its registered members, while members are obligated to purchase through the union and display a license and an ID card. The parties also agree to ongoing meetings on a quarterly basis. Interestingly, the MOU commits the Ministry of Commerce and Industry to assist NAPETUL members in formalizing their businesses through registration at the Liberian Business Registry. The MOU has, in practice, helped formalize some NAPETUL members who have become taxpayers.

Other Achievements

While the MOU represents a substantial victory for the union, it is modest compared to the overall goals of the organization, which include organizing, protecting, and elevating the status of street vendors through the country. The gains NAPETUL has achieved from collective negotiation have been few and far between. NAPETUL's governance structures have improved, and its members are much more aware of their rights.

In the early days of the negotiations with the city, NAPETUL leadership was largely reactive to events as they occurred. Most of the meetings that were held were initiated by the MCC, which would set the agenda as to what was to be discussed. Over time, NAPETUL became more proactive. NAPETUL did and still does provide regular feedback to its members through meetings, but the lack of clearly identifiable success in negotiations at first resulted in some members questioning the ability of the union to represent their interest. The NAPETUL leadership recognized this risk and intensified its interaction with the rank and file to ensure it had a full appreciation of the efforts being made. To further the objectives of NAPETUL, the leadership registered the union with the Ministry of Labor and joined the Liberia Labor Congress in 2012.

Despite all the challenges that NAPETUL has faced, it has made several other significant achievements. The organization has grown substantially and developed a formal structure befitting a national rather than local organization. Branches were established in thirteen counties in 2013 and early 2014 before the outbreak of the Ebola crisis. Elections for coordinators were conducted in all thirteen counties. At the time of this writing, NAPETUL had conducted leadership training for its officials in eight counties.

NAPETUL has also become networked globally. Representatives attended an International Labor Organization (ILO) conference in Geneva in June 2014. It has become active in StreetNet, an international network of street vendor organizations. NAPETUL attended the StreetNet International Convention in Santiago, Chile, in 2013, with Ms. Doryen heading the delegation. Doryen also attended

StreetNet's International Leadership Training Workshop in 2012, and StreetNet then sponsored leadership training for NAPETUL officials in "Enhancing Negotiation Skills" in 2013. In addition to the StreetNet training, NAPETUL has also participated in training offered by the international network WIEGO in 2011 and in Realizing Rights International Leadership Training.

The organization has identified ongoing training needs as an important component of its development. This training will enhance and improve the operations and make the leadership more effective, efficient, and accountable to its members, local and international partners, and sponsors. The topics identified are negotiation, financial management, accounting (QuickBooks), reporting and communication, record keeping and filing, basic Word and Excel, monitoring and evaluation, and business proposal/plan writing skills. Many of these skills meet the needs of NAPETUL members as microentrepreneurs as well as the needs of the organization and its leadership. NAPETUL has also worked on obtaining loans for its members from the Central Bank of Liberia in 2012, 2013, and 2014 (before the Ebola crisis).

Cities around the world face the challenge of what to do with the large numbers of persons who earn their livelihoods by selling goods and services on the streets. Evicting street vendors and confiscating their goods is a common short-term response by cities, but such measures are not legal under the constitutions of many countries, which mandate the right to work, and they do not resolve the longer-term development challenge of protecting the informal livelihoods of the urban working poor in cities that do not generate enough formal jobs.

In this case from Monrovia, Liberia, vendors organized themselves into a single organization that could speak with one collective voice with municipal authorities, and they engaged in direct actions that motivated those authorities to engage in negotiations. At first, NAPETUL lacked negotiation skills; the leadership took a lot of what was said and agreed to it at face value, no one took minutes of meetings, and there were no follow-up letters to document what was agreed to. This was understandable given the limited education and experience of the union's leadership, all of whom were themselves street vendors. As NAPETUL began engaging with international organizations and in particular began to access training, leaders grew in effectiveness as they added negotiating skills and strategy development to their natural leadership skills.

NAPETUL was also able to take advantage, at times, of the different interests within the government. In the period before the MOU was signed, the union had more success in dealing directly with the police. In particular, NAPETUL was able to take advantage of the police interest in maintaining order during the 2010 holiday season and was then able to continue direct communication and develop understandings with the police in an ongoing way. There is no doubt that the government also recognized the political clout the street vendors have given their numbers. While the mayor was likely less concerned about this, as she was appointed and not elected, her political bosses may have been a bit more circumspect. As a result, when there has been a strong push by the city government and a pushback by the vendors, the national government cautioned that negotiations must continue. And eventually, the president appointed a new mayor who was able to finally reach an agreement with the vendors.

This case illustrates that it is possible and of critical importance for city authorities to engage with organizations of street vendors to find solutions to their mutual challenges. It also illustrates that street vendors, and other groups of urban informal workers, need to collectively bargain or negotiate with city officials and other local authorities and that to do so effectively they need training in effective bargaining. NGOs played a crucial role in providing training and advice and support throughout the prolonged negotiations between NAPETUL and representatives of the city of Monrovia. But most importantly the working poor in the urban informal economy need to be recognized for their contributions to the city and be involved in decisions that affect their livelihoods. Bargaining platforms with cities are for urban informal workers the equivalent of bargaining agreements with employers for formal wage and salaried workers.

LIST OF PERSONS INTERVIEWED

NAME	INSTITUTION	POSITION
Boyenneh, Prince B.	Monrovia City Corporation	Former legal counsel
Doryen, Comfort	NAPETUL	Chairperson
Fahnbulleh, Delux	NAPETUL	Secretary general
Fidelis, M. O.	NAPETUL	Asst. treasurer
Konah, Charles	Small Business Alliance	Former co-chairperson
Kpeh, Nelson P.	NAPETUL	Asst. secretary general
Krah, Frank A.	Monrovia City Corporation	Senior advisor to the mayor
Nyipon, Theresa	NAPETUL	Treasurer
Page, Caroline	Monrovia City Corporation	Environmental director
Peters, G. William	NAPETUL	Block leader/Mechlin Street
Thabafre, Masa	Monrovia City Corporation	Sanitation director
Tweh, Seyon	Small Business Alliance	Former chairperson

SOURCES

- Articles of Amendment of the Articles of Incorporation of National Petty Traders Union of Liberia. Deputy Minister of Commerce and Industry, letter to NAPETUL, February 4, 2010.
- Director of the Liberia National Police, letter to NAPETUL, December 6, 2011.
- MCC, letter to NAPETUL, September 23, 2010.
- Minister of State for Presidential Affairs/Chief of President's Office Staff, letter to NAPETUL, August 9, 2010.
- Municipal Government of Monrovia, Ordinance No. 1 (Revised).
- Municipal Government of Monrovia, Ordinance No. 3. NAPETUL Annual Report, 2010.
- NAPETUL Annual Report, 2011.
- NAPETUL, letter to Mayor Mary Broh, November 28, 2009.
- NAPETUL, letter to Mayor Mary Broh, December 8, 2009.
- NAPETUL, letter to Mayor Mary Broh, December 15, 2009.
- NAPETUL, letter to Mayor Mary Broh, December 20, 2010.
- NAPETUL, letter to Mayor Mary Broh, March 12, 2011.
- NAPETUL, letter to Monrovia City police. July 12, 2010.
- NAPETUL, letter to President Ellen Johnson Sirleaf, July 21, 2010.
- *National Chronicle*, "Mary Broh Threatens to Sue Petty Traders," January 20, 2011.

Conclusion

EXPANDING THE BOUNDARIES OF LABOR ORGANIZING AND COLLECTIVE BARGAINING

Susan J. Schurman, Adrienne E. Eaton, and Martha A. Chen

Capitalism has been on the move before, and with very similar ideas. It has also been halted before, and forced to concede the public spaces and social protections that make human life tolerable.[1]

In this chapter we compare the findings and summarize the lessons from the nine case studies. In brief, our study suggests that there is no "best way" for labor to respond to the changes in work and employment associated with changes in trade, technology, the globalization of the economy, and neoliberal policies. Rather there are a variety of alternatives based on the circumstances each group of workers confronts.

Understanding the Bargaining Transaction: A Framework for Comparing Cases

As described in the introduction, the case studies that form this volume were conducted by different research teams with little coordination between them except for the Solidarity Center's guidance stemming from the terms of their USAID grant. When we (the three editors) initially started work on the book, two of us (Eaton and Schurman), whose work is based in traditional industrial and labor relations, objected to describing the campaigns by self-employed workers that did not involve employers as "collective bargaining." In our view collective bargaining has a well-established definition, contained in International Labor Organization (ILO) Convention 154, as recurrent negotiations between workers or their unions and employers, resulting in written, legally enforceable agreements. Moreover, the literature on trade unions' efforts to organize informal workers makes clear that the dominant approach has been to seek reformalization and collective bargaining with an employer. Chen, a leading expert on informal work and workers' organizing, disagreed, pointing to WIEGO's (Women in Informal Employment: Globalizing and Organizing) research on and experience in creating "representational systems" or "forums" in local governments in which informal workers were engaged in collective negotiations.[2]

After reading all the case reports it was clear that all the campaigns in this volume culminated in some type of collective *negotiation*, either with employers or with a government entity. From these discussions we were drawn to early industrial relations theory, in particular to John R. Commons' critique of orthodox economics having failed to understand the phenomenon of "collective action" and, hence, having no way of theorizing how conflicts of interest among individuals can be transformed into collective interests or groups. Commons argued that "negotiating transactions" form the framework for collective action and the vehicle through which conflicts are settled. In his "institutional economics" he proposed that institutions, defined as "collective action exercised in control, liberation and expansion of individual action," are the means through which conflicts of interest are negotiated.[3]

Through the course of analyzing the findings from the cases, we recognized the need to redefine the unit of analysis at the center of the cases. At the outset our implicit unit of analysis was the campaign. As we struggled with the challenge of comparing the cases, however, we came to understand that focusing on the nature of the negotiating or bargaining transactions as our unit of analysis provided a sharper lens through which to examine the most important strategic choices of each campaign: who to organize, what form of organization to create or join, what gains to bargain or negotiate for, and what entities hold the power to agree to the campaigns' demands.

Table 10.1 displays a framework for comparing and contrasting the cases on seven factors: (1) the source or basis of the threat or exploitation faced by the workers; (2) the goal, issues, or interests at stake; (3) the organizing strategy and type of organizational formation created; (4) the methods of struggle employed; (5) the political opportunity structure of the country or region; (6) the major actors in the negotiating transaction; and (7) the significant outcomes achieved.

Nature of Threat or Constraint

With the exception of the domestic workers in Uruguay, each of our cases involves workers facing threats or exploitation stemming from some combination of globalization, neoliberal economic restructuring, and technological advances. Some, like the South African hospitality workers, find themselves steadily replaced by

TABLE 10.1

CASE	THREAT OR EXPLOITATION	GOALS AND INTERESTS	ORGANIZING STRATEGY / FORM	FORMS OF STRUGGLE	POLITICAL OPPORTUNITY STRUCTURE	ACTORS IN NEGOTIATING TRANSACTION	OUTCOMES
Colombia—port workers	Neoliberal policy regime outsources port workers to labor intermediaries	Restore formal employment and collective bargaining; guaranteed hours, higher wages, contributions to social benefits	Organize workers "committed to the cause" into new independent union with assistance of largest Central Labor Federation and Solidarity Center; recruit machine operators with structural power	Raise worker expectations through "rights" education; mount public protests; assert pressure for adoption of Labor Action Plan in US-Colombia FTA; eventually strike	Political opportunity due to regime change and negotiations with the United States over the Free Trade Agreement; but Ministry of Labor aligned with employers	Employers especially at top of the industry	Formal labor contracts and benefits for crane operators only
South Africa—retail and hospitality workers	Employers introduce part-time and contingent workers at lower pay and benefits	Maintenance of full-time, permanent jobs; conversion of informal to formal employment; pay and benefits equitable for informal workers	Existing union convinces members to organize informal workers; alternative structures set up that facilitate organizing; strengthen role of shop stewards	Educational campaign with formal union members to include informal workers and accept concessions in order to raise their standards	National Labor Code legislating minimum labor standards undermines what can be achieved through collective bargaining	Employer; Government	Partial wins especially around conversion; set minimum hours; some benefits equity while continuing to allow informal employment

(Continued)

TABLE 10.1 (Continued)

CASE	THREAT OR EXPLOITATION	GOALS AND INTERESTS	ORGANIZING STRATEGY/ FORM	FORMS OF STRUGGLE	POLITICAL OPPOR- TUNITY STRUCTURE	ACTORS IN NEGOTIATING TRANSACTION	OUTCOMES
Dominican Republic— immigrant workers multiple sectors	Public policy regarding all workers of Haitian background no matter their birthplace places them in informal status	Improve working conditions and/ or change national immigration policy	Existing unions reach out to work with Haitian workers although formal membership prohibited by law	Leadership changes within unions, both Dominican and US (leading to change in Solidarity Center program and support); international pressure on government of the Dominican Republic	Government of Dominican Republic vulnerable to international criticism for treatment of Haitian migrants	N/A (Thus far, no negotiations with employer or state)	Some traditional unions in Dominican Republic include workers with Haitian background
Uruguay— domestic workers	Lack of workers' rights and recognized employer	Recognition as workers; regular wage increases; payment for overtime; fewer work hours, more rest; protection against dismissal	Organize first as association then as union.	Central Labor Federation starts organizing, revives occupational union; pressures friendly political regime	Longstanding political democracy	Government; Housewives League (established to represent employers)	National collective bargaining agreement covering domestic workers; domestic workers included in the labor laws and represented in Wage Councils
Cambodian beer promotion workers	Mismatch between employer and workplace: beer companies informally employ beer promoters to work in restaurants and bars	Formalization with employment contracts; recognition of independent union as bargaining agent; higher wages and improved conditions, especially regarding control over customer interactions	Achieve formal status with employment contracts followed by organizing of workers by independent union and campaign for traditional collective bargaining	NGOs and international or foreign unions pressure industry to develop a code of conduct which includes sexual abuse/HIV as focal issue; rights and vocational education for workers; union recruiting; strike	Cambodian state plays little role; alleged "yellow" union allied with ruling political party constitutes obstacle to recognition of independent union	Domestic beer producers (employers) and their foreign owners	Industry code of conduct; formalization for some workers bringing contracts, higher and more regular wages (vs commission); inclusion in social benefits

Tunisia—subcontracted government employees	Government as employer outsources low wage workers	End subcontracting in public and private sectors; raise labor standards	Existing National Labor Federation	Support regime change; pressure new regime through political alliances and direct action by workers including strikes, street protests	Arab Spring regime change	State as employer	60,000 workers contracted in by various public-sector agencies
Georgia—transport workers	Exploitation by route owners and operators; competition from new, formal route owners; exclusion from work as a result of vehicle safety requirements	Maintain employment; improve wages/income, and working conditions	Organize as an affiliate of an existing sectoral union; ally with particular political parties at the municipal level; support from NGOs; street protests; strikes or strike threats	Ally with particular political parties at the municipal level; support from NGOs; street protests; strikes or strike threats	Regime change; Rose Revolution; developing social dialogue in transport sector at national level; political alliances at the municipal level	Route owners and operators; municipal governments; national Unified Transport Ministry	Union representation on tendering commissions; inclusion of labor protections in tender for minibus operators (job security, medical insurance, working hours, paid annual leave, safety); collective agreements with operators covering similar issues

(Continued)

TABLE 10.1 (Continued)

CASE	THREAT OR EXPLOITATION	GOALS AND INTERESTS	ORGANIZING STRATEGY/ FORM	FORMS OF STRUGGLE	POLITICAL OPPOR-TUNITY STRUCTURE	ACTORS IN NEGOTIATING TRANSACTION	OUTCOMES
Brazil—waste pickers	Entry into recycling market by formal sector firms. Drives down prices; increases competition among self-employed waste pickers and with formal sector waste recyclers	Fair prices and regular payment; recognition as providing public service; integration into municipal waste collection systems; elimination of intermediaries; safe working conditions	Social movement initiates organizing into cooperatives and associations	Political pressure on friendly political regime	Regime change; Brazilian Workers Party elected, responsive to social movement pressure	House of Representatives of State of Minas Gerais Brazil; formal recycling companies; recycling dealers	"Recycling Bonus Law" establishing monetary incentive paid to waste pickers who are members of coops or associations
Liberia—street vendors	Street vendors present a challenge to policy imperative to "clean up" the city; police remove vendors and confiscate goods.	Ability to work without police harassment; training in business skills; access to loans; recognition as workers contributing to the economy	Organize into associations; associations merged to create a single voice to negotiate with municipal and national authorities and police; street protests	Political organizing	Regime change; Realizing Rights movement; election of Ellen Sirleaf Johnson; change in appointed mayor	Municipal government; national government; police	Agreements with police followed by a written MOU regularizing the status of vendors who operate in designated spaces; training; access to loans

part-time workers whose terms of employment render them informal, thus setting up a potential competitive relationship inside the firm between formal and
informal workers; others, like the Colombian port workers, find their jobs outsourced to labor intermediaries who siphon off a portion of their wages. Still
others—the Brazilian waste pickers and the Georgian minibus drivers—face
threats to their livelihoods due to changes in the structure of the industry. The
Uruguayan domestic workers confronted the challenge of individual bargaining
with each employer. Each of these situations requires a strategy that organizes
collective power and creates an appropriate organizational form suited to the
constraints and players in the context.

Goals and Interests

The next three factors in our analysis follow to some extent Richard Hyman's
three questions for identifying union "types": What constituencies are included?
What are the objectives? What are the methods of struggle?[4] We first address the
question of objectives. The goal of each campaign discussed in the case studies is,
broadly speaking, the improvement of the workers' conditions and, in particular,
their income. In a number of the cases a first step on the path to improved conditions was to gain recognition as workers who play an important role in their
sector, their society, or the economy. In the cases involving informal wage earners
and traditional unions, one essential vehicle for achieving this goal is to seek a
degree of reformalization of employment relations. This makes these cases quite
different from those discussed by Agarwala, in which informal wage workers
in India accepted their informal employment status but sought improvements
in their lives through government benefits including housing, health care, and
increased access to education for their children.[5]

The meaning of formalization to different groups of informal workers is
important. In advance of the standard-setting discussion on formalization at the
2014 and 2015 International Labor Conferences (ILC), the WIEGO network, in
partnership with local worker organizations, organized three regional workshops
at which participating organizations of informal workers expressed what they
mean by formalization.[6] In brief, for all informal workers, legal recognition as
workers/economic agents, organization and representation, and access to social
protection are key dimensions of formalization. Other key dimensions of formalization tend to be sector-specific. In return for registration and taxation, the
informal self-employed want sector-specific legal, policy, and programmatic support. Considered another way, formalization to informal workers should mean
the reduction of the decent work deficits of informal workers as framed in the

ILO report for the 2002 ILC: deficits in terms of economic opportunities, economic rights, social protection, and social dialogue.[7]

This broad understanding of formalization is present in all of the nine cases. For instance, formalization for the Cambodian beer promoters meant bringing them more clearly and explicitly under the labor code, which in turn meant, among other things, that they could be organized by a traditional union and engage in collective bargaining. For the self-employed Brazilian waste pickers, formalization has meant organization into registered cooperatives that are then recognized as part of the public waste-management system and are eligible for state-paid bonuses for their work in that system.

Beyond these broad dimensions of formalization, each group of workers also sought to raise standards for their work. Typically this included raising income through different pathways, including higher wages (South African hospitality and Uruguayan domestic workers); annual bonuses (the waste pickers); shift from commissions to wages (Cambodian beer promoters); elimination of intermediaries (Georgian minibus drivers, Tunisian public-sector workers); and reduced harassment and threat of evictions (Liberian street vendors). In the case of most of the waged workers, raised standards also meant inclusion in government or employer-provided social benefits and improved working conditions.

These campaigns also sought improved work security, although again this took different forms. As above, both the Brazilian waste pickers and the Georgian minibus drivers sought to protect their livelihoods (their "jobs") in the face of government moves to formalize their sectors or seek other service providers. Similarly, a central goal of the Liberian street vendors was a space to trade free of police harassment. For waged workers, a central feature of formalization is an elimination of the casual nature of their employment.

Organizational Form

Here we address Hyman's question of the constituencies included. The definition—or redefinition—of who should be included constitutes the most dramatic and essential change for the traditional trade unions in our cases. Deciding to include informal workers as vital to achieving or maintaining collective power, instead of viewing them as competition, is, by design, at the core of the cases focused on waged workers (South African hospitality workers, Tunisian public employees, Georgian minibus drivers, Haitian migrants in the Dominican Republic). These cases were either initiated by existing trade union organizations or involved the creation of new unions within the existing trade union structure in their countries (Colombian port workers and Uruguayan domestic workers). The Cambodian beer promoters were assisted by an independent union competing with a more established but yellow union. Of the remaining two cases, the Liberian street vendors created a membership-based organization (MBO) that describes itself as a union and is affiliated with the national union federation but negotiates with the government rather than an employer. The Brazilian waste pickers are organized as a cooperative but one that engages in collective bargaining with the state. This is because the waste pickers have to first bargain to secure a government contract and then provide waste collection and recycling services. Our findings lend support to Theron's argument that traditional union forms can work for informalized waged workers but that the self-employed require different organizational forms geared to the nature of their work and the entities with whom they have to bargain to make their claims or demands. The Georgian minibus drivers straddle this divide; although some are ostensibly self-employed, they are dependent on the new bus systems and route operators. The Liberian case makes clear, however, that nontraditional union forms may affiliate with more traditional forms.[8]

Methods of Struggle

Our cases reveal a number of ways in which informal workers, whether organized as unions or in other forms of membership-based organizations, whether part of traditional union campaigns or in self-organized campaigns, are combining traditional trade union tactics with new tactics imported from new social movements.[9] Sidney Tarrow describes the tactics of new social movements as "the new repertoire of contentious collective action."[10]

FRAMING PROCESSES

Social movement scholars assert the importance of "*frames*" that justify, dignify, and animate collective action.[11] Framing involves "the strategic creation and manipulation of shared understandings of the world and its problems as well as viable courses of action."[12] A common thread running through our cases is the use of what Gumbrell-McCormick and Hyman call "moral" or "communicative" power as the stimulus for collective action.[13] Moral power is rooted in shared values and beliefs. Labor's historic commitment to equality and justice for all workers provides a powerful and transcendent frame for most of these campaigns.

In his chapter on Colombia, Hawkins refers to the importance of raising the consciousness, not only of workers themselves, but also of the broader society, that degraded working conditions should not be accepted. Similarly, Ryklief describes a "values-based" campaign encapsulated in the slogan "Unity, Democracy and Socialism," terms that have particular resonance in postapartheid South Africa and that helped to persuade the members of the South African Commercial, Catering, and Allied Workers Union (SACCAWU) that it was both economically and morally right to make some concessions in order to include the new workers in the union and maintain core standards for everyone. In Cambodia, the Cambodian Food Service Workers' Federations was able to reach the conscience of the Danish and international communities by highlighting the disparity between Danish values regarding working conditions and the degraded and sexualized nature of the work of the beer promoters. In Tunisia, the revolution itself, along with Union Général Tunisienne du Travail's long-term efforts on behalf of workers, helped to raise expectations for increased political and economic justice. For the Uruguayan domestic workers, obtaining recognition as workers with the right to be included in the labor movement served as a moral claim. Likewise, the Liberian street traders demanded to be treated as workers contributing to the economy, rather than lawbreakers subject to police harassment. Dominican Republic union members were persuaded to include domestic workers and Haitian migrants based on values of justice; the domestic workers campaign in turn centered their efforts on a "We Are Workers" campaign that sought recognition of their status and their accompanying rights. The Brazilian waste pickers have attempted to link their claims for recognition as workers who need to earn a living for themselves and their families and as crucial public service providers in the waste-management system. The Georgian minibus drivers demanded recognition as public service providers.

Starting with few resources other than a moral claim rooted in a transcendent ideology, these campaigns laid a foundation for successful collective action by "framing" their cause in ways that resonate with international or local norms of justice and fairness. Moral power forms the trigger that can spur individuals to support a cause and, for some, to participate in collective action.

NARROW UNION VERSUS BROADER MOVEMENT STRATEGIES

For decades, scholars and activists have urged unions to embrace "social movement unionism" (SMU) as the key to restoring labor's power.[14] Definitions of SMU vary, resting largely on two major critiques of traditional unionism. The earliest of these, rooted in a neo-Marxist or socialist perspective, advocates social and political unionism, in which trade unions explicitly align with anticolonial, antiglobalization, and antineoliberal movements.[15] The second critique, originated primarily in the United States, theorizes that unions should transform themselves from "business" unions—narrow, economic, rent-seeking organizations—into social movement unions through increased internal democracy, activation of the rank and file, autonomy from political parties, and alliances with community-based labor and human rights organizations.[16] To date, there is little evidence that unions have embraced the SMU prescription. Although a growing number of unions have incorporated initiatives to encourage increased rank-and-file activism, often referred to as "the organizing model," few have embraced the full SMU program or sought to broaden the scope of their organizing campaigns to include informal workers.[17]

Our cases suggest that the debate about narrow economic versus social movement unionism is a false dichotomy. Most of these cases involved traditional unions. And many organizations of informal workers are registered trade unions in their countries. Each of these campaigns was "economic" in the sense that the goal was an improvement in the workers' pay and working conditions, and each, eventually and by design, employed some type of collective negotiation. Each campaign also included "movement" dimensions, both in terms of framing the campaigns (as discussed above) and in terms of tactics and strategies used.

What is "new" in many of these campaigns, therefore, is the incorporation of both traditional trade union economic tactics as well as tactics from the social movement repertoire. This synthesis of old and new strategies and tactics has enabled each of these campaigns to develop sufficient organized collective power to induce more powerful actors to enact or grant tangible improvements in the terms and conditions of work. Rather than contrast economic and social movement forms of unionism as either/or ideological choices—the one "right way" to organize—we find it more helpful to think in terms of the alternative power *resources* and power *formations* best suited to the context of the campaign in its successive stages of development.[18] In particular our cases highlight the importance of two sources of workers' collective power: moral and structural, and two different formations or strategies: movements and institutions.

Historically, workers have used these different power resources and formations repeatedly to adapt to changing economic and political conditions. As the power of existing institutional arrangements wanes, workers search for new ways to organize dissent. We agree with Van Holdt's insight that trade unionism is "characterized by a constant tension between movement and the institutionalization and routinization of industrial relations."[19]

> Many, if not most, trade unions arise out of highly contentious challenges to oppressive workplace or political regimes. Even when highly institutionalized, trade unions tend to retain an element of social movement in their ability to undertake industrial action or mobilize support for collective bargaining or social proposals. Nor is institutionalization a one-way process: trade unions like other social movements go through "cycles of contention" . . . when their movement dimensions are revitalized in response to changing historical conditions.[20]

The informal workers in our study, whether in trade unions or in alternative MBOs like cooperatives, illustrate this cycle of contention combining movement and union power formations, drawing from the repertoires of both to fit the circumstances. For example, both the Brazilian waste pickers' cooperative and the Liberian street vendors' association developed processes of collective negotiations with government entities. Meanwhile, in the South African hospitality case, Ryklief tells us that, unique among South African trade unions, SACCAWU has created "platforms of self-organization," semiautonomous company-level councils that report directly to members, expanded the role of shop stewards, and, in general, granted a high level of autonomy from national union officials or staff. She hypothesizes that this decentralized and democratic structure helps to overcome members' tendency to perceive informal workers as "other" and to support including them in the union. The Colombian port workers' newly formed union looks more like an MBO than a traditional union.

LEVERAGING NEW SOURCES OF STRUCTURAL POWER

In addition to mobilizing moral power, a number of these campaigns were able to exploit their members' structural power, that is, the power possessed by workers, individually or collectively, by virtue of their location within the firm, the supply chain, or the economic system.[21] Workers with hard-to-replace skills, competencies, or talents, or who occupy a critical role in the production process, possess a potentially high level of bargaining power that can command better terms and conditions. Historically, as Gumbrell-McCormick and Hyman point out, workers who possess both forms of structural power—skill and location in the production process—have been able to establish strong unions. But their example of skilled typographers in the printing industry also points to the vulnerability of both forms of structural power in the face of technological or organizational change. Likewise, the massive displacement of manufacturing workers in the United States over the past two decades demonstrates the vulnerability of mass organizations based on location in the production process when globalization and trade policies facilitate moving or outsourcing production to lower-wage countries. At the same time, such changes can create new sources of structural power for workers, requiring new organizing and bargaining approaches. Informal workers—both waged and self-employed—possess sources of structural power that can be mobilized by campaigns.

In the South African case, for example, the formal and informalized workers were located in the same worksite and performing the same tasks, which served to highlight the inequality between the two forms of employment. Initially, the informal workers represented competition with the formal workers; they were replacing some of their jobs. Such arrangements often result in the remaining core (formal) employees, and even union representatives, aligning their interests with the employer, since they may view the informal workforce, with its generally lower terms and conditions, as a buffer protecting their own job security and working conditions.[22] Against great odds, the union, SACCAWU, was able to overcome this problem by persuading the core employees that their own structural power was being progressively reduced by the addition of informal workers and that, eventually, they too would be replaced. In Colombia, Union Portuaria was able to exploit the structural power of the crane operators, which included both skill and location in the labor process, to reformalize their jobs. The Brazilian waste pickers' cooperatives, Liberian street vendors' union, and Georgia minibus drivers in the Transport and Road Building Workers Trade Union all built their campaign strategies around their self-employed members' role in the respective service delivery processes.

THE IMPORTANCE OF ASSOCIATIONAL POWER

Our cases also highlight the limitations of individual campaigns in the absence of broader associational power. Eric Wright defines associational power as "the various forms of power that result from the collective formations of workers. This includes such things as unions and parties but may also include a variety of other forms, such as works councils or forms of representation by workers on boards of directors in schemes of worker codetermination or even, in certain circumstances, community organizations."[23] As our findings show, associational power also includes networks of informal workers' organizations.

Despite SACCAWU's success in organizing and bargaining, Ryklief expresses pessimism about the long-term prospects for the union's efforts unless the current national labor policy of "regulated flexibility" is abandoned. This is unlikely unless the entire South African trade union structure makes it a priority. Hawkins predicts that Portuaria's failure, thus far, to expand bargaining coverage to other categories of port workers will render the union's "success" tenuous and perhaps unsustainable. He quotes an expression in Spanish, "hecha la ley, hecha la trampa," meaning that every law has its loophole; in other words, the content of the law also contains the way to circumvent it without further enforcement. Evans argues that improvements in the status and conditions of Cambodian beer promoters has shifted some of the burden of exploitation to the unorganized hostesses who work directly for the same bars and restaurants where the beer promoters ply their trade. The Tunisian labor movement, which achieved the broadest victory among our cases, has not been able to replicate that victory for subcontracted private-sector workers. The small-scale successes in our cases will remain small-scale in the absence of broader associational power.[24] Neither movement nor institutional power is sufficient unless it is linked to other organizational actors in ways that can be used to the mutual benefit of all the actors.

Traditional unions have built associational power by forming national and international confederations. Recently, the traditional trade union structures have begun to emphasize the importance of including previously excluded categories of workers, including the unemployed, and expanding their relationships with other organizations that share their broader mission of creating social and economic justice for workers. There is also a growing movement of organizations of informal workers, including the wage employed, self-employed, and those in intermediary categories such as industrial outworkers. It is inspired in part by the Self-Employed Women's Association (SEWA) of India, a trade union of nearly two million women informal workers, and supported by the WIEGO network. This movement includes StreetNet International, an international alliance of street vendor organizations with forty-nine affiliates in forty-five countries; three regional networks of organizations of home-based workers, both self-employed and subcontracted, with forty-nine affiliates in eight South Asian countries, seven affiliates in seven Southeast Asian countries, and thirteen affiliates in thirteen Eastern European countries; a regional network of organizations, often cooperatives, of waste pickers, with seventeen affiliates in seventeen countries in Latin American and the Caribbean; and an International Domestic Workers' Federation with fifty-seven affiliates in fifty-eight countries.[25] Most of the street vendors and waste pickers, and many of the home-based workers, are self-employed.

Associational power permits labor organizations to exercise workers' collective political as well as economic power. In Brazil, for example, the Movimento Nacional dos Catadores de Materials Reciclaveis (MNCR) was able to mobilize the potential political power of waste pickers in addition to their structural power to persuade the state to negotiate. Likewise, the Liberian street vendors' were able to combine political and structural power as was the Georgia Trade Union Confederation on behalf of minibus drivers.

As Gumbrell-McCormick and Hyman, along with many other industrial relations scholars, have observed, "Trade unions are primarily national organizations and became consolidated in the 20th century as interlocutors of nationally based employers and national governments; but . . . [now] they act within an economy that is increasingly integrated internationally."[26] Our cases reflect the important role that cross-national associational power can play. With a couple of exceptions, each of the campaigns described in this volume received crucial assistance either from national trade unions in other countries, a Global Union Federation (GUF), or the regional, national, or international networks of informal worker organizations mentioned above and supported by the WIEGO network. The Cambodian beer promoters' campaign could not have happened without the moral outcry from international HIV/AIDS organizations along with the power of the Danish union representing Carlsberg workers, the Solidarity

Center, and from the International Union of Food and Allied Workers, a Global Union Federation. The Dominican Republic labor federation and the Colombian port workers received crucial support from the Solidarity Center as did some of the other campaigns. In addition to support from MNCR, which is part of the WIEGO-supported Global Alliance of Waste Pickers, the Brazilian waste recyclers in Minas Gerais also received support from the United Nations Children's Fund (UNICEF). The Liberian street vendors' union is a member of StreetNet International, and the Uruguay union is a member of the International Domestic Workers' Federation. The minibus drivers in Georgia received strong support from the Georgia Trade Union Confederation. Conversely, as Hawkins states in the Colombian port workers' case, the International Transport Workers Federation (ITF) did not provide support to Union Portuaria's campaign. Our cases make clear that there is growing associational power at an international level and that it arises from both traditional union forms and other types of membership-based organizations, many of them now linked internationally through networks and all working toward the same ends.

Political Opportunity Structure

Research on social movements and collective action emphasizes the important role of *political opportunity structures*: "a set of formal and informal political conditions that encourage, discourage, channel and otherwise affect movement activity."[27] Political opportunity structures have been shown to affect the strategy, structure, and success of social movements.[28] The political circumstances in which these cases unfolded vary considerably. All the countries are at least nominal democracies but with current regimes that range from progressive, "pro-poor" parties to deeply corrupt and autocratic politics. These politics determine, to some extent, the available space for civil society organizations, including unions, and informal workers themselves to act and to act successfully. While each of the countries included in the study has its own political dynamics, all have experienced liberalization of their economies and in most cases that liberalization is ongoing. Liberalization has been a driving force, either indirectly or directly—as well as trade and technology trends—to the informalization of previously formal workers. At the same time, the fact that each country is at least nominally democratic clearly made it possible, in the majority of the cases, to leverage workers' and labor organizations' associational power along with workers' structural and political power.

While a detailed consideration of the role of political opportunities in these cases is beyond the scope of this chapter, it is clear that the political context was a major factor in each campaign. In Tunisia, the revolution created an opportunity that the UGTT was well-prepared to exploit. In Colombia, a change in the government, and in particular the inclusion of stronger labor rights in a trade agreement with the United States, created the opportunity for the port workers to organize their new union. In Georgia, the new labor codes adopted after the change to a market economy and the election of a new political regime created opportunity. In Brazil, the election of the Workers Party created an opportunity to use political leverage with a friendly regime to negotiate the "recycling bonus." In Liberia, police harassment of the street traders reached a level that triggered a protest, but it ultimately took the appointment of a new mayor to successfully negotiate an agreement. Ironically in South Africa, a country with the world's strongest labor code, the labor code itself, with the best of intention to ensure a minimum wage, presents a serious constraint on the union's options for continuing to maintain or raise standards through collective bargaining.

Emphasizing the importance of at least friendly political regimes does not negate the movement dimensions of these campaigns. As with most successful social movements, the agitation for change by people and organizations forced the presiding political and economic powers to sit down to the negotiating table. We would add that the organizations involved in the narrowly focused campaigns described in this volume are generally part of larger political forces that led to regime change in the first place. In other words, these labor organizations are not just passive recipients of regime change but are actors in the change process. That is most evident in the Tunisian case, where the UGTT had been a major force for change for many years and had helped to create the context in which the regime change led to reinstatement of the informalized workers.

Actors in the Negotiating Transaction: Expanding the Boundaries of Collective Bargaining

These cases illustrate many of the limitations of traditional collective bargaining that numerous scholars have described for decades.[29] Both the strength and the weakness of traditional collective bargaining is the highly prescribed nature of the process. In the context of informal workers, both the range of "bargainable" issues (either legally or normatively) and the definition of actors in the bargaining transaction need to be broadened. Even countries that permit a wide scope of bargaining nonetheless have labor codes with highly prescribed rules governing the process, at the center of which is the concept of an employer and a labor union.

The cases in this volume point to alternative forms of negotiation between a worker organization and the state or the market. In the two campaigns of purely self-employed workers, the Liberian street vendors engaged in complex negotiations with the Monrovia municipal government, its police administration, and the national government; the Brazilian waste pickers negotiated with the House of Representatives of the state of Minas Gerais, as well as recyclers up the chain and formal recycling companies.

In their campaign to improve conditions for the minibus drivers, the Georgian transport union had to confront the twin facts that, at least at the start of the case, there was no employer as such to bargain with and that the state, at different levels, indirectly influenced employment opportunities and conditions in the sector. The resulting process of negotiations reveals some of the trade-offs and dilemmas that unions face when they seek to organize and bargain for informal workers. In Tbilisi, where the campaign was most successful, the union elected to focus on the drivers and to align itself with the municipal government's effort to rationalize and formalize the tender-awarding process, thereby eliminating the primary intermediaries: route owners and operators.[30] The union negotiated at first with municipal authorities to assert their particular interests in the tendering and rule-setting process and then later with the new private route operators. Likewise in Uruguay, in order for the domestic workers to engage in collective bargaining, an employer entity had to be created. The negotiating process to achieve this result first involved the state in the creation of the League of Housewives.

While the campaign for equal status for workers of Haitian origin is directed at the state, the campaign to improve standards for domestic workers has been directed at both the state, in an effort to include domestic workers in the labor code and to ratify the ILO convention, and at individual employers of those workers to recognize the rights that exist under current laws.

In the cases where workers had been most clearly informalized from above, and where the negotiations were between an employer and the union, the state nonetheless plays a large role but in two different ways. In Tunisia, for example, the state is both the entity with the power to legislate a change of status from informal to formal and also the ultimate employer. In the other cases, state policy loomed large in the background, so much so that the likelihood of longer-term success through traditional organizing and collective bargaining seems remote without significant change in both labor codes and enforcement. Our findings underscore the need for a broader conception of collective bargaining. In particular, the role of employers in the bargaining process needs to be augmented by the inclusion of other entities with the power to negotiate and to agree to workers' demands.

The Past as Prologue

During the course of this study we have been especially struck by the many ways the stories in this volume echo some of the patterns that characterized the formative years of the labor movements in the Global North, before the modern global trade union movement crystallized into the post–World War II model. At the dawn of the twentieth century, the great American labor economist, John R. Commons, published his famous study of changes in the shoemaking trade and corresponding changes in the shoemakers' union in late eighteenth- and early nineteenth-century America.[31] Relying on court records and minutes from employers' and union meetings, Commons follows the shoemaker as he evolves, over the course of the nineteenth century, from subsistence peddler making shoes in customers' homes using material supplied by the family in exchange for room and board, to self-employed artisan selling shoes to customers through advance orders, and ending up as a low-wage factory worker in danger of being supplanted by women and children and unable to support a family. Along the way, Commons notes, a new market entrant appears—a "middleman"—what we termed in the introductory chapter a "labor intermediary," sometimes called a "labor broker." The intermediary extracts his profit from workers' wages. Each of these stages of development, Commons argues, can be traced to changes in the market and, eventually, technology, which provide the low-cost producer with an outsized influence on the price of the product and hence the compensation to labor, whether waged or self-employed. Commons argued that at different stages of development, different entities presented a "competitive menace," or threat focused on lowering the product cost through lowering the quality of the product or exploiting labor. Workers at each stage organized in different formations to confront the organization of the market at the moment.

This classic work of early industrial relations scholarship reminds us that the changing dynamics of markets—in our cases, the shift from formal to informal wage employment and the shift largely toward services rather than goods, although some of the services involve the movement of goods—call for different adaptive strategies as workers seek to organize. Rather than clinging to forms of organization geared to conditions of the past, or engaging in theoretical arguments about the "right" response, adaptation requires a new analysis of the forms of competition, exploitation, or exclusion posed by changes in markets and in regulatory policy regimes. The path of change from informal self-employment to informal waged employment to formal wage employment and back again is a characteristic of changing market conditions. If the goal is to control the terms and conditions of work and employment, then the strategy must be aligned with labor market structure and conditions.[32]

Likewise the Webbs, writing in the same era as Commons, elaborated on the well-known "three methods" of trade unions we discuss in the introduction—collective bargaining, legal enactment, and mutual insurance—by distinguishing two "devices" by which unions could achieve collective bargaining power: the first they termed "restriction of numbers," the second, "the common rule." The former seeks to achieve favorable terms and conditions for workers in particular occupations (or labor markets) by excluding competition from new entrants willing to work for lower standards; the latter tries to regulate competition in labor markets for the benefit all workers by establishing "a minimum standard below which no employer may descend, never a maximum beyond which he may not, if he chooses, offer better terms."[33] Each of these strategies represents an analysis of the most effective way to limit labor market competition, eliminate non-value-adding intermediaries, and raise standards for workers. Shoemakers' unions and their counterparts in other trades in the nineteenth and early twentieth centuries in the United States and Western Europe attempted—often successfully—to eliminate undercutting competition through legal prohibitions or limitations on women's and child labor. More recently, the first strategy of unions—again often successfully in many countries in Western Europe—was to prohibit informal or "atypical" work.[34]

Neither the Webbs nor Commons could have foreseen how globalization and changes in trade and technology in the twenty-first century would lead to the deconstruction of the industrial production systems that were emerging in their era and the reinsertion of middlemen, who may or may not add some value to the market but who certainly take their own cut and leave little for the actual worker.[35] In the very industry that so interested Commons, as globalization has advanced, another stage of shoemaking has developed that looks very much like an early stage: namely, the outsourcing of production to industrial outworkers, many of whom are home-based, through intermediary contractors.[36] From our cases, the public sector workers in Tunisia, port workers in Colombia, some of the Georgian minibus drivers, and South Africa hospitality workers employed via brokers are all fighting for the removal of middlemen, a greater share of the value added, or direct employment at higher standards than they currently experience. Haitian day laborers in the construction industry are also largely hired by subcontractors, but their focus does not appear to be on eliminating those middlemen but rather on raising the standards for their work. As best we can tell, the beer promoters are not employed by middlemen. Instead, they are a kind of marketing intermediary, dispatched workers who are paid on commission and work in bars or restaurants that are not their source of payment. And although most domestic workers are waged workers, in a sense their problems too result from an insufficiently developed market. Employed by households to work in households, there are extreme pressures to keep their wages low and their work hours long, and typically there is no institution that collectivizes the employers and their interests. Where collective bargaining has been enabled for domestic workers, it has had to solve—as in our Uruguayan case—the problem of interest representation on the employer side of the table.

Our findings suggest that for informal waged workers, the Webbs' two devices still apply, depending on the labor market to be organized. Restriction in numbers, however, can easily lead to viewing informal workers in the same labor market as competition to be excluded, as has been a major problem in the building and construction trade unions in the United States. And the common rule can lead to a failure to recognize informal self-employed workers as workers requiring different organizational forms and new forms of collective bargaining. Successfully organizing informal workers requires recovering all three of the Webbs' methods and adapting them to the new realities of a global economy: new forms of organization to engage in new forms of collective bargaining, political action, and mutual aid.

The Path Forward: From Competition and Exclusion to Solidarity and Inclusion

The findings from these cases provide vivid examples that informal workers can and are engaging in collective action. The cases also demonstrate that when unions decide to organize informal workers, they have the capacity to do so and that many informal workers—both waged and self-employed—desire to be part of the trade union movement. Eight of these nine campaigns involve either organizing by unions or informal workers creating a union. As Table 10.1 shows, while many of the outcomes achieved in these cases are both modest and fragile, each campaign was able to achieve meaningful, tangible improvements for at least some of their members. The tenuous nature of these outcomes notwithstanding, these cases add to mounting evidence that the global labor movement is learning how to adapt to the twenty-first-century globalized economy.

Our findings also make it clear, however, that the likelihood of sustaining these gains increases dramatically as more workers organize and engage in collective action. To that end, as unions make the transition from viewing informal workers as competitors or buffers or not recognizing them as workers at all, to embracing them as an important, perhaps the majority, of the new global working class, the number of successful campaigns will grow. These nine campaigns contain important lessons. Each was the result of a long-term strategy built on a powerful moral claim as well as the structural power of the workers in their respective economies. Each benefited from the associational power of the labor movement and other progressive organizations. Each combined traditional economic union and social movement tactics. Each created an appropriate organizational form geared to the type of negotiations that would yield results.

There are clear signs that this transition is under way. In the United States, for example, the growing number of worker centers serving informal workers have received support from many unions as well as from the AFL-CIO. The Taxi Workers Alliance, representing many self-employed drivers, has affiliated with the AFL-CIO. Various unions are attempting to organize Uber and other car service drivers who have been defined as self-employed. Some have suggested that in the course of this transition, collective bargaining may fall away as the central strategy of labor organizations; interestingly, our cases suggest less a disappearance and more a broadening and reshaping of collective bargaining.[37]

History suggests that workers will develop new forms of collective action to adapt to the twenty-first-century economy as their parents and grandparents did in the twentieth century. The campaigns described in this study are part of this larger pattern. Telling their stories will hopefully inspire others to follow their example.

Notes

ACKNOWLEDGMENTS

1. The Solidarity Center is a nongovernmental organization associated with the major US labor federation, the American Federation of Labor/Congress of Industrial Organizations. It is a 501(c)(3) nonprofit organization funded by grants.

2. The USAID grant listed seven "required" countries: Ukraine, Bangladesh, Honduras, Mexico, Cambodia, Georgia, and South Africa. The final three are represented in our study. The grant also listed eleven optional countries: El Salvador, Nicaragua, Guatemala, Democratic Republic of Congo, Sri Lanka, Ecuador, Tanzania, Mozambique, Brazil, Dominican Republic, and Liberia; the final three are included in this study.

INTRODUCTION

1. From Daniel Hawkins, "Port Workers in Colombia: Reinstatement as Formal Workers," chapter 1 in this volume.

2. Rina Agarwala, *Informal Labor, Formal Politics, and Dignified Discontent in India* (Cambridge: Cambridge University Press, 2013); Christine Bonner, "History of the Formation of StreetNet, IDWN, Global Alliance of Waste Pickers, and HomeNet South Asia" (unpublished manuscript, 2013); Christine Bonner and Françoise Carre, "Global Networking: Informal Workers Build Solidarity, Power, and Representation through Networks and Alliances" (WIEGO Working Paper, no. 31 (2013)).

3. Brandon Ambrosino, "The Gig Economy Is Coming. You Probably Won't Like It," *Boston Globe Magazine*, April 20, 2016; Noam Scheiber, "Growth in the 'Gig Economy' Fuels Work Force Anxieties," *New York Times*, July 12, 2015; Gerald Friedman, "The Rise of the Gig Economy," *Dollars and Sense*, March/April 2014.

4. Steven Greenhouse, "Uber: On the Road to Nowhere: Uber Drivers Are Getting Creative in Their Fight for Basic Workplace Rights," *American Prospect*, Winter 2016; Johnathan Chew, "How Uber and Lyft Drivers Could Get a Lot More Bargaining Power," *Fortune*, December 14, 2015; Noam Scheiber, "Uber Drivers and Others in the Gig Economy Take a Stand," *New York Times*, February 2, 2016.

5. David Weil, *The Fissured Workplace: Why Work Became So Bad for So Many and What Can be Done to Improve It* (Cambridge, MA: Harvard University Press, 2014); Ruth Milkman and Ed Ott, *New Labor in New York: Precarious Workers and the Future of the Labor Movement* (Ithaca, NY: Cornell University Press, 2014).

6. Exceptions include Bonner, "History of the Formation of StreetNet"; Bonner and Carre, "Global Networking"; Pat Horn, "Voice Regulation in the Informal Economy and New Forms of Work" (International Labor Organization, 2006), http://wiego.org/publications/voice-regulation-informal-economy-and-new-forms-work.

7. Paul E. Bangasser, "The ILO and the Informal Sector: An Institutional History" (International Labor Organization Employment paper, 2000), http://www.ilo.int/wcmsp5/groups/public/@ed_emp/documents/publication/wcms_142295.pdf.

8. Gundula Fischer, "Revisiting Abandoned Ground: Tanzanian Trade Unions' Engagement with Informal Workers," *Labor Studies Journal* 38, no. 2 (2013): 139–60. Tanya Goldman, "Organizing in South Africa's Informal Economy: An Overview of Four Sectoral Case Studies" (Small EnterpriseE Development (SEED) Working Paper, no. 60 (2004)): 1–78, http://www.ilo.org/empent/Publications/WCMS_117671/lang--en/index.htm; Tanya Goldman, "Organizing in the Informal Economy: A Case Study of the Building Industry in South Africa" (SEED Working Paper, no. 38 (2003)): 1–79, http://www.ilo.org/empent/Publications/WCMS_093977/lang--en/index.htm; Jane Barrett,

"Organizing in the Informal Economy: A Case Study of the Minibus Taxi Industry in South Africa" (SEED Working Paper, no. 39 (2003)): 1–59, http://www.ilo.org/empent/Publications/WCMS_117698/lang--en/index.htm; Mark Bennett, "Organizing in the Informal Economy: A Case Study in the Clothing Industry" (SEED Working Paper, no. 37 (2003)): 1–57, http://www.ilo.org/empent/Publications/WCMS_117699/lang--en/index.htm; Kwasi Adu-Amankwah, "Organizing Informal Workers Requires Nurturing Dynamic Links with the Relevant Public Authorities and Institutions, both National and International, That Can Provide the Necessary Support," in *Trade Unions in the Informal Sector: Finding Their Bearings, Nine Country Papers* (Labour Education Working Paper 116, 2001), 1–14.

9. *Trade Unions in the Informal Sector: Finding Their Bearings, Nine Country Papers*, Labour Education Working Paper 116, 1999, 1–148; Bangasser, "The ILO and the Informal Sector."

10. Christine Bonner and Dave Spooner, "Organizing in the Informal Economy: A Challenge for Trade Unions," *International Politics and Society* 2, no. 11 (2011).

11. Susan Schurman and Adrienne Eaton, "Organizing Workers in the Informal Economy: A Review of the Literature on Organizing in Africa, Asia, Latin America, North America, and Western, Central and Eastern Europe" (report to the Solidarity Center, January 2012).

12. Martha Chen et al., *Membership Based Organizations of the Poor* (London: Routledge, 2007).

13. Celia Mather, "The Transformation of Work: Challenges and Strategies: Informal Workers' Organizing" (report to the Solidarity Center, February 2012), http://www.solidaritycenter.org/wp-content/uploads/2014/11/WIEGO.Informal-Workers-Organizing.pdf.

14. Agarwala, *Informal Labor*.

15. Diego Coletto, *The Informal Economy and Employment in Brazil: Latin America, Modernization and Social Changes* (Basingstoke: Palgrave Macmillan, 2010).

16. C. Tilly et al., "Informal Workers' Organizing as a Strategy for Improving Subcontracted Work in the Textile and Apparel Industries of Brazil, South Africa, India and China" (UCLA Working Paper, September 2013), http://www.irle.ucla.edu/ publications/documents/Informalworkerorganizingintextilesandgarments-UCLAReport-9-2013.pdf.

17. International Conference of Labour Statisticians, "Resolution Concerning Statistics of Employment in the Informal Sector" (15th International Conference of Labour Statisticians, 1993), referenced in Bangasser, "The ILO and the Informal Sector."

18. Ibid.; International Conference of Labour Statisticians, "Guidelines Concerning Statistics on Informal Employment" (17th International Conference of Labour Statisticians, 2003).

19. Martha A. Chen, "The Informal Economy: Definitions, Theories and Policies" (WIEGO Working Paper, no. 1 (2012)), http://wiego.org/sites/wiego.org/files/publications/files/Chen_WIEGO_WP1.pdf; Joann Vanek et al., "Statistics on the Informal Economy: Definitions, Regional Estimates and Challenges" (WIEGO Working Paper (Statistics), no. 2 (2014)), http://wiego.org/sites/wiego.org/files/publications/files/Vanek-Statistics-WIEGO-WP2.pdf.

20. Jan Theron, "Informalization from Above, Informalization from Below: The Options for Organization," *African Studies Quarterly* 11, nos. 2–3 (2010): 112–13; Zoran Slavnic, "La Informalizacion y la Economia Politica de la Reestructruacion (Informalization and Political Economy of Restructuring)," *Migracion y Desarrollo*, no. 13 (2009).

21. John Atkinson and Nigel Meager, *Changing Work Patterns: How Companies Achieve Flexibility to Meet New Needs* (London: National Economic Development Office, 1986).

22. This distinction can be blurred if the self-employed person is stuck in a constrained relationship with a single supplier or single customer.

23. David Weil, *The Fissured Workplace: Why Work Became So Bad for So Many and What Can be Done to Improve It* (Cambridge, MA: Harvard University Press, 2014). It is interesting to note that Canadian labor laws actually recognize and cover a category of workers called "dependent contractors." For the seminal article that led to this change, see Harry Arthurs, "The Dependent Contractor: A Study of the Legal Problems of Countervailing Power," *University of Toronto Law Journal* 16, no. 1 (1965): 89–117.

24. Slavnic, "La Informalizacion," 7; Weil, *The Fissured Workplace.* Weil also discusses outsourcing chains in the United States that may end in the use of individual "independent contractors," misclassified or not.

25. Barrett, "Organizing in the Informal Economy;" Adu-Amankwah, "Organizing Informal Workers Requires Nurturing Dynamic Links." Barrett describes organizing taxi drivers, many of whom had been formally employed by the South African Transport and Allied Workers' Union. Adu-Amankwah describes efforts by the Ghana Private Road Transport Union to organize and assist truck drivers of all types: "hired drivers" in both formal and informal employment arrangements, owner-drivers and vehicle owners who employ others.

26. Dorothy Sue Cobble, "Gender Equality and Labor Movements: Toward a Global Perspective" (report to the Solidarity Center, funded by the Office of Democracy and Governance, Bureau for Democracy, Conflict, and Humanitarian Assistance, US Agency for International Development, under the terms of Award No. AID-OAA-L-00001, 2012), http://smlr.rutgers.edu/research-centers/research-partnership-with-solidarity-center. Cobble juxtaposes traditional unions with "'new unions,' which may or may not rely on collective bargaining as their principal strategy. Taking a page from labor's past, these organizations might constitute themselves primarily as mutual aid organizations or as community or political entities concerned with changing labor and social policy or with democratizing the larger society. Many may also call themselves associations and not unions," 7.

27. Aelim Yun, "Building Collective Identity: Trade Union Representation of Precarious Workers in South Korean Auto Companies," *Labour, Capital and Society* 44, no. 1 (2011): 155–78; Edmund Heery, "Trade Unions and Contingent Labor: Scale and Method," *Cambridge Journal of Regions, Economy and Society* 2, no. 3 (2009): 429–42; Emma Cerviño, "Trade Union Strategies Towards Atypical Workers" (working paper, Juan March Institute, Madrid, 2000). Cerviño talks about exclusion, partial inclusion, and total inclusion.

28. Rodolfo Elbert, "How Do Unions Respond to Nonstandard Work Arrangements? Relations Between Core and Non-core Workers in a Food Processing Factory," *Journal of Workplace Rights* 14, no. 1 (2010): 387–98.

29. Fischer, "Revisiting Abandoned Ground."

30. Vanek et al., "Statistics on the Informal Economy," 7.

31. In fact, the Dominican Republic case was not originally constructed with either protocol but was done as part of a series with yet another protocol, a series specifically focused on traditional unions' relationships to immigrant workers in four different countries. Samanthi J. Gunawardana, "The Transformation of Work: Challenges and Strategies: Labor Movement Responses to International Labor Migration in Sri Lanka" (report to the Solidarity Center, January 2014), http://www.solidaritycenter.org/wp-content/uploads/2015/09/Labor-Movement-Responses-to-Migration-in-Sri-Lanka.report.1.2014.pdf; Janice Fine, "The Transformation of Work: Challenges and Strategies: Restriction and Solidarity in the New South Africa: COSATU's Complex Response to Migration and Migrant Workers in the Post-Apartheid Era" (report to the Solidarity Center, January 2014), http://www.solidaritycenter.org/wp-content/uploads/2015/09/Restriction-and-Solidarity-in-New-South-Africa-migration-report.1.2014.pdf.

32. R. K. Yin, *Case Study Research: Design and Methods* (Los Angeles: Sage, 2013).

33. Sidney Webb and Beatrice Webb, *Industrial Democracy* (London: Longmans, Green, 1902); Sidney Webb and Beatrice Webb, *The History of Trade Unionism* (New York: Longmans, Green, 1920).

34. Adrienne E. Eaton and Paula B. Voos, "Managerial Unionism: Prospects and Forms," *Labor Studies Journal* 29, no. 3 (2004): 25–56.

35. Samuel B. Bacharach, Peter A. Bamberger, and William J. Sonnenstuhl, *Mutual Aid and Union Renewal* (Ithaca, NY: Cornell ILR Press, 2001); Paul Jarley, "Unions as Social Capital: Renewal through a Return to the Logic of Mutual Aid?" (unpublished manuscript, University of Kentucky, 2003).

36. Agarwala, *Informal Labor.*

37. Judy Fudge, "Little Victories and Big Defeats: The Rise and Fall of Collective Bargaining Rights for Domestic Workers in Ontario," in *Not One of the Family: Foreign Domestic Workers in Canada,* ed. Abigail B. Bakan and Davia Stasiulis (Toronto: University of Toronto Press Incorporated, 1997), 119–46.

38. Martha Chen, Christine Bonner, and Françoise Carre, "Organizing Informal Workers: Benefits, Challenges and Successes" (background paper for Human Development Report 2015, New York; New York: UN Human Development Report Office, 2016).

39. Pat Horn, "New Forms of Collective Bargaining: Adapting to the Informal Economy and New Forms of Work," *Labour, Capital and Society* 38, nos. 1–2 (2005); "The Transformation of Work: Challenges and Strategies: Informal Workers and Collective Bargaining: Case Studies from India, Georgia, Brazil, Liberia, and Uruguay" (report to the Solidarity Center, 2013), http://www.solidaritycenter.org/wp-content/uploads/2014/11/WIEGO.Informal-Workers-and-Collective-Bargaining.pdf.

40. Debbie Budlender, "Informal Workers and Collective Bargaining: Five Case Studies" (WIEGO Organizing Brief, no. 9 (2013)), http://wiego.org/sites/wiego.org/files/publications/files/Budlender-Informal-Workers-Collective-Bargaining-WIEGO-OB9.pdf; "The Transformation of Work" (report to the Solidarity Center, 2013).

41. Rebecca Gumbrell-McCormick and Richard Hyman, *Trade Unions in Western Europe: Hard Times, Hard Choices* (Oxford: Oxford University Press, 2013); Immanuel Ness, ed., *New Forms of Worker Organization: The Syndicalist and Autonomist Restoration of Class Struggle Unionism* (Oakland: PM Press, 2014).

42. Kim Moody, *Workers in a Lean World: Unions in the International Economy* (London: Verso, 1997); Peter Waterman, *Globalization, Social Movements and the New Internationalism,* 2nd ed. (London: Continuum, 2001); Lowell Turner, Harry Katz, and Richard Hurd, eds., *Rekindling the Movement: Labor's Quest for Relevance in the 21st Century* (Ithaca, NY: Cornell University Press, 2001); Gumbrell-McCormick and Hyman, *Trade Unions in Western Europe,* chap. 6.

43. Steven Lopez, "Contesting the Global City: Pittsburgh's Public Service Unions Confront a Neoliberal Agenda," in *Global Ethnography: Forces, Connections, and Imaginations in a Postmodern World,* ed. M. Burawoy et al. (Berkeley: University of California Press, 2000), 268–98.

1. PORT WORKERS IN COLOMBIA

1. "Balance Preliminar de las Economias de America Latina y el Caribe, 2011," Economic Commission for Latin America and the Caribbean (CEPAL), 2012. In 2011 the regional unemployment average for Latin America was 6.8 percent.

2. Alejandro Portes, "By-Passing the Rules: The Dialectics of Labor Standards and Informalization in Less Developed Countries," in W. Sengenberger and D. Campbell, *International Labor Standards and Economic Interdependence* (Geneva: Institute for Labor Studies, 1994), 159–76; Marta A. Chen, "Rethinking the Informal Economy: Linkages with the Formal Economy and the Formal Regulatory Environment" (Research Paper 2005/010, Helsinki: UNU-WIDER, 2005).

3. "Departamento Administrativo Nacional de Estadistica," Departamento Administrativo Nacional de Estadistica, www.dane.gov.co.

4. DANE's measurement of informality only considers the size of enterprise as a determining factor (five persons or less). For 2013, the national level of informality, measured according to whether occupied workers were affiliated to the pension or health social security regimes, came to 64.6 percent, a total of 13,590,000 workers who remained outside the formal systems of these two basic protection schemes.

5. Maria I. Casas, *Imperceptiblemente nos encerraron: Exclusion del sindicalismo y logicas de la violencia antisindical en Colombia, 1979–2010* (Bogotá: Comisión Colombiana De Juristas, 2012), 37–43.

6. Of the 4,492 unions registered in the country (2014), 3,594 have fewer than one hundred members.

7. In Colombia there are three formal types of collective contracts: collective bargaining agreements (CBAs), collective pacts, and union contracts (*contratos sindicales*). It is important to note that only CBAs imply a process of deliberation and collective negotiation between union representatives and employers.

8. Mauricio Cárdenas, "Treinta Años de Sindicalismo en Colombia: Vicisitudes de una Transformación," in *En La Encrucijada: Colombia en el Siglo XXI,* ed. F. L. Buitrago (Bogotá: Grupo Editorial Norma, 2006), 233–60.

9. Luisa Gomez, "Hitos del viacrucis para el TLC con Estados Unidos," *Portafolio,* September 12, 2011, http://www.portafolio.co/negocios/empresas/hitos-viacrucis-tlc-estados-unidos-124568.

10. Mark Anner, *Solidarity Transformed: Labor Responses to Globalization and Crisis in Latin America* (Ithaca, NY: Cornell ILR Press, 2011).

11. "El Estado Colombiano utiliza su agenda de inteligencia departamento administrativo de seguridad—DAS—contra las organizaciones de derechos humanos," *CAJAR,* http://justiciaypazcolombia.com/IMG/pdf/Documento_seguimientos_al_CCAJAR_x_parte_del_DAS_junio_2509.pdf.

12. Stefano Farne, "Las cooperativas de Trabajo asociado en Colombia: Balance de la politica gubernamental, 2002–2007," *Revista de la Economia Institucional* 10, no. 18 (2008): 261–85.

13. According to the Confederation of Colombian Cooperatives (Confecoop).

14. Especially in the health industry, after Decree 536 of 2004, which opened up the possibility that state-owned social enterprises could utilize third-party contracts with external operators.

15. Farne, "Las cooperativas," 267.

16. In Colombia, los parafiscales are contributions made by workers and employers towards three entities: SENA (technical college for Colombian workers), Cajas de Compensación (systems that offer recreational and familial activities for Colombian workers), and Instituto Colombiano de Bienestar Familiar (state entity that offers protection and preventive well-being to infants, children, and adolescents).

17. As well as the SPR terminal, there are also three other specific port terminals with their respective regional port societies. This study concentrates solely on the main port society, the SPRBuen and the labor relations found there.

18. Superintendencia de Industria y Comercio, "Estudios de mercado: Sector Portuario Colombiano e incidencia de las Polìticas Pùblicas en la SPRBUN," 29, http://www.sic.gov.co/drupal/recursos_user/documentos/promocion_competencia/Estudios_Economicos/Estudios_Economicos/Estudios_Mercado_Puertos.pdf.

19. A relatively new industrial union of the transport sector, SNTT, National Union for Transport and Service Workers in the Transport Industry, began to organize in the port sector in mid-2015, managing to negotiate and sign a CBA for direct employees of one of the principal port operating firms, Compas, in early 2016. This chapter does

not deal directly with SNTT as it only emerged in the port sector after the period dealt with here.

20. Sintraalpar is a union in name only. It has no elected directive board and no formally affiliated members. Simbraseim is also in reality but a semblance of a union as its members are not formally affiliated and aren't required to pay dues.

21. It is important to specify that the *contrato sindical* (literally union contract) in Colombia is not a collectively bargained agreement. It is a mode of labor intermediation officially backed by the leadership of a firm-level union.

22. Jhon Jairo Castro (president of UP-Buenaventura), interview by author, October 3, 2012; Fabio Arias (fiscal of the CUT-National), interview by author, October 9, 2012; Jose Luciano Sanin (general director of the ENS), interview by author, October 12, 2012. Comment by Castro during interview and reiterated during interviews with Arias and Sanin.

23. "Plan Nacional de Expansión Portuaria 1993–1995," Documento Conpes 2680, Ministerio de Transporte, Republic of Colombia, 1993.

24. "Privatizacion de los puertos: A toda vela," *El Tiempo*, March 2, 1993, http://www.eltiempo.com/archivo/ documento/MAM-60678. According to Colombia's leading national newspaper, as of 1993, 7,700 port workers had been retrenched and a further 2,740 were awaiting retrenchment.

25. The ENS survey and fieldwork was conducted between April and September 2011. In total, port workers from the following cities filled out 699 conditions of decent work surveys: Buenaventura (195); Barranquilla (188); Santa Marta (186); and Cartagena (130).

26. Ibid.

27. "XE Currency Converter," XE Currency Converter, www.xe.com/ucc/convert/? Amount=535.600&From=COP&TO=USD. This sum is equal to the equivalent of roughly US $293.50.

28. "Ley No 50: por la cual se introducen reformas al Código Sustantivo del Trabajo y se dictan otras disposiciones," *Diario Oficial*, no. 39.618 (1990), http://www.alcaldiabogota. gov.co/sisjur/normas/Norma1.jsp?i=281; "Decreto 4369: Por el cual se reglamenta el ejercicio de la actividad de las empresas de servicios temporales y se dictan otras disposiciones," *Diario Oficial*, no. 46.472 (2006), http://www.minproteccionsocial.gov.co/ Normatividad/ DECRETO%204369%20de%202006.pdf.

29. Group interview #1, interview by author, October 2, 2012.

30. Port machine operator, interview by author, October 2, 2012.

31. Sanin, interview, October 12, 2012; Castro, interview, October 3, 2012.

32. Castro, interview, October 3, 2012.

33. Stevedore/member of the UP, interview by author, October 3, 2012.

34. Especially the labor clauses or side agreements that form part of the NAFTA of 1993 (Mexico, Canada, and the USA), and the MERCOSUR (originally Brazil, Argentina, Paraguay, and Uruguay) signed in 1991, as well as the Chile-US FTA (signed in 2003). In Central America, local and US unions came together to vociferously complain about the systematic violation of worker rights in export-processing zones, pressure which eventually led to the inclusion of a labor chapter to the FTA.

35. WOLA (Washington Office on Latin America) is an NGO that seeks to promote human rights, democracy, and social justice. The main Colombian actors involved in the opposition movement to the US-Colombia FTA were the Polo Democratico (the leftist political opposition party), the three Colombian union confederations (CUT, CGT, and CTC), the ENS, as well as a number of diverse social movement groups and NGOs such as RECALCA, CENSAT Agua Viva, among others.

36. Edward Webster (WITS University emeritus professor of sociology), comments made during a teleconferencing lecture, transmitted to the faculty of the Department of Labor Studies and Employment Relations, Penn State University, October 18, 2012.

37. The US-Colombia FTA was formally approved by the US Congress (both the House and the Senate) on October 12, 2011. It then received the presidential sanction on October 21, 2011. In May 2012, the FTA formally came into effect.

38. Jose Luciano Sanin Vasquez, "El Plan de Acción sobre Derechos Laborales. Una nueva frustración?" *ENS*, 2011; "Action Plan Santos-Obama," *Mintrabajo*, April 6, 2012, www.mintrabajo.gov.co/index.php/tlc-plan-de-accion-laboral/314-documentos/370-action-plan-santos-obama.html?showall=1.

39. These sectors were selected for special attention and protection due to the multiple and continual labor rights' violations found in each of these industries. The Colombian labor movement and its US counterparts argued that unionists in these five sectors required additional protection.

40. "Decreto No. 1228: Por el cual se modifica la planta de personal del Ministerio de la Protección Social," (2011), http://wsp.presidencia.gov.co/Normativa/Decretos/2011/Documents/Abril/15/dec122815042011.pdf.

41. David Luna (former vice minister for labor relations), interview by author, October 10, 2012.

42. Donatella Della Porta and Sidney Tarrow, *Transnational Protest and Global Activism* (Lanham, MD: Rowman & Littlefield, 2005).

43. "Sistema de informacion laboral y sindical: Reporte a Diciembre 2013," *ENS*, 2014, http://ens.org.co/apc-aa-files/40785cb6c10f663e3ec6ea7ea03aaa15/11_SISLAB_2013_2.pdf.

44. Please note that the author of this text is an employee of the ENS, although he had no direct involvement in the mentioned training workshops.

45. Interviewee 6, interview by author, October 4, 2012.

46. Interviewee 4, interview by author, October 4, 2012.

47. According to the labor advisor to the vice president of Colombia, Oscar Gutierrez, whenever a member of the UP wished to organize a meeting with port management, the Vice Presidency would have to intervene and attempt to negotiate the visit. In his words, in the port sector "it has not been possible that the employers accept, in real terms, union activity. Formally, they say that the workers can unionize but if they do so, the following day they discover that they no longer have a job." Mr. Gutierrez also affirmed that efforts by the CUT to establish an ongoing dialogue with the SPRBuen and the main operating firms had not come to fruition.

48. This was confirmed during the author's fieldwork at the port. During a near day-long informal tour/scout of the port terminal from the inside, the author managed to speak with and interview workers from a variety of occupations: stevedores, cleaners (male and female), grain distributors, tallywomen, as well as management security. All of the workers with whom the author spoke complained about the pay, the forms of hiring and firing, the arbitrary disciplinary procedures, the stress and intensity of working shifts and hours, among other aspects.

49. Focus group, interview by author, October 3, 2012. Comments made during a focus group session with thirty-two members of the UP-Buenaventura.

50. "SENA," *SENA*, www.sena.edu.co. SENA is the National Training Service. It is the state entity in charge of vocational training and educational courses.

51. Focus group, interview, October 3, 2012. According to workers in the focus group session with UP members, which included approximately eight newly formalized TECSA machine operators, prior to even hearing about the creation of UP, these workers had attempted, unsuccessfully, to discuss and improve their working conditions and pay scale with the TECSA management.

52. Ibid. Comments made by Jhon Jairo Castro during the focus group session.

53. "En el Puerto de Buenaventura se dan primeros pasos para la formalizacion laboral," *ENS*, February 9, 2012, http://ens.org.co/index.shtml?apc=Na--;27;-;-;&x=20166857.

54. Interviewee 4, interview, October 4, 2012.

55. Interviewee 6, interview, October 4, 2012.

56. Stella Salazar, interview by author, October 8, 2012.

57. Luna, interview, October 10, 2012.

58. In this context, many CTAs had begun the process of changing their juridical name and business model (*su razón social*).

59. Arias, interview, October 9, 2012. The vice minister of labor relations, David Luna, stated that as part of the ministry's policy of promoting respect for unions and encouraging social dialogue, there had been a number of social dialogue meetings both in Bogota as well as in diverse departments. If a union requests the ministry to pressure the firm in question to negotiate, the ministry is now authorized to order firms to do so. Nonetheless, according to Arias, the tripartite meetings organized by the ministry had been nothing but a display of "discursive commitment to social dialogue. . . . The business sector had refused to negotiate the implementation of concrete policies aimed at formalizing working relations in the port sector and especially at Buenaventura."

60. "Punto para los trabajadores," *Semana*, June 18, 2011, http://www.semana.com/economia/articulo/punto-para-trabajadores/241500-3.

61. Tallywomen, interview by author, October 3, 2012.

62. Due to the prevalence of intermediation at the port and firms hiring workers on a "per shift" or "per ship" basis, most workers pay for an entry card that permits them to enter the terminal, after which they can search for work. This system is the basis through which intermediation thrives and survives, despite the many normative changes that were pushed through as part of the Labor Action Plan.

63. Jhon Jairo Castro, interview by author, August 16, 2013.

64. UP National Directive Board, interview by author, September 12, 2013.

65. Andrew Schrank, "Professionalization and Probity in a Patrimonial State: Labor Inspectors in the Dominican Republic," *Latin American Politics and Society* 51, no. 2 (2009): 91–115.

66. Mark Anner, "Meeting the Challenges of Industrial Restructuring: Labor Reform and Enforcement in Latin America," *Latin American Politics and Society* 50, no. 2 (2008): 33–65; Layna Mosley, *Labor Rights and Multinational Production* (Cambridge: Cambridge University Press, 2010).

67. Dimitris Stevis, "International Framework Agreements and Global Social Dialogue: Parameters and Prospects," ILO Employment Working Paper, no. 47 (2010).

68. Jhon Jairo Castro (president of UP-Buenaventura), e-mail correspondence with the author, January 4, 2013. Based on an e-mail correspondence, it appears there is a new-found consensus among the UP to push for its affiliation with the ITF.

69. Sanin, interview, October 12, 2012.

70. Arias, interview, October 9, 2012.

2. RETAIL AND HOSPITALITY WORKERS IN SOUTH AFRICA

1. "Bertelsmann Stiftung," Bertelsmann Stiftung, http://www.bertelsmann-transformation-index.de/60.0.html?L=1.

2. "Statistical Release P0302: Mid-Year Population Estimates, 2014," Statistics South Africa, July 31, 2014, http://beta2.statssa.gov.za/publications/P0302/P03022014.pdf.

3. "GINI Index (World Bank Estimate)," World Bank, http://data.worldbank.org/country/south-africa. At 65, the highest on the Gini index (2011); Sampie Terblanche, *Lost in Transformation: South Africa's Search for a New Future since 1986* (Sandton: KMM Review Publishing, 2012).

4. National Labour and Economic Development Institute (NALEDI), "Country Analysis Report," prepared for Mondiaal FNV (2010), 9, https://www.fnv.nl/site/over-de-fnv/

internationaal/mondiaal-fnv/documenten/english/monitoring-reports-2010/Monitoring_
report_2010_South_Africa.pdf.

5. "South Africa GDP Growth Rate, 1993–2016," Trading Economics, http://www.
tradingeconomics.com/south-africa/gdp-growth.

6. "African Statistical Yearbook: 2014," African Development Bank Group (AfDB),
the African Union Commission (AUC) and the United Nations Economic Commission for Africa (ECA), 2014, http://www.afdb.org/fileadmin/uploads/afdb/Documents/
Publications/African_Statistical_Yearbook_2014.pdf.

7. Franco Barchiesi, "Informality and Casualization as Challenges to South Africa's
Industrial Unionism: Manufacturing Workers in the East Rand/Ekurhuleni Region in the
1990s," *African Studies Quarterly* 11 (2010): 67–85.

8. Devan Pillay, "Globalisation and the Informalisation of Labor: The Case of South
Africa," in *Labor and Challenges of Globalisation: What Prospects for International Solidar-
ity?* ed. A. Bieler, I. Lindberg, and D. Pillay (Scottsville: University of KwaZulu-Natal Press
Press, 2008), 49–52.

9. "Statistical Release P0211: Quarterly Labour Force Survey, Quarter 4 2013" (Statistics
South Africa, February 11, 2014), http://www.statssa.gov.za/publications/P0211/P02114th
Quarter2013.pdf.

10. Ibid.; "Statistical Release P0211.5: Quarterly Labour Force Survey, Historical Revi-
sions of the QLFS 2008 to 2013" (Statistics South Africa, February 11, 2014), http://www.
statssa.gov.za/publications/P02115/P021152013.pdf.

11. Vulnerable includes, among others, contract cleaning workers, domestic workers,
farm workers, forestry workers, workers in the hospitality sector, civil engineering, and
taxi drivers. Child performers would be an example of a special sector.

12. Unions need to prove representation of 50 percent of workers in the sector to bring
employer bodies to the negotiating table through the setting up of a sectoral bargaining
council.

13. "Labour Research Service," Labour Research Service, www.lrs.org.za. Wage data
demonstrates the large differentials between sectoral minima and collective agreements
on an annual basis.

14. Professionals are excluded from these protections through an exemption of anyone
above a ceiling of annual earnings, but they are also subject to regulation. With higher
earners such as office workers, management staff members, and professionals, the number
of hours per week is specified in the employment contract and any time that is worked over
this limit is classified as overtime. This overtime does not distinguish between after-hours,
Sundays, or public holiday work, and the employment contract could specify whether the
employee agrees up front to do some overtime work when required. No compensation is
required from the employer, but unless urgent and due to unforeseen circumstances, the
employee is entitled to refuse to work overtime.

15. "Trade Unions in South Africa," South Africa.info, October 8, 2015, http://www.
southafrica.info/business/economy/policies/tradeunions.htm#.VQcMsE1WEcM; "Establishment," CONSAWU, http://consawu.co.za/establishment/. COSATU claims 2.2 million
members. SACOTU is a confederation made up of the two federations, FEDUSA, which
claims 375,000 members, and NACTU, which claims 400,000. CONSAWU claims 290,000
members.

16. Pillay, "Globalisation and the Informalization of Labour," 55.

17. "Findings of the COSATU Workers' Survey, 2012," COSATU, http://www.cosatu.
org.za/docs/reports/2012/final%20workers%20surveys%20results%20August%20
2012.pdf, 35–6. COSATU is facing a potential split after dismissing its general secretary
(Zwelinzima Vavi) in 2015 and expelling its largest affiliate, NUMSA, in 2014. The dispute
involves several other unions in the federation and is still in progress.

18. Labour Relations Act, no. 66 of 1995, Ch. 9, Sec. 198 (2)–(4). Labor brokers, sometimes called service contractors or temporary employment services, are a particular form of outsourcing in southern Africa, providing low-skilled, casual labor to companies. Companies hire the labor broker to provide workers rather than hire the workers themselves. Workers who sign on with labor brokers have no fixed hours or benefits and are paid much less than those directly employed by the company. They provide labor for certain jobs (like cleaning and gardening services) and for peak periods and antisocial hours. Labor brokers are still subject to the BCEA and the sectoral determinations in the industry. In August 2009, COSATU presented a submission on labor brokers to the parliamentary portfolio committee on labor and launched its campaign to ban labor brokers. Current South African legislation bestows employer status on the labor broker but joint responsibility on the both labor broker and its client, making them both liable for any contraventions of CBAs, sectoral determinations, or the BCEA. Further changes to the Labour Relations Act that came into effect on January 1, 2015, give added protection to employees on fixed-term contracts through a new section that reduces the period before a casual employee has to be made permanent from six to three months, but it does nothing to clarify the mutual liability.

19. Michelle Taal, "Organising in the Hospitality Sector of South Africa," Labor Research Service, 2012, http://www.lrs.org.za/docs/2012%20Hospitality%20South%20 Africa%202012.pdf.

20. "The Retail Industry on the Rise in South Africa," *Gauteng Province Quarterly Bulletin* 3 (2012), http://www.treasury.gpg.gov.za/Documents/QB1%20The%20Retail%20 Industry%20on%20the%20Rise.pdf.

21. Taal, "Organising in the Hospitality Sector," 4.

22. "SACCAWU," SACCAWU, http://www.saccawu.org.za/. Union membership is a constitutional right in South Africa, and trade unions are free to sign up members without impediment. On demonstration of registration and being "sufficiently representative" the union can receive access to the workplace and conduct shop steward elections and negotiations on behalf of its members.

23. Edward Webster, et al., *Working in the Hospitality Industry in Gauteng* (South Africa: Society, Work and Development (SWOP) Institute of the University of the Witwatersrand, 2012).

24. B. Kenny, "The Market Hegemonic Workplace Order in Food Retailing," in *Beyond the Apartheid Workplace: Studies in Transition*, ed. Edward Webster and Karl Von Holdt (Scottsville: University of KwaZulu-Natal Press, 2005). Shoprite, Checkers, and Pick n Pay, all organized by SACCAWU, shared approximately 95 percent of the market in formal food retailing.

25. Shane Godfrey, Jan Theron, and Margareet Visser, "The State of Collective Bargaining in South Africa: An Empirical and Conceptual Study of Collective Bargaining" (DPRU working paper 07/130, UCT, 2007).

26. "Annual Report, 1998," Central Statistical Services/Statistics South Africa, 1998, http://www.gov.za/sites/www.gov.za/files/statssa_annualreport1998.pdf; "Annual Report, 2002/2003," Statistics South Africa, 2003, http://www.statssa.gov.za/publications/Annual Report/AnnualReport2002.pdf; R. Rees, "Flexible Labour: Meeting the Challenge," *South African Labour Bulletin* 21, no. 5 (1997): 30–36; B. Kenny, "Divisions of Labour, Experiences of Class: Changing Collective Identities of East Rand Food Retail Sector Workers through South Africa's Democratic Transition" (PhD diss., University of Wisconsin, 2004), 488; Kenny, "The Market Hegemonic Workplace Order in Food Retailing." Official estimates put casual and temporary labor by the late 1990s somewhere between 17 and 20 percent of the total formal retailing workforce, up from 11 percent in the late 1980s. Independent case study research, however, has found much higher rates of casualization, ranging from 45 percent to 65 to 70 percent at store levels in specific regions

27. See SACCAWU statement on labor brokers in Appendix 2.2.

28. The union is one of the supporting unions in the dispute between COSATU and NUMSA, which was expelled from COSATU in 2014. SACCAWU is also experiencing financial and legal problems due to irregularities in the management of its National Provident Fund (a type of pension fund), which was put under a court-appointed curatorship. The union has signed an agreement to pay back R30 million it owes to the fund.

29. B. Kenny, "Militant Divisions, Collective Possibilities: Lessons for Labour Mobilization from South African Retail-Sector Workers," *LABOUR Capital and Society* 38, no. 1 and 2 (2005): 157–83.

30. Webster, et al., *Working in the Hospitality Industry in Gauteng.*

31. Ibid.

32. In 2012, the Labour Research Service (LRS) held focus group sessions with SACCAWU hospitality and catering workers in three provinces. Two were held in Cape Town, one in Durban, and one in Johannesburg.

33. Ibid.

34. Taal, "Organising in the Hospitality Sector."

35. Ibid.

36. "Gender at Work," Gender at Work, http://www.genderatwork.org/saccawu. SACCAWU has been active in the Gender at Work project, which encourages women in the retail sector to stand as shop stewards.

37. Patricia Petersen and Trenton Elsely, "Drivers and Obstacles to Organizing Vulnerable Workers" (Labour Research Service Report, 2012).

38. "Pick n Pay Integrated Annual Report" (Pick n Pay, 2014), http://www.picknpayinvestor.co.za/downloads/2014/Pick _n_Pay_IAR_2014.pdf.

39. S/St7, interview by author, November 23, 2012.

40. "Notes to the Annual Financial Statements, 2011" (Pick n Pay, 2011), http://www.financialresults.co.za/2011/ pnp_ar2011/afs_stores_note04.html.

41. T/U O3, interview by author, November 23, 2012.

42. M. Clarke, "Global Commodity Chains and Lean Retailing: The Growth of Precarious Work in South Africa's Retail Sector" (paper presented at the annual convention of the ISA, Chicago, Illinois, USA, February 28–March 3, 2007); M. J. Mathekga, "The Political Economy of Labour Market Flexibility in South Africa" (master's thesis, Stellenbosch University, December 2009).

43. Nonunion members pay a similar fee as union member dues into a fund that is used to support collective bargaining activities.

44. The union is currently negotiating for a "closed shop" agreement. This is possible if 75 percent of the workforce belongs to the union.

45. TU/O3, interview.

46. S/St.1, S/St.6, and S/St.7, interview by author, November 23, 2012; TU/O2, interview by author, November 23, 2012.

47. A term coined by TU/O3 to describe the multiple employment categories in various collective bargaining agreements signed by the union.

48. A provident fund is a retirement scheme that varies slightly from a pension in that employees are paid a portion as a lump sum immediately on retirement and the balance as a monthly allowance. It is preferred by low-paid workers who often have a limited life expectancy.

49. The rationale for the exclusion of casuals to stand for shop stewards is that unions negotiate time off for union business for shop stewards, including full-time shop stewards who are paid by the company but do union work exclusively, in the recognition agreement. Employers are reluctant to give time off to casuals who only work to schedules, so unions have signed agreements that exclude casuals from receiving these concessions.

50. S/St.7, interview; TU/O2, interview.

51. "The Impact of Casualisation on Wages," *SACCAWU Blogspot,* July 7, 2005, http:// saccawublog.blogspot.com. "Pick n Pay pays a fulltime Cashier an entry minimum of R25.95 per hour whilst a non-fulltime Cashier is paid R13.24 an hour for a minimum guaranteed 85 hours per month. Although the Pick n Pay does contribute to the Provident Fund for non-fulltimers, the other benefits are pro-rata." Verified by TU/O2.

52. K. Forrest, "SACCAWU: 30 Years On, More of the Same," *South African Labour Bulletin* 29, no. 5 (2005): 65–66.

53. SACCAWU was demanding a 12 percent increase in wages, or R400 per month, while Pick n Pay was offering 7.9 percent, or R310 per month, backdated to March 2005. The union settled at R325.

54. TU/O2, interview.

55. TU/O2, interview.

56. "Sun International Integrated Annual Report, 2014," Sun International, 2014, http://www.suninternational.com/content/dam/suninternational/corporate/investors/ documents/integrated-annual-report-2014.pdf.

57. "About Sun International," Sun International, http://www.suninternational.com/ corporate/.

58. "Sun International Integrated Annual Report, 2014."

59. Nonunion members pay a similar fee as union member dues into a fund that is used to support collective bargaining activities as agreed by both union and company management.

60. S/St.1, interview by author, November 23, 2012.

61. Ibid.

62. "Sun International Integrated Annual Report, 2011," Sun International, 2011, http://www.suninternational.com/content/dam/suninternational/Corporate/investors/ documents/sun-international-integrated-ar-2011.pdf.

63. S/St.1, interview. The union reports that the first two disputes had not been resolved by 2014.

64. Ibid.

65. Nompumelelo Magwaza, "Hotels Firm Plans Taking Back Units," *Business Report,* February 24, 2015, 17.

66. S/St.1, interview.

67. The Employment Conditions Commission was established by the terms of section 59 (1) of the Basic Conditions of Employment Act, 1997 (BCEA). It advises the minister of labour on the making of sectoral determinations and any matter concerning basic conditions of employment including the effect of government policies on employment.

68. Petersen and Elsely "Drivers and Obstacles."

69. FG2, interview by author, November 23, 2012.

70. TU/O2, interview.

71. Ibid.

72. As in the SISA discussions for incorporation of contract workers.

73. TU/O2, interview. All shop stewards interviewed.

74. Ibid.

75. S/St.1 and S/St.2, interview by author, November 23, 2012; TU/O1, interview by author, November 23, 2012. As in the case of Sun International Grand West. A majority of cleaners at the Grand Hotel employed by a contract cleaning company were recruited to the union, but management halted shop steward elections by refusing to allow another company's workers to meet on their premises.

76. FG1, interview by author, November 23, 2012.

77. FG2, interview. All shop stewards interviewed.

78. Ibid.

79. Y. Momomiat, "A Labouring Behemoth Finally Reaches the Crossroads," *Mail and Guardian*, December 21, 2012–January 3, 2013, 34–35.

80. FG2, interview. All shop stewards interviewed.

81. TU/O2, interview.

82. Ibid.

3. HAITIAN MIGRANT WORKERS IN THE DOMINICAN REPUBLIC

1. Cathy Feingold, interview by author, December 6, 2012. The Solidarity Center's full name is the American Center for International Labor Solidarity. It is an independent organization affiliated with US labor federation, the AFL-CIO, which provides resources, staff, training, and other support to labor organizations in the Global South.

2. Jose Itzigsohn, *Developing Poverty: The State, Labor Market Deregulation, and the Informal Economy in Costa Rica and the Dominican Republic* (University Park: Penn State Press, 2000), 106–10. In fact, as a consequence of poor working conditions and social security benefits and salaries that could not guarantee basic subsistence, many skilled workers preferred temporary jobs in the informal economy over stable jobs in the formal sector.

3. Douglas S. Massey, "Why Does Immigration Occur? A Theoretical Synthesis," in *The Handbook of International Migration: The American Experience*, ed. Charles Hirschman, Philip Kasinitz, and Josh DeWind (New York: Russell Sage Foundation, 1999), 34–52; Saskia Sassen-Koob, "Notes on the Incorporation of Third World Women Into Wage Labor through Immigration and Offshore Production," in Saskia Sassen-Koob, *Globalization and Its Discontents* (New York: New York Press, 1998), 111–31.

4. "The Promotion of Migrant Workers Rights in the Dominican Republic" (Solidarity Center internal document), 2.

5. Bridget Wooding, interview by author, January 8, 2013.

6. "In Search of Decent Work: Labor Experiences of Immigrant Workers in Construction in the Dominican Republic" (Solidarity Center and CNUS Report, 2009).

7. Ibid. The Solidarity Center and CNUS also helped a nascent market vendor organizing effort to establish an organizing and policy presence. This effort is beyond the scope of this chapter.

8. Research methods include primary source materials from the Solidarity Center including internal memos and reports, historical documents, foundation and NGO research reports, scholarly articles, press statements, and many interviews with key stakeholders.

9. Rosario Espinal, "Between Authoritarian and Crisis-Prone Democracy: The Dominican Republic after Trujillo," in *Society and Politics in the Caribbean*, ed. Colin Clarke (London: Macmillan, 1991), 145–65.

10. Ibid.; Eulogia Familia, interview by author, January 9, 2013.

11. "Annual Survey of Violations of Trade Union Rights: Dominican Republic—2012," ITUC, 2012, http://survey.ituc-csi.org/Dominican-Republic.html?lang=en.

12. "Labour Overview Latin America and the Caribbean, Committee of Experts Report, Freedom of Association and Protection of the Right to Organise in the Dominican Republic" (ILO, 2011), http://www.ilo.org/wcmsp5/groups/public/---ed_norm/---relconf/documents/meetingdocument/wcms_174843.pdf. These include the following requirements: at least 40 percent membership in an institution in order to form a public employee association and twenty workers to establish a trade union; an absolute majority of workers in an enterprise or branch of activity in order to engage in collective bargaining; and a two-thirds vote of trade union members in order to form federations at the municipal, provincial, regional, or national levels.

13. Itzigsohn, *Developing Poverty*, 109.

14. Ibid., 113.

15. Ibid., 50.

16. Bridget Wooding and Richard Moseley-Williams, *Needed but Unwanted; Haitian Immigrants and Their Descendants in the Dominican Republic* (London: Catholic Institute for International Relations, 2004).

17. Ibid., 18.

18. James D. Fearon and David D. Laitin, "Ethnicity, Insurgency, and Civil War," *American Political Science Review* 97, no. 1 (2003): 11.

19. Howard J. Wiarda, "The Development of the Labor Movement in the Dominican Republic," *Journal of Interamerican Economic Affairs* 20 (1966): 43.

20. Ibid., 21.

21. Allison Petrozziello, Hintzen Amelia, and Juan Carlos Gonzalez Dias, *Género y el riesgo de apatridia para la población de ascendencia haitiana en los bateyes de República Dominicana* (Gender and the Risk of Statelessness for the Population of Haitian Descent in the Bateys of the Dominican Republic) (Santo Domingo: Observatorio Migrantes del Caribe (OBMICA), 2014).

22. Stacie Kosinski, "State of Uncertainty: Citizenship, Statelessness and Discrimination in the Dominican Republic," *Boston College International and Comparative Law Review* 32, no. 2 (2009).

23. Petrozziello, Amelia, and Gonzalez Dias, *Género y el riesgo de apatridia.*

24. Ibid., 390.

25. Ibid., 383, 390. The Dominican Supreme Court upheld the constitutionality of the law, ruling that Haitian workers were to be considered "in transit" and that their offspring were therefore not entitled to citizenship.

26. Allison J. Petrozziello, "Haitian Construction Workers in the Dominican Republic: An Exploratory Study on Indicators of Forced Labor" (report prepared by the Observatorio Migrantes del Caribe (OBMICA) for ICF International, Santo Domingo, Dominican Republic, September 2012), 15.

27. "In Search of Decent Work," 16.

28. Familia, interview, January 9, 2013, 1.

29. Lisa McGowan, now head of the Women's Division at Solidarity Center, is credited for being the key thinker within the organization who forged the conceptual framework.

30. The US Department of State's Office to Monitor and Combat Trafficking in Persons used the acronym "G/TIP" until 2011, when it was changed to "J/TIP" due to a reorganization at the State Department.

31. These two paragraphs are drawn from Solidarity Center 2007–2008, 2009–2010, and 2011–2012 S-SGTIP Reports on Combating Trafficking into and from the Dominican Republic.

32. Ibid.

33. Eulogia Familia, interview by author, November 29, 2012, 2.

34. As the work progressed, CNUS and the Centro Bonó, a key Jesuit NGO that works with migrants, formed a reciprocal relationship where labor lawyers train the migrant rights community in labor law to help them address migrant-related labor cases and migrant rights lawyers work with labor lawyers to better understand the migrant rights regime.

35. Eulogia Familia, quoted in "Solidarity Center: Promoting Worker Rights Worldwide, 2011 Annual Report" (Solidarity Center, 2011), 11.

36. Geoff Herzog, interview by author, February 2, 2015. Although employers are expected to pay into a special pension fund that was created in 1986 for construction workers, the fund was not operationalized until 2006 (undocumented workers are not included). Part of the pension fund goes to the union for social programs to benefit their members. FENTICOMMC has repeatedly protested that employers are not paying into it, while employers have repeatedly sought to have it ruled unconstitutional.

37. Petrozziello, "Haitian Construction Workers," 1–2.

38. Ibid., 38.

39. Ibid., 39.

40. Pedro Julio Alcantara, interview by author, December 13, 2012, 14.

41. Ibid., 7.

42. Boca Chica, Juan Dolio, San Pedro de Macoris, and La Romana.

43. The sample included some with Dominican documents, some without Dominican documents but with Haitian documents, some immigrant temporary workers lacking Dominican documents, and some Haitian Dominicans who were born in the DR of Haitian parents but often still did not have Dominican documents.

44. "In Search of Decent Work," 2.

45. Ibid., 8.

46. Alcantara, interview, December 13, 2012, 5.

47. Ibid., 11.

48. Geoff Herzog, interview by author, November 29, 2012. More up-to-date data was not made available by the union.

49. Isis Duarte, "Household Workers in the Dominican Republic: A Question for the Feminist Movement," in *Muchachas No More: Household Workers in Latin America and the Caribbean*, ed. Elsa M. Chaney and Mary Garcia Castro (Philadelphia: Temple University Press, 1989), 202–3.

50. "Anuario Estadístico de la Comisión Económica para América Latina y el Caribe (Statistical Yearbook for Latin America and the Caribbean)," CEPAL, 2011, http://interwp. cepal.org/anuario_estadistico/anuario_2011/.

51. Wilfredo Lozano, *Inmigración, Género y Mercado de Trabajo en la República Dominicana: Estudios Complementarios ENI—2013* (Santo Domingo: Fondo de Población de las Naciones Unidas (UNFPA), 2013). Survey on Haitian immigrants in the DR conducted by the IOM and FLACSO (16 percent figure); National Immigrants Survey (ENI), 7.2 percent figure.

52. Olimpia Torres, *La Institucionalización sociocultural y jurídica de la desigualdad: el trabajo doméstico remunerado: resúmenes de estudios de la sv región de Centroamérica y República Dominicana* (San Salvador: Secretaría Jurídica del Sistema de la Integración Centroamericana (SG-SICA), 2010).

53. Ibid., 21.

54. Feingold, interview, 6.

55. Bridget Wooding and Alicia Sangro, "La presencia de las mujeres migrantes haitianas en el servicio doméstico en la República Dominicana." Movimientos migratorios desde y hacia la República Dominicana, Ministerio de Economía, Planificación y Desarrollo, Fondo para el Fomento de la Investigación Económica y Social (FIES) (2011), 1.

56. Victoria Garcia, interview by author, January 4, 2013.

57. Wooding, interview, 4. Bridget Wooding, perhaps the most highly respected researcher on migrant and domestic workers in the DR, credits the SC with strengthening ATH. Wooding reports that "at the time SC came on the scene, suddenly ATH emerged from the woodwork and also began to encourage Haitian women into their ranks."

58. Maria Jean Louis, interview by author, December 17, 2012, 7.

59. Ibid., 3.

60. Tamara Normil, interview by author, December 17, 2012, 9.

61. Among other findings was a surprising level of reported abuse. Some women reported being regularly verbally harassed and physically abused by their bosses, while others recounted working for practically nothing and being forbidden from leaving the homes in which they worked for up to a month at a time.

62. Normil, interview, 7.

63. Feingold, interview, 10.

64. Ibid.

65. Elena Pérez García, interview by author, 14.

66. Alicia Sangro Blasco, "Buenas Practicas en Planes de Regularización" (IOM workshop on the role of civil society in the Regularization Plan, Juan Dolio, Dominican Republic, February 20, 2014).

67. Pérez García, interview, 16.

68. Ibid., 5.

69. The organization also participates in the Coordinadora Intersindical de Mujeres Trabajadoras (CIMTRA), which brings together the women from all three labor confederations.

70. Jean Louis, interview, 8.

71. "Lanzan campaña regional para reconocer derechos de trabajadoras domésticas," *El Caribe*, June 18, 2014, http://www.elcaribe.com.do/2014/06/18/lanzan-campana-regional-para-reconocer-derechos-trabajadoras-domesticas#sthash.Hzd1AKU2.dpuf.

72. Familia, interview, November 29, 2012, 5.

73. Familia, interview, January 9, 2013, 18.

74. Hilda Sanchez Martinez, "Dominican Republic: Unions Support Haitian Migrant Workers," *ILO News*, September 3, 2012, http://www.ilo.org/global/docs/WCMS_189185/lang--en/index.htm.

75. Janice Fine and Daniel J. Tichenor, "An Enduring Dilemma: Immigration and Organized Labor in Western Europe and the United States," in *The Oxford Handbook of Politics and International Migration*, ed. Marc R. Rosenblum and Daniel J. Tichenor (New York: Oxford University Press, 2012).

76. "CNUS Communicado a Las: Autoridades Gubernamentales Dominicanas, a Los: Empleadores/as, a la: opinion publica nacional e internacional," *Hoy*, February 12, 2011.

77. Anbareli Espinoza, "Haitianos Protestan en Embajada Piden Reabran Pidih," *Hoy*, February 25, 2015, http://hoy.com.do/haitianos-protestan-en-embajada-piden-reabran-pidih/.

78. Daniel J. Cantor and Juliet B. Schor, *Tunnel Vision: Labor, the World Economy, and Central America* (Boston: South End Press, 1987).

79. Janice Fine and Daniel J. Tichenor, "A Movement Wrestling: American Labor's Enduring Struggle with Immigration, 1866–2007—Erratum/Corrigendum," *Studies in American Political Development* 23, no. 2 (2009): 218–48.

80. Marshall Ganz, "Resources and Resourcefulness: Strategic Capacity in the Unionization of California Agriculture, 1959–1966," *American Journal of Sociology* 105, no. 4 (2000): 1015.

81. Ibid., 1010–17.

82. John D. McCarthy and Mayer N. Zald, "The Enduring Vitality of the Resource Mobilization Theory of Social Movements," in *Handbook of Sociological Theory*, ed. Jonathan H. Turner (New York: Kluwer Publisher, 2001), 533–65.

83. Geoff Herzog, interview by author, April 9, 2015.

84. Resolution 3, Trade Union Organizing and Self-Reform, Second TUCA Congress, April 2012.

85. J. W. Kingdon, *Agendas, Alternatives and Public Policies*, 2nd ed. (New York: Harper Collins, 1995).

86. Wooding, interview, 10.

87. Geoff Herzog, interview by author, February 2, 2015.

88. This issue is not unique to low-wage worker organizations in the Dominican Republic. In the United States, worker centers have also struggled with financial sustainability.

89. Tambora, "Dominican Republic Cannot Harbor Two Poor Nations: President," *Dominican Today*, April 10, 2015, http://www.dominicantoday.com/dr/poverty/2015/4/10/54760/print.

4. DOMESTIC WORKERS IN URUGUAY

1. Broad Front.

2. Sole Union of Domestic Workers and League of Housewives, Consumers and Users of Uruguay (henceforth referred to as the Liga de Amas de Casa or the Liga), respectively.

3. "Uruguay en Cifras, 2013," Instituto Nacional de Estadística (INE, National Institute of Statistics), August 26, 2013, http://www.ine.gub.uy/documents/10181/39317/Uruguay+en+cifras+2013.pdf/5d3469e9-3c7f-4f6a-9f81-d7ce83f87a65.

4. Khalid Malik, "Human Development Report 2014, Sustaining Human Progress: Reducing Vulnerabilities and Building Resilience," United Nations Development Programme (UNDP), 2014, http://hdr.undp.org/sites/default/files/hdr14-report-en-1.pdf. The Human Development Index (HDI) takes into account life expectancy at birth, mean and expected years of schooling, and gross national income per capita, while the inequality-adjusted HDI considers the disparities in these dimensions among the population. The Gender Inequality Index is calculated on the basis of maternal mortality, adolescent fertility, educational attainment, the share of parliamentary seats, and labor force participation.

5. Originally made up of Christian Democrats, socialists, communists, and other leftist groups.

6. Daniel Buquet, "El irresistible ascenso de la izquierda al gobierno en Uruguay," in *La nueva política en América Latina. Rupturas y continuidades*, ed. Carlos Moreira, Diego Raus, and Juan Carlos Gómez Leyton (Montevideo: Flacso, Universidad Nacional de Lanús, Universidad Arcis and Ediciones Trilce, 2008), 251–72.

7. Martin Pintos, *Poder sindical: Historias de conflictos, ocupaciones y desbordes* (Montevideo: Editorial Fin de Siglo, 2012), 226–27. Interunion Assembly of Workers—National Convention of Workers. Recently relations have cooled a bit as the labor central became critical of the new FA president, Jose Mujica, for not continuing the social programs initiated by Vázquez. The PIT-CNT was founded in 1983 with the merger of the Plenario Intersindical de Trabajadores and the Convención Nacional de Trabajadores. It is guided by the principles of radical internal democracy and independence from the state and parties; it operates as an assembly, not a rigid organization.

8. The general minimum wage and adjustments for those groups of workers that are included in wage councils are established through tripartite negotiation. For those groups of workers who are not included in wage councils, the executive branch establishes a general minimum wage and wage adjustments that apply nationwide.

9. Guillermo Alves et al., "La desigualdad del ingreso en Uruguay entre 1986 y 2009" (working paper no. 3, Instituto de Economía. Montevideo: Universidad de la República, 2010).

10. Social Security Institute.

11. Elizabeth Tinoco, "Reduction of Informal Employment in Uruguay: Policies and Outcomes," ILO, 2014, 4, http://www.ilo.org/wcmsp5/groups/public/---americas/--rolima/documents/publication/wcms_245894.pdf.

12. Ibid., 9–10.

13. Association of Professional Prostitutes of Uruguay.

14. Association of Fried Bread Makers and the Union of Hot Dog Vendors, respectively.

15. Union of Urban Solid Waste Sorters and Ministry of Labor and Social Security, respectively.

16. Ministerio de Trabajo y Previsión Social and Consejo de Salarios, files for Grupo 21.

17. *El Diario*, *El País*, and *La República* were consulted during the periods in which domestic work was incorporated into the wage councils, collective agreements were negotiated, and Domestic Workers' Day, August 19, was created.

18. Verónica Amarante and Alma Espino, "Situación del servicio doméstico en Uruguay," in *Uruguay: Ampliando las oportunidades laborales para las mujeres* (Montevideo:

INAMU-Banco Mundial, 2008), 60–83; Laura Triaca, "Trabajo Doméstico e Impacto de las Políticas en Uruguay: Evolución Reciente" (Ministerio de Trabajo y Seguro Social, Unidad de evaluación y monitoreo de relaciones laborales y empleo, 2013); Karina Batthyány, "Estudio sobre trabajo doméstico Uruguay, Serie Condiciones de Trabajo y Empleo, no. 34" (ILO, 2012). All the authors consulted referred to three categories of domestic workers that are registered by the Encuesta Continúa de Hogares (ECH, Continuing Survey of Households): child caregivers, persons who care for the sick in private households, and domestic staff (cooks, cleaners, and general domestic workers). The description of domestic workers in this chapter refers largely to studies that use data for all three categories of workers for 2006, 2009, and 2012. The study by Batthyány is excellent, but she excludes caregivers from her calculations.

19. Triaca, "Trabajo Doméstico," 2013.

20. Ibid., 16.

21. The low percentage of men who are domestic workers can be attributed at least in part to the exclusion of chauffeurs and gardeners from the statistical estimates and from the law; these are covered by other wage councils.

22. "La situación de mujeres en el sector del trabajo doméstico en Uruguay 2012," Instituto Nacional de las Mujeres, Ministerio de Desarrollo Social and Ministerio de Trabajo y Seguridad Social, 2013, http://www.inmujeres.gub.uy/innovaportal/file/23681/1/cuadriptico_domesticasweb.pdf.

23. Fabio Guerra, "Domésticame: Un vistazo a la subjetividad en el servicio doméstico," in *Pequeños demonios y otros ensayos históricos y socio-políticos: primer concursos de ensayos, Fondo histórico cultural Hugo Cores,* ed. Gerardo Albistur (Montevideo: Trilce, 2009), 67–86.

24. Oscar Ermida Uriarte, "La nueva legislación laboral uruguaya," *IUS Labor* 4 (2006).

25. "Ley No. 18.065: Dispónese normas para la regulación del trabajo doméstico. (2.048*R)," *Diario Oficial,* no. 27.133 (2006), http://www.impo.com.uy/copetes/pdf/20061205/documentos.pdf.

26. "Decreto 224/007: Reglaméntase la Ley 18.065 relativa a trabajo doméstico. (1.212*R)," *Diario Oficial,* no. 27.268 (2007), http://www.impo.com.uy/copetes/pdf/20070629/documentos.pdf.

27. Leticia Pugliese and Silvia Santos, "Situación del trabajo doméstico en el Uruguay: Actualización del informe," in *Comentarios de Seguridad Social* (Montevideo: Banco de Previsión Social, Asesoría General en Seguridad Social, 2010).

28. Ariel Ferrari and María Celia Vence, "Avances del sector doméstico uruguayo," in Mary R. Goldsmith Connelly, et al., *Hacia un fortalecimiento de derechos laborales en el trabajo de hogar: algunas experiencias de América Latina* (Montevideo: Friedrich Ebert Stiftung, 2010), 55–89.

29. The inspectors requested documents but did not enter the households.

30. Nora Pacheco, "Historia del Sindicato Único de Trabajadoras Domésticas" (unpublished manuscript, Montevideo: SUTD-PIT-CNT, 2010), 2; Lorena García Mourelle, *La experiencia de la Juventud Obrera Católica Femenina en Uruguay (1944–1960)* (Montevideo: OBSUR Observatorio Del Sur, Centro De Documentación, Investigación Y Promoción Social, 2010). During the 1930s and 1940s, there were precedents for domestic workers' organizations: Iris Cabral, an Afro-Uruguayan activist and herself a domestic worker, organized the sector as well as demanding domestic workers' right to unionization, pensions, and workplace safety. In the 1940s, a group of domestic workers tried to form a mutual aid society and fought for the extension of labor rights to domestic workers. As far as could be ascertained, there is no relation between these early organizations and those that emerged later. The JOC's activities with domestic workers date from the 1950s.

31. National Association of Private Household Employees.

32. Young Catholic Workers.

33. Labor Association of Domestic Service and Related Employees.

34. Pacheco, "Historia," 2010, 4.

35. Asociaciones Profesionales Bill, 1981, Ley 15.137 (May 21, 1981). In 1981, professional associations (named labor organizations when they were formed by workers and which even could negotiate with employers) were granted legal status.

36. Noelia Ojeda Rodríguez, "Análisis comparado de Políticas públicas laborales: El caso del sector doméstico (1985–1990) y (2005–2009)" (BA thesis, Universidad de la República, 2010). Various explanations have been given for this period of dormancy, including the failure to achieve policy gains, workers' reluctance to join the union for fear of reprisals by employers, and health and family problems of the leaders.

37. Mariselda Cancela, interview by author, November 26, 2012.

38. Ibid.

39. Graciela Mazzuchi "Labor Relations in Uruguay: 2005–2008," Working Papers No. 6, Industrial and Employment Relations Department, ILO, 2009, 50.

40. Pintos, *Poder sindical,* 2012, 12. Thirty-nine laws were approved during Tabaré Vázquez's presidency.

41. Ibid., 23.

42. Maite Burgueño et al., "Puertas adentro: el trabajo doméstico, sus condiciones y organización político gremial," in *Pensamiento crítico y sujetos colectivos en América Latina, perspectivas interdisciplinarias,* ed. Yamandú Acosta et al. (Montevideo: Espacio Interdisciplinario, Universidad de la República Uruguay y Ediciones Trilce, 2011), 271–90.

43. The Sole National Union of Construction and Annexes.

44. Tripartite Committee for Equal Opportunity and Treatment at Work; National Women's Institute; and Chamber of Commerce and Industry, respectively.

45. Merike Blofield, *Care Work: Domestic Workers' Struggle for Equal Rights in Latin America* (University Park: Penn State University Press, 2012); "Proyecto que regula el trabajo domestic," *El País,* March 8, 2008, http://historico.elpais.com.uy/06/03/08/pnacio_205188.asp.

46. Two members of the SUTD did attend the 100th International Labor Conference that adopted ILO Convention 189, Decent Work for Domestic Workers.

47. Amarante and Espino, "Situación del servicio doméstico en Uruguay," 70.

48. Consejo de Salarios, 1943, Ley 10.449, Senate and House of Representatives of the Oriental Republic of Uruguay (November 12, 1943). Wage Councils. The tripartite wage councils were established in 1943.

49. Mazzuchi, *Labor Relations in Uruguay.*

50. Cristina Otero, personal interview, November 21, 2012, Montevideo.

51. This came after the Chamber of Commerce withdrew from participation.

52. Surprisingly there was very little press coverage of the negotiations. The decision by the Liga, Consumidores y Usuarios to participate in the wage councils, however, was the subject of various newspaper articles.

53. Clasificacion de los Grupos de Actividad de los Consejos de Salarios, 2008, Decree 326/008 (July 7, 2008).

54. Mazzuchi, *Labor Relations in Uruguay.*

55. Matilde Castillo, personal interview November 21, 2012, Montevideo.

56. Cristina Otero, interview by author, November 21, 2012.

57. Libertad Sindical Normas para su Protección, 2006, Ley 17.940 Article 2 (January 2, 2006).

58. "Presentación de categorías de sector doméstico," SUTD, September 6, 2010. Wages are included in US dollar equivalent in this chapter as a consideration to readers from other countries.

59. Forty-four hours per week and twenty-five workdays per month.

60. Mabel Lorenzo de Sánchez, interview by author via telephone, May 18, 2015.

61. This section is developed in less detail given that the field research for this study focused on the emergence of Group 21 and the negotiation of the first two collective agreements.

62. Declarase de Interes Publico la Prevencion de Canceres genito-mamarios, 2000, Ley 17.242 (June 20, 2000).

63. On November 27, 2015, the congress passed Law 19353, which created a national system of care aimed at enhancing the autonomy and providing assistance to persons in situations of dependency (children under twelve years of age, persons with disability, and the elderly). Although traditionally, many domestic workers have cared for children, the elderly, and persons with disability, often in conjunction with the realization of other tasks, it is not clear how they will be affected by this new law. It still is not determined whether care workers will be included within the wage council for domestic workers or for another occupational sector.

64. At forty-four hours per week and twenty-five workdays per month.

65. The Uruguayan peso underwent considerable devaluation over the past two years, thus the increase in the equivalent wages in dollars is minimal.

66. Department of Labor Inspection.

67. "XXVI Reunión especializada de la mujer del MERCOSUR. III Mesa técnica: reunión de la mesa asesora de género, trabajo e integración económica" (MERCOSUR/ REM/MT- GTIE/ACTA, no. 02/11, November 9, 2011), http://www.mercosurmujeres. org/userfiles/file/files/rem2011%202/REM_2011_ACTA02_ANE09_ES_Mesa_Tecn_ Genero_Trabajo_e_Integracion_Economica.pdf.

68. Ernesto Murro and Guillermo Miranda, "Manual de buenas prácticas para traba-jadoras y empleadoras de servicio doméstico" (ILO, 2013), http://www.ilo.org/wcmsp5/ groups/public/---americas/---ro-lima/---sro-santiago/documents/publication/wcms_ 219955.pdf.

69. Ximena Ruy Lopez (delegate for the Ministry of Labor and Social Security, Group 21 of the wage council), interview by author, November 23, 2012.

70. Batthyány, "Estudio sobre trabajo doméstico Uruguay," 14. Batthyány made a simi-lar observation when she stated that both the Liga and the SUTD share the conviction that housework should be valued and made visible.

71. Triaca, "Trabajo Doméstico," 13.

72. Murro and Miranda, "Manual de buenas practices." Hugo A. Barone, lawyer at the Liga through the BPS agreement, in his introduction indicates that one of the challenges that the Liga faces is to make employers aware that they are involved in a work relation-ship. He found that many employers often get involved in resolving the personal problems of the domestic worker, but at the same time do not respect their labor rights.

73. Alexandra Rizio et al., "Domestic Workers Worldwide. Four Collective Bargain-ing Models" (report prepared by the Fordham University School of Law for the National Domestic Workers' Alliance, 2011); Claire Hobden, "Domestic Workers Organize—But Can They Bargain? Mapping Collective Bargaining and Other Forms of Negotiation in the Domestic Work Sector" (ILO's Work in Progress, February 2015), http://www.ilo. org/wcmsp5/groups/public/---ed_protect/---protrav/---travail/documents/publication/ wcms_345704.pdf.

5. BEER PROMOTERS IN CAMBODIA

1. "Labor law" or the "Labor Code" in this chapter refer to the Labour Code of the Kingdom of Cambodia. The law excludes many categories of formal workers, for instance, judges, civil servants, police, military, air/transport, and domestic/household workers.

2. Worker associations provide support and education for workers that are normally excluded from joining unions. Associations are registered with the Ministry of the Interior instead of with the Ministry of Labor.

3. Organizations of street vendors, waste pickers, home-based workers, and others may "bargain" with government authorities. See the introduction to this volume for a discussion of the nature of bargaining by informal workers and their organizations.

4. "Beer promoters" and "beer promoter women" are used interchangeably. They are women who are hired to promote a specific brand of beer.

5. "Cambodia Socio-economic Survey Report (CSES), 2012," National Institute of Statistics (NIS), Ministry of Planning, 2012, http://www.nis.gov.kh/nis/CSES/Data/CSES_ Labour.html.

6. "Country Profile, Cambodia," United Nations, http://www.un.org.kh/index.php? option=com_content& view=article&id=47&Itemid=66.

7. "Minimum Wage for the Garment and Shoe Industry in Cambodia w.e.f. October 1, 2010 to 2014," WageIndicator Foundation, http://www.wageindicator.org/main/ salary/minimum-wage/cambodia. All monetary values are in US dollars unless otherwise noted. Although Cambodia has its own currency, called the Riel, the US dollar is just as commonly used and is sometimes preferred. US $1 = 4054 Riel. The only established minimum wage in Cambodia is in the garment industry. In 2012, the minimum was the equivalent of US $66 per month and was increased, after a campaign by workers, unions, and other activists, to first $80 (2013) and then US $128 USD.

8. The standard of living in Cambodia has increased overall due to the rise in per capita income. As more foreign investments, businesses, NGOs, and labor activists have flooded the country, the salaries of many educated English-speaking workers have seen an increase.

9. "Cambodia Socio-Economic Survey (CSES), 2013" (report by National Institute of Statistics (NIS), Ministry of Planning, Phnom Penh, July 2014), http://www.nis.gov.kh/ nis/CSES/Final%20Report%20CSES%202013.pdf.

10. Economic Institute of Cambodia (EIC), *Handbook on Decent Work in the Informal Economy in Cambodia* (Bangkok: International Labour Office, 2006), http://www.ilo. org/wcmsp5/groups/public/---asia/---ro-bangkok/documents/publication/wcms_bk_ pb_126_en.pdf.

11. Ulla Heinonen, "The Hidden Role of Informal Economy: Is Informal Economy Insignificant for Phnom Penh's Development?" in *Modern Myths of the Mekong: A Critical Review of Water and Development Concepts, Principles, and Policies*, ed. Matti Kummo, Marko Keskinen, and Olli Varis (Espoo: Helsinki University of Technology, 2008). Even within the government's own research, the number varies. Other research done by foreign scholars estimate 60 percent to 90 percent, which is a wide variation gap on the statistics.

12. "CSES, 2013," NIS.

13. "CSES, 2012," NIS; "Cambodia Socio-economic survey report (CSES), 2011" (National Institute of Statistics (NIS), Ministry of Planning, 2011); "Cambodia Socio-economic survey report (CSES), 2009" (National Institute of Statistics (NIS), Ministry of Planning, 2009); "Cambodia Socio-economic survey report (CSES), 2004" (National Institute of Statistics (NIS), Ministry of Planning, 2004). All these are available at http:// www.nada-nis.gov.kh/index.php/catalog/CSES.

14. Labour Code of the Kingdom of Cambodia, 1997, Ch. IV, Article 65, 1st Legislature, 7th Sess.

15. Labour Code of the Kingdom of Cambodia, 1997, Ch. IV, Article 67, 1st Legislature, 7th Sess. A contract of a fixed duration must be in writing. If not, it becomes a labor contract of undetermined duration.

16. Labour Code of the Kingdom of Cambodia, 1997, Ch. IV, Article 74, 1st Legislature, 7th Sess. Undetermined duration contracts can also be referred to as unspecified duration contracts.

17. Labour Code of the Kingdom of Cambodia, 1997, Art. 67.

18. When a contract is signed for a fixed period of less then two years, but the work tacitly and quietly continues after the end of the fixed period, the contract becomes a labor contract of undetermined duration.

19. Labour Code of the Kingdom of Cambodia, 1997, 1st Legislature, 7th Sess.

20. United Nations Development Fund for Women (UNIFEM), the World Bank (WB), the Asian Development Bank (ADB), the United Nations Development Programme (UNDP), and the Department for International Development of the United Kingdom (DFID/UK), *A Fair Share for Women: Cambodia Gender Assessment* (Phnom Penh: UNIFEM, WB, ADB, UNDP, DFID/UK, 2004), 24, 27.

21. Beer workers in Phnom Penh, interviews by author, Phnom Penh, Cambodia, September 2012.

22. Cambodian male and female citizens, interviews by author, Phnom Penh, Cambodia, September 2012. Interviews in reference to women who work and how they are viewed.

23. Michelle Green and Ian Lubek, "Health, Safety and Security for Cambodian Women Beer Sellers were Substandard in 2009: Urgent Actions Are Still Required by All Major Brewers (AB/INBEV, Carlsberg, HEINEKEN/ Asia Pacific Breweries, SAB/Miller, Guinness, San Miguel, Bavaria, Asahi, etc.)" (prepared on behalf of SiRCHESI, NGO # 704, Cambodia, revised April 20, 2010).

24. Mark Anthony White, "Cambodia HIV/AIDS Strategic Plan 2002–2005" (United States Agency for International Development (USAID), Office of Public Health, March 2004), http://www.hivpolicy.org/Library/HPP000433.pdf.

25. Joseph J. Zasloff, "Emerging Stability in Cambodia," *Asian Affairs* 28, no. 4 (2002): 187–200.

26. Veasna Nuon and Melisa Serrano, *Building Unions in Cambodia: History, Challenges, Strategies* (Singapore: Friedrich-Ebert-Stiftung Office for Regional Cooperation in Asia, 2010), 19. Unions were a part of Cambodia as early as 1954, but very little is known about them before 1979.

27. Zasloff, "Emerging Stability." During the period of rule by the Kampuchean People's Revolutionary Party (PRPK) and its successor the Cambodian People's Party (CPP) (1979 on), the Cambodian Workers Union Federation (CWUF) operated on the standard communist "transmission belt" model. Its main function was to establish a mechanism of communication between the workers, the employers, and the government as a means to "transmit government and party doctrine in order to create" an ideology for workers.

28. Ibid.

29. "Solidarity Center in Cambodia, Country Overview" (Solidarity Center), http://www.solidaritycenter.org.kh/country-overview.html#_ftn1.

30. Nuon and Serrano, *Building Unions in Cambodia*, 25.

31. "Solidarity Center in Cambodia, Country Overview"; Nuon and Serrano, *Building Unions in Cambodia*.

32. Having multiple unions within a single workplace normally confuses the workers by creating doubt and challenges for the independent nonaffiliated unions.

33. "Yellow unions" are important actors in Cambodian labor relations. They are usually identified as unions where the union leadership is also a part of the management's team or where a sweetheart deal exists. NACC and CCTU in particular are considered "yellow unions" due to their affiliation with the government.

34. Nuon and Serrano, *Building Unions in Cambodia*.

35. Sweetheart deals are common between management and unions where affiliations exist.

36. Nuon and Serrano, *Building Unions in Cambodia*.

37. "Cambodian Labor Federation," Cambodian Labor Federation, http://clccambodia. org/en/history.html.

38. It is unclear as to the exact number of local unions that it takes in order to be considered a federation since there are no definitive data on this.

39. "Cambodia—Labour Market Profile 2014" (Ulandssekretariatet LO/FTF Council, 2014), http://www.ulandssekretariatet.dk/sites/default/files/uploads/public/PDF/LMP/lmp_cambodia_2014_final_version_revised.pdf. There is no consistent method of tracking union membership.

40. Yon Sineat (former ACILS/Solidarity Center employee and currently employed with LO/FTF Council in Phnom Penh), discussion with the author via Skype, January 9, 2013; "Cambodia—Labour Market Profile 2014."

41. Numbers were estimated by calculating the total number of union federation and confederation leaders who were male versus female.

42. The Constitution of the Kingdom of Cambodia, 1993, Ch. II and III, Const. Assembly, 2nd Sess.

43. The Constitution of the Kingdom of Cambodia, 1993, Chs. VIII–X, Const. Assembly, 2nd Sess.

44. The Constitution of the Kingdom of Cambodia, 1993, Ch. III, Article 31, Const. Assembly, 2nd Sess.

45. The Constitution of the Kingdom of Cambodia, 1993, Ch. III, Article 36, Const. Assembly, 2nd Sess.

46. The Constitution of the Kingdom of Cambodia, 1993, Ch. III, Article 37, Const. Assembly, 2nd Sess.

47. The Constitution of the Kingdom of Cambodia, 1993, Ch. IV Article 51, Const. Assembly, 2nd Sess.; the Constitution of the Kingdom of Cambodia, 1993, Ch. V, Article 56, Const. Assembly, 2nd Sess.

48. The Constitution of the Kingdom of Cambodia, 1993, Ch. III, Article 45, Const. Assembly, 2nd Sess.

49. Labour Code of the Kingdom of Cambodia, 1997.

50. Nuon and Serrano, *Building Unions in Cambodia*.

51. "The Arbitration Council," the Arbitration Council, http://www.arbitration council.org/. It is interesting to note that Cambodia currently has no labor court system.

52. Details of the research methods are discussed in the methodological appendix.

53. "Carlsberg Annual Report, 2011," Carlsberg Group, http://www.carlsberggroup. com/investor/downloadcentre/Documents/Annual%20Report/Carlsberg_2011%20 Annual_report_English.pdf.

54. Yon Sineat and Mora Sar, e-mail message to author, December 2012.

55. Horng Vuthy, "Challenges for Organizing the Beer Promotion Women in Cambodia" (Asia Monitor Resource Centre, September 1, 2010), http://www.amrc.org.hk/content/challenges-organizing-beer-promotion-women-cambodia.

56. "Private Sector Partnerships: A Case Study Documenting CARE Cambodia's Partnership with Heineken International, 2003–2005" (CARE International in Cambodia report, 2005).

57. BP1 through BP8 (see methodological appendix), interviews by author, Phnom Penh, Cambodia, September 2012.

58. BP3, in discussion with the author, Phnom Penh, Cambodia, September 2012. BP3 was relating a story she witnessed.

59. Beer promoters focus group 1 (see methodological appendix), in discussion with the author, Phnom Penh, Cambodia, September 2012; "Private Sector Partnerships," CARE International.

60. Beer promoters, interview by author, Phnom Penh, Cambodia, September 2012.

61. EIC, *Handbook on Decent Work in the Informal Economy.*

62. Sineat, discussion with the author, January 2013.

63. CFSWF union membership data provided by CFSWF to author.

64. Labour Code of the Kingdom of Cambodia, 1997.

65. "Cambodian Food and Service Workers' Federation (CFSWF)" (Cambodian Food and Service Workers' Federation (CFSWF)), http://www.cfswf.org/khmer/.

66. Ian Lubek et al., "Collaboratively Confronting the Current Cambodian HIV/AIDS Crisis in Siem Reap: A Cross-Disciplinary, Cross-Cultural 'Participatory Action Research' Project in Consultative, Community Health Change," *Asian Psychologist* 3, no. 1 (2002): 21–28; Richard Sine, "Sex Trade Lures Cambodia's 'Beer Girls,'" *Boston Globe*, September 22, 2002, http://www.fairtradebeer.com/reportfiles/bgc220902.html.

67. Ingrid Quinn, "Selling Beer Safely, a Baseline Survey and Needs Assessment of Beer Promoters in Phnom Penh" (CARE International in Cambodia, September 2003), http://www.fairtradebeer.com/reportfiles/CARE/ingridquinnCARE2003.pdf.

68. "Private Sector Partnerships."

69. Louise Bury, "A Report on the Situation of Beer Promoter Women in the Workplace, Cambodia: Results of a Harassment and Abuse Survey" (CARE International in Cambodia, Spring 2005), http://www.fairtradebeer.com/reportfiles/CARE/louisebury CARE2005.pdf.

70. Ibid.

71. Ibid.

72. Ian Lubek, "Cambodian 'Beer Promotion Women' and Corporate Caution, Recalcitrance or Worse?" *Psychology of Women Section Review* 7, no. 1 (2005): 2–11.

73. "ACTU Looks to Help Asian Beer Sales Girls," ABC News, May 27, 2006, www.abc.net.au/news/2006-05-27/actu-looks-to-help-asian-beer-sales-girls/1763554.

74. Alison Tate, "Media Coverage Re.: Cambodian Beer Promotion Women," *Australian Council of Trade Unions (ACTU)*, May 22, 2008, http://www.actu.org.au/our-work/international/news/media-coverage-re-cambodian-beer-promotion-women.

75. "Union Aid Aboard, APHEDA," Union Aid Aboard, APHEDA, www.apheda.org.au.

76. Green and Lubek, "Health Safety and Security for Women Beer Sellers."

77. "Beer Sellers Industry Cambodia (BSIC): Code of Conduct for Beer Promoters" (Fair Trade Beer, October 2006), http://www.fairtradebeer.com/reportfiles/breweries/codeofconduct25oct2006.pdf.

78. Kristof Racz and Sam Grumiau, "Promoting Decency? Report on the Situation of Beer Promotion Work in Cambodia" (Stichting Onderzoek Multinationale Ondernemingen (SOMO) Centre for Research on Multinational Corporations, 2012).

79. "CFSWF," CFSWF.

80. Green and Lubek, "Health Safety and Security for Women Beer Sellers."

81. Ibid.

82. Mora Sar, in discussion with the author via Skype, December 2012.

83. BP1, interview by author, Phnom Penh, Cambodia, September 29, 2012. Discussion on why she was initially afraid to talk to Mora.

84. Beer promoters focus group 1, September 2012.

85. Ibid.

86. Mora Sar, interview by author, Phnom Penh, Cambodia, October 1, 2012.

87. The Trade Union Workers Federation of Progress and Democracy is in the CCWR confederation and under NACC. CFSWF alleges that TUPWPAB was formed by TUWFPD, where management of Cambrew is affiliated, in order to thwart its ability to collectively bargain and represent the beer promoters through the MRS.

88. Former TUPWPAB/TUWFPD members, interview by author, September 2012.

89. BP2, BP3, and BP4, interview by author, Phnom Penh, Cambodia, September 2012. All stated that they had been threatened and that others workers had tried to dissuade them from joining the union.

90. Beer promoters focus Group 3 (see methodological appendix), in discussion with the author, Phnom Penh, Cambodia, September 2012.

91. Beer promoters focus group 2 (see methodological appendix), in discussion with the author, Phnom Penh, Cambodia, September 2012.

92. Mom Kunthear and Vincent MacIsaac, "Beer Girl Exploitation Revealed," *Phnom Penh Post*, July 22, 2011, http://www.phnompenhpost.com/national/beer-girl-exploitation-revealed.

93. Khuon Leakhana, "Angkor Protestors Slighted," *Phnom Penh Post*, July 26, 2011, http://www.phnompenhpost.com/index.php/2011072650621/National-news/angkor-protesters-slighted.html.

94. CFSWF Union Leader, interview by author, Cambrew Beer Factory, Cambodia, 2012.

95. Tep Nimol, "One Week Deadline for Beer Strike Resolution," *Phnom Penh Post*, August 5, 2011, http://www.phnompenhpost.com/index.php/2011080550878/National-news/one-week-deadline-for-beer-strike-resolution.html.

96. Sar, interview, October 2012.

97. Beer promoters focus group 3, September 2012.

98. ACILS Solidarity Center, interviews by author, Cambodia, 2012. Interview in reference to trying to obtain the MOU between Cambrew and TUWFPD.

99. Mora Sar, discussion with the author via Skype, January 2013.

100. Simon Lewis and Kuch Naren, "Beer Promoters Allege Bias Following Strike," *The Cambodia Daily*, February 29, 2012.

101. Ben Sokhean, "Angkor Brewery Agree to Strikers Demands," *The Cambodia Daily*, May 12, 2014.

102. Sar, discussion via Skype, January 2013.

103. Shane Worrell, discussion with the author via Skype, February 24, 2015; Shane Worrell and Mom Kunthear, "Beer Promoters Sees Change," *Phnom Penh Post*, January 16, 2015.

104. Shane Worrell, "Reforms Not Reaching Hostesses," *Phnom Penh Post*, January 20, 2015, http://www.phnompenhpost.com/national/reforms-not-reaching-hostesses-researcher; Racz and Grumiau, "Promoting Decency?"; Yang Yi, "Cambodia Unveils Regulation to Protect Entertainment Workers," Xinhuanet, October 8, 2014, http://news.xinhuanet.com/english/world/2014-10/08/c_133699392.htm; Wendy Zeldin, "Cambodia: New Regulation to Protect Workers," the Law Library of Congress, http://www.loc.gov/ lawweb/servlet/lloc_news?disp3_l205404161_text. Hostesses could potentially be protected under a new regulation proposed by the Ministry of Labor with input from the ILO, called Working Conditions, Occupational Safety and Health Rules of Entertainment Service Enterprises, Establishment and Companies. The new regulation seeks to give entertainment workers who work outside the formal economy, such as hostesses, rights under the labor law.

6. INFORMALIZED GOVERNMENT WORKERS IN TUNISIA

1. UGTT leaders, interview by author, Tunisia, October 2012.

2. The author would like to acknowledge the research assistance of Wafa Ben Slimane.

3. The head of the UGTT spoke of allies within the transitional government.

4. Sana Sbouai, "Informal Work, or Evidence of the State's Incompetence," *Nawaat*, May 9, 2012, http://nawaat.org/portail/2012/05/09/informal-work-or-evidence-of-the-states-incompetence/.

5. Ibid.

6. "Arab Countries in Transition: Economic Outlook and Key Challenges" (International Monetary Fund, October 9, 2014), http://www.imf.org/external/np/pp/eng/2014/100914.pdf.

7. Susan J. Schurman and Adrienne E. Eaton, "Trade Union Organizing in the Informal Economy: A Review of the Literature on Organizing in Africa, Asia, Latin America, North America and Western, Central and Eastern Europe" (report to the American Center for International Labor Solidarity, January 2012); Guy Standing, "Globalization, Labor Flexibility, and Insecurity," *European Journal of Industrial Relations* 3, no. 1 (1997): 7–37.

8. Mohamed-Salah Omri, "The UGTT Labor Union: Tunisia's Powerbroker," Tunisia-live: Living Tunisia, January 22, 2014, http://www.tunisia-live.net/2014/01/22/the-ugtt-labor-union-tunisias-powerbroker/; Chris Toensing, "Tunisian Labor Leaders Reflect Upon Revolt," Middle East Research and Information Project, http://www.merip.org/mer/mer258/tunisian-labor-leaders-reflect-upon-revolt-0.

9. Mediouni Lassad, "Government-Labor Power Struggle Set to Continue," IPS-Inter Press Service, December 23, 1985.

10. Ibid.

11. Sadri Khiari et Olfa Lamloum, "Tunisie des elections en trompe-l'oeil," *Politique Africaine* 4, no. 76 (1999): 112.

12. Ibid.

13. Ismail Sahbani, secretary general of the UGTT, speaking to the UGTT national assembly of 1992, quoted in Christopher Alexander, "State Labor and the New Global Economy in Tunisia," in *North Africa: Development and Reform in a Changing Global Economy*, ed. Dirk Vandewalle (New York: St. Martin's Press, 1966), 177.

14. UGTT leaders and public sector workers, interview by author, Tunisia, October 2012.

15. Ibid.

16. This lack of specific law governing subcontracting was the subject of a 2012 round table conference held by the Centre Tunisien des études économiques (CTEE) and the Institut Arabe des Chefs D'entreprises (IACE). At the conference, some attendees mentioned that legal tribunals tasked with hearing appeals of disputes relating to subcontracting under current Tunisian law issued widely divergent decisions and appealed in an oblique manner to the Code du Travail and the law of contracts and obligations.

17. The sources for this paragraph are interviews conducted by the author with UGTT leaders and subcontracted workers in October 2012.

18. The source for the following paragraphs and the quotes therein is an interview by author with subcontracted workers, Tunisia, October 2012.

19. UGTT leaders, interview.

20. Subcontracted workers, interview.

21. The source for this entire section is UGTT leaders, interview.

22. Omri, "The UGTT Labor Union: Tunisia's Powerbroker;" Toensing, "Tunisian Labor Leaders Reflect Upon Revolt."

23. Ibid.

24. "Le Sifflet . . . des Femmes de Ménage," Documentary, Facebook, https://www.facebook.com/video.php?v=1413294290497. The direct actions that took place as part of this campaign often involved blowing whistles to bring attention to the abusive practices.

25. Interview with UGTT leader.

26. Ibid.

27. UGTT staff, written communication to author, October 2012.

28. "Tunisie: Le principal syndicat veut des negociations sociales 'rapides,'" *Star Africa*, October 2, 2011, http://fr.starafrica.com/actualites/tunisie-le-principal-syndicat-veut-des-negociations-sociales-rapides-146858.html.

29. Ibid.

30. Female subcontracted workers, interview by author, Tunisia, October 2012.

31. Subcontracted workers interview.

32. UGTT leaders, interview.

33. Omri, "The UGTT Labor Union: Tunisia's Powerbroker."

7. MINIBUS DRIVERS IN GEORGIA

1. "The World Factbook: Middle East: Georgia" (Central Intelligence Agency, 2012), https://www.cia.gov/library/publications/the-world-factbook/geos/gg.html, retrieved June 10, 2012. GDP (PPP) Total—$37.27 billion.

2. "GeoStat Georgia, Census 2014" (GeoStat), www.geostat.ge.

3. Women accounted for 62.2 percent of the membership and those under thirty-five accounted for 15.1 percent.

4. *Freedom of Association: Digest of Decisions and Principles of the Freedom of Association Committee of the Governing Body of the ILO* (Geneva: International Labour Office, 2006).

5. "Ratification and Promotion of Fundamental ILO Conventions" (International Labour Office Governing Body, Committee on Legal Issues and International Labour Standards, October 2, 2006), http://www.ilo.org/wcmsp5/groups/public/---ed_norm/---relconf/documents/meetingdocument/wcms_gb_297_lils_6_en.pdf, accessed October 2, 2013.

6. The European Social Charter (Revised), Decree # 1876, Parliament of Georgia (July 1, 2005).

7. Lawson Trade Unions, Parliament of Georgia (1997).

8. Right to Organise and Collective Bargaining Convention, 1949, Convention 98, Article 4, International Labor Organization (July 1, 1949).

9. "The European Social Charter (revised): 7th National Report on the Implementation of the Revised European Social Charter submitted by the Government of Georgia (Articles 2, 4, 5, 6, 26, and 29)" (report registered by the Secretariat November 21, 2013), https://rm.coe.int/CoERMPublicCommonSearchServices/DisplayDCTMContent?documentId=0900001680489fbb. The code is also contrary to EU standards and the European Social Charter 7, of which Georgia has ratified Articles 2, 4, 5, 6, 26, and 29. Article 2(1) is breached because an employed individual may agree to an agreement that will not limit the maximum working hours. Article 4(2) is breached because employer and employee may agree on unlimited overtime. Further, the Labor Code does not ensure additional payment or compensatory leave for overtime. Article 4(4) is contrary to the charter because preliminary warning to an employee in case of his or her dismissal is not prescribed. Article 5 is breached because an excessive number of members is required for founding a trade union. Further, employment contracts can specify that the person may not join a trade union. Article 6(2) is breached because an employer may unilaterally ignore a collective bargaining agreement and because collective agreements are not encouraged.

10. The term "wages" is used here because the union views the drivers as employees. Indeed, part of the struggle between the drivers and the route owners and municipal authorities is the drivers' employment status.

11. The titles listed were the individuals' titles at the times they were interviewed. Many of the people listed no longer hold these titles.

8. WASTE PICKERS IN BRAZIL

1. Sonia M. Dias, "Overview of the Legal Framework for Inclusion of Informal Recyclers in Solid Waste Management in Brazil," *WIEGO Policy Brief (Urban Policies)*, no. 6 (2011): 1.

2. Sonia M. Dias, "Trajetórias e Memórias dos Fóruns Lixo e Cidadania no Brasil: Experimentos Singulares de Justiça Social e Governança Participativa" (doctoral thesis, Universidade Federal de Minas Gerais, 2009).

3. "Diagnóstico dos Resíduos Sólidos Urbanos—Relatório de Pesquisa, Brasília, 2012" (IPEA, 2012), http://www.ipea.gov.br/agencia/images/stories/PDFs/relatoriopesquisa/121009_relatorio_residuos_solidos_urbanos.pdf.

4. Sonia M. Dias, "Statistics on Waste Pickers in Brazil," *WIEGO Statistical Brief*, no. 2 (2011).

5. Waste pickers very often work as family units.

6. Sonia M. Dias and Fabio C. G. Alves, "Integration of the Informal Recycling Sector in Solid Waste Management in Brazil" (study prepared for Deutsche Gesellschaft für Technische Zusammenarbeit (GTZ) GmbH, 2008), 14.

7. Open dumps are unsanitary sites where waste is dumped with no treatment whatsoever, as opposed to sanitary landfills, where waste is disposed of in a site where environmental measures are applied to minimize impacts to the environment.

8. Sonia M. Dias, "Construindo a Cidadania: Limites e Avanços do Projeto de Coleta Seletiva em Parceria com a Asmare" (master's thesis, Universidade Federal de Minas Gerais, 2002).

9. Ibid.

10. For instance, PNAD is a household survey, which means that pickers of recyclables who work and live by dumpsites will not be captured in this figure.

11. Dias, "Construindo a Cidadania."

12. Sonia M. Dias, "Integrating Informal Workers into Selective Waste Collection: The Case of Belo Horizante, Brazil," *WIEGO Policy Brief (Urban Policies)*, no. 4 (2011). Lists main characteristics on this city's recycling system in partnership with the waste picker cooperative Asmare. Belo Horizonte at that time was the most advanced city in terms of formal recognition of waste pickers, and it inspired many cities in Brazil and elsewhere.

13. Sonia M. Dias, "Waste and Citizenship Forum's Trajectories—Achievements and Challenges" (conference paper for IPSA Congress Proceedings, Montreal, Canada, July 19–24, 2014).

14. Patrick Heller, "Moving the State: Politics of Democratic Decentralization in Kerala, South Africa, and Porto Alegre," *Politics and Society* 29, no. 1 (2001): 131–63, a discussion on how the nature of the politically transformative project of the state of the Workers Party and the dynamics of party-social movement interactions has created a window of opportunity for social inclusion and participation.

15. Dias and Alves, "Integration of the Informal Recycling Sector."

16. Dias, "Construindo a Cidadania"; Chris Birkbeck, "Self-Employed Proletarians in an Informal Factory: The Case of Cali's Garbage Dump," *World Development Journal* 6, no. 9–10 (1978): 1173–85; Marcel Bursztyn, "Capitulo 1: Da pobreza à miséria, da miséria à exclusão: o caso das populações de rua," in Marcel Bursztyn and Elimar Nascimento, *No meio da rua—nômades, excluídos e viradores* (Rio de Janeiro: Garamond, 2000).

17. Sonia M. Dias, "Waste and Citizenship Forum—Achievements and Limitations," paper no. 11 presented at CWG—WASH Workshop, Kolkatta, India, February 1–6, 2006; Dias, "Trajetórias e Memórias." A forum is a participatory arrangement where public matters can be talked over and argued about. It convenes different organizations to discuss, in the case presented here, the issue of how waste management can be associated with the extension of an important social citizenship right: the right for work, which means the right for waste pickers to earn their living through collection and processing of wastes as well as the improvement of their working conditions.

18. Membership rose to fifty-six entities in the years to come.

19. Dias, "Waste and Citizenship Forum"; Dias, "Waste and Citizenship Forum's Trajectories."

20. Claus Offe, "A atribuição de status público aos grupos de interesse," in Claus Offe, *Capitalismo desorganizado* (São Paulo: Brasiliense, 1994). Referring to the institutional forms and practices made available by the political system to groups of interest that confers a particular status to their basis of operation.

21. Dias and Alves, "Integration of the Informal Recycling Sector," 16.

22. "Diagnóstico dos Resíduos Sólidos Urbanos," IPEA, 2012.

23. "National Survey of Basic Sanitation, 2008," IBGE, 2010, http://ibge.gov.br/english/estatistica/populacao/condicaodevida/pnsb2008/default.shtm#sub_pesquisas.

24. This is a broad characterization. There are many variations depending on the number of cooperative members and the existence of municipal programs for selective waste collection, among other factors.

25. Dias, "Construindo a Cidadania."

26. Dias and Alves, "Integration of the Informal Recycling Sector;" Melanie Samson, "Wasted Citizenship? Reclaimers and the Privatized Expansion of the Public Sphere," *Africa Development* XXXIV, no. 3 and 4 (2009): 1–25. Examples of different agreements and contracts cooperatives are integrated in formal solid waste systems.

27. It might be owned by the cooperative or rented or built by the municipality; it might be obtained via agreements with supporting NGOs or built with resources available from federal government lines; or it might be built in an occupation of public land.

28. A. Scheinberg, J. Anschütz, and A. van de Klundert, "Waste Pickers—Poor Victims or Waste Management Professionals?" (paper no. 56 presented at CWG—WASH International Workshop, Calcutta, India, February 1–5, 2006); Samson, "Wasted Citizenship"; Jo Beall, "Dealing with Dirt and the Disorder of Development: Managing Rubbish in Urban Pakistan," *Oxford Development Studies* 34, no. 1 (2006): 81–97.

29. Sonia M. Dias and Ana C. Ogando, "Mujeres 'catadoras': Construyendo una agenda de gênero em las organizaciones catadoras," in *Genero, Pobreza et Medio Ambiente*, ed. Fernando López Castellano (Granada: Spanish Foundation IPADE, 2013).

30. "2010 Population Census" (IBGE, 2010), http://www.ibge.gov.br/english/estatistica/populacao/censo2010/.

31. Worth mentioning here is that the center's executive director from 2008 to 2014 was a former member of the Catholic Church's organization *Pastoral de Rua*, which was instrumental in the initial mobilization of waste pickers in Belo Horizonte in the early 1990s. He was a prominent leader of the Waste and Citizenship Forums at the national and state levels. He was also one of the founding members of the NGO INSEA; he left the NGO when he took the position of executive director of CMRR.

32. Sonia M. Dias, "The Municipal Waste and Citizenship Forum: A Platform for Social Inclusion and Participation," *WIEGO Policy Brief (Urban Policies)*, no. 5 (2011).

33. The CMRR registered cooperatives/associations in the state for the purpose of having a central databank for the recycling bonus.

34. "Movimento Nacional dos Catadores de Materiais: Reciclaveis," Movimento Nacional dos Catadores de Materiais:Reciclaveis, www.mncr.org.br.

35. Social movements experience a permanent tension of its two arenas of action: social and political-institutional. The greatest challenge for social movements is to have an offensive strategy without losing its identity. So far, the waste pickers' movement has been able to achieve this balance.

36. Dias, "Construindo a Cidadania," 163–70.

37. Dias and Alves, "Integration of the Informal Recycling Sector," 75.

38. Ibid.

39. Ibid., 76; Peter Evans, *Embedded Autonomy: States and Industrial Transformation* (Princeton, NJ: Princeton University Press, 1995). Evans' concept of "embedded autonomy" throws a light on how some ties between individuals across the public-private divide might be used as catalyst for social development, which might help understand the role of these leaderships in the Brazilian case. Evans argues that the existence of ties connecting public officials and representatives of civil society cannot only necessarily be associated with rent-seeking behavior. It might, in some cases, act as a repository of social capital that foments social development.

40. Dias and Alves, "Integration of the Informal Recycling Sector," 76.

41. Ibid., 77.

42. This section is based on desktop review and on semistructured interviews carried out with key actors in solid waste management. In addition, it relies on fieldwork notes from WIEGO's Informal Economy Monitoring Study (IEMS). Documents consulted are listed in Appendix I.

43. PSDB, the Social Democrat Party.

44. Minas Gerais, Law no. 19.823, approved on November 22, 2011.

45. Waste picker leader for MNCR and Redlacre (Latin American Waste Pickers network), interview by author, January 17, 2015. Government planning in Brazil is structured around three instruments: the "Plano Plurianual" (PPA, in Minas Gerais PPAG), a multiyear plan; the Lei de Diretrizes Orçamentárias (LDO), the law that establishes the budgetary guidelines; and the Lei Orçamentária Anual (LOA), the annual budget law. Financial resources from the recycling bonus comes from what is called parliamentary budget ("emenda parlamentar"), which means it has be approved year by year instead of being included in the multiyear plan called PPAG in Portuguese.

46. Waste picker leader of Redesol, interview by author, January 23, 2014.

47. Ana C. Ogando et al., "Informal Economy Monitoring Study: Waste Pickers in Belo Horizonte, Brazil," WIEGO Informal Economy Monitoring Survey (IEMS) (2013). These are results from focus groups that were part of WIEGO's Informal Economy Monitoring Study for Belo Horizonte. Specifically, they classified the recycling bonus as the second most important positive force in the sector.

48. These negotiations bring together people from the state government, representatives of municipal governments, waste pickers' representatives, and representatives of the private sector specializing in solid waste management.

49. MNCR has fought incineration of waste in one of its fiercest struggles. The 2010 National Policy framed incineration as a last resource technology, but the lobby for waste-to-energy technologies is powerful and requires strong mobilization to fight the adoption of these "magical solutions" that may harm the environment and the livelihoods of informal recyclers.

50. Leader from the Minas Gerais Chapter of the MNCR, interview by author, January 10, 2015.

51. Private-public partnerships. Waste pickers oppose this kind of arrangement as they see it as a way for the government to open the door for big private contractors to introduce waste-to-energy technologies. Waste pickers argue that the way the PPP is drafted leaves it open to the discretion of the contractor to decide on the method for final disposal of waste. It is feared that incineration will be favored over recycling.

52. Waste picker leader who sits on the coordinating committee, interview by author, January 10, 2015.

53. "Relatório de Prestação de Contas da Bolsa Reciclagem" (internal document, CMRR, 2014).

54. Four million reals (rate as of January 26, 2015).

55. Dias, "Trajetórias e Memórias."

56. Dias, "Waste and Citizenship Forum's Trajectories."

57. Dias, "Trajetórias e Memórias."

9. STREET VENDORS IN LIBERIA

1. Sally Roever, "Street Vendor Sector Report: Informal Economy Monitoring Study," WIEGO, 2014, http://wiego.org/sites/wiego.org/files/publications/files/IEMS-Sector-Full-Report-Street-Vendors.pdf.

2. Javier Herrera et al., "Informal Sector and Informal Employment: Overview of Data for 11 Cities in 10 Developing Countries," WIEGO, 2012, http://wiego.org/sites/wiego.org/files/publications/files/Herrera_WIEGO_WP9.pdf.

3. Roever, "Street Vendor Sector Report."

4. Ibid.

5. Ibid.

6. "World Factbook, 2013, Africa: Liberia" (Central Intelligence Agency), https://www.cia.gov/library/publications/the-world-factbook/geos/li.html, accessed September 31, 2013.

7. Darlington Porkpa, "Decent Work Bill Finally Goes into Law" (Government of Liberia, Ministry of Information, May 26, 2015), http://www.micatliberia.com/index.php/blog/item/3655-decent-work-bill-finally-goes-into-law.html.

8. National Petty Traders Union of Liberia (NAPETUL) Constitution, 2009, and Article of Incorporation.

9. Realizing Rights was founded in 2002 by Mary Robinson, former president of Ireland (1990–1997) and former United Nations High Commissioner for Human Rights (1997–2002).

10. NAPETUL was scheduled to hold its first Congress in May 2015.

11. "Mary Broh Threatens to Sue Petty Traders," *National Chronicle* (Liberia), January 20, 2011, 8.

12. Frank Krah, interview by author, September 18, 2012, at MCC.

13. Comfort Doryen, interview by author, September 18, 2012, at NAPETUL office on Second Street, Sinkor.

14. The authors of this chapter are signatories to the MOU.

CONCLUSION

1. Francis Fox Piven and Richard A. Cloward, *The Breaking of the American Social Compact* (New York: New Press, 1997), 14.

2. Debbie Budlender and Jeremy Grest, "Summary Report: Case Studies of Collective Bargaining and Representative Forums for Street Traders" (StreetNet International, 2012), http://www.streetnet.org.za/docs/research/2012/en/composite.pdf.

3. John R. Commons, "Institutional Economics," *American Economic Review* 21 (1931): 648–57; Francis M. McLaughlin, "John Rogers Commons: Are His Insights Important in Teaching Modern Labor Economics? (paper prepared for the 37th Annual Lonergan Workshop, Boston College, June 20–25, 2010).

4. Richard Hyman, "Trade Unions and Interest Representation in the Context of Globalization," *Transfer* 3, no. 3 (1997): 3515–33; Robert Hoxie, *Trade Unionism in America: General Character and Types* (Chicago: University of Chicago Press, 1917).

5. Rina Agarwala, *Informal Labor, Formal Politics, and Dignified Discontent in India* (Cambridge: Cambridge University Press, 2013).

6. International Labour Organization, "The Transition from the Informal to the Formal Economy: Report V (Brown Report)" (prepared for International Labour Conference, 104th Session, Geneva, Switzerland, 2015); "WIEGO Network Platform: Transitioning from the Informal to the Formal Economy in the Interest of Workers in the Informal Economy" (prepared through a participatory process with informal workers and distributed at the International Labour Conference 2014).

7. *Decent Work and the Informal Economy* (Geneva: International Labour Organization, 2002).

8. Leah F. Vosko, "Representing Informal Economy Workers: Emerging Strategies and Their Lessons for North American Unions," in *The Sex of Class: Women Transforming*

American Labor, ed. Dorothy S. Cobble (Ithaca, NY: Cornell University Press, 2007). The two-million-member Self Employed Women's Association, a hybrid organizational form combining union and cooperative forms and activities and affiliated with the Indian Trade Union Congress, is an exemplar of this point.

9. Peter Waterman, *Globalization, Social Movements and the New Internationalism*, 2nd ed. (London: Continuum, 2001); Immanuel Ness, ed., *New Forms of Worker Organization: The Syndicalist and Autonomist Restoration of Class Struggle Unionism* (Oakland: PM Press, 2014).

10. Sidney Tarrow, *Power in Movement: Social Movements, Collective Action and Politics* (Cambridge: Cambridge University Press, 1998), 2.

11. Ibid., 22.

12. John L. Campbell, "Where We Stand: Common Mechanisms in Organizations and Social Movements Research," in *Social Movements and Organization Theory*, ed. Gerald F. Davis et al. (New York: Cambridge University Press, 2005), 49.

13. Rebecca Gumbrell-McCormick and Richard Hyman, *Trade Unions in Western Europe: Hard Times, Hard Choices* (Oxford: Oxford University Press, 2013), 31.

14. Kim Moody, *Workers in a Lean World: Unions in the International Economy* (London: Verso, 1997); Lowell Turner, Harry Katz, and Richard Hurd, eds., *Rekindling the Movement: Labor's Quest for Relevance in the 21st Century* (Ithaca, NY: Cornell University Press, 2001).

15. Peter Waterman, "Social Movement Unionism: A New Model for a New World" (working paper no. 110, Institute for Social Studies, The Hague, Switzerland, 1993); Peter Waterman, "Social Movement Unionism: The Case of South Africa," *Work, Employment and Society* 16 (2002): 283–304.

16. Moody, *Workers in a Lean World*; Turner, Katz, and Hurd, *Rekindling the Movement*.

17. In the US, SEIU, AFSCME, AFT, and CWA have all organized government-subsidized home-based care givers, in the process bringing higher wages, improved standards, and greater formalization to a sector characterized by a great deal of informality. The Teamsters Union has also worked with various groups of drivers—port truck, delivery service, and even Uber—who are typically defined, correctly or not, as self-employed.

18. Rebecca Gumbrell-McCormick and Richard Hyman, *Trade Unions in Western Europe: Hard Times, Hard Choices* (Oxford: Oxford University Press, 2013), chap. 2; Gumbrell-McCormick and Hyman, *Trade Unions in Western Europe*, chap. 3.

19. Karl Van Holdt, "Social Movement Unionism: The Case of South Africa," *Work, Employment and Society* 16, no. 2 (2002): 298.

20. Ibid.

21. Erik O. Wright, "Working Class Power, Capitalist Interests and Class Compromise," *American Journal of Sociology* 105, no. 4 (2000): 962.

22. Aelim Yun, "Building Collective Identity: Trade Union Representation of Precarious Workers in South Korean Auto Companies," *Labour, Capital and Society* 44, no. 1 (2011): 155–78.

23. Wright, "Working Class Power," 962; Gumbrell-McCormick and Hyman, *Trade Unions in Western Europe*, 31. Authors prefer the term "institutional power."

24. Paul Osterman et al., *Working in America: A Blueprint for the New Labor Market* (Cambridge, MA: MIT Press, 2001). This problem of scaling successful "experiments" in raising labor market standards is a central conclusion of the seminal review of those experiments in the United States.

25. "WIEGO Individual Members," WIEGO, http://wiego.org/wiego/wiego-individual-members. Provides profiles of these organizations.

26. Gumbrell-McCormick and Hyman, *Trade Unions in Western Europe*, 158; Wright, "Working Class Power," 962.

27. Campbell, "Where Do We Stand?" 44.

28. Ibid., 45.

29. Raymond A. Friedman, *Front Stage, Backstage: The Dramatic Structure of Labor Negotiations* (Cambridge, MA: MIT Press, 1994).

30. Interestingly, drivers in the city of Batumi decided their interests were aligned with those of the intermediaries.

31. John R. Commons, "American Shoemakers, 1648–1895: A Sketch of Industrial Evolution," *The Quarterly Journal of Economics* 24 (1909): 39–83.

32. We use the term labor market competition here to include product or service market competition for the self-employed since their products are the result of their own labor.

33. Sidney Webb and Beatrice Webb, *Industrial Democracy* (London: Longmans, Green, 1902), 715; Gumbrell-McCormick and Hyman, *Trade Unions in Western Europe*, 1. The Webbs use the term "device" to refer to these two strategies.

34. Gumbrell-McCormick and Hyman, *Trade Unions in Western Europe*; Edmund Heery, "Trade Unions and Contingent Labor: Scale and Method," *Cambridge Journal of Regions, Economy and Society* 2, no. 3 (2009): 429–42; Emma Cerviño, "Trade Union Strategies Towards Atypical Workers" (working paper, Juan March Institute, Madrid, 2000); Yun, "Building Collective Identity."

35. David Weil, *The Fissured Workplace: Why Work Became So Bad for So Many and What Can Be Done to Improve It* (Cambridge, MA: Harvard University Press, 2014).

36. Lauren A. Benton, "Homework and Industrial Development: Gender Roles and Restructuring in the Spanish Shoe Industry," *World Development* 17, no. 2 (1989): 255–66.

37. Harold Meyerson, "The Seeds of a New Labor Movement," *American Prospect*, October 30, 2014, http://prospect.org/article/labor-crossroads-seeds-new-movement.

Notes on Contributors

Gocha Aleksandria has been vice president of the Georgian Trade Union Confederation (GTUC) since 2005. He is trained as an engineer-metallurgist and joined the Chemical Industry Trade Union of Georgia in 1996 while working at a chemical plant in Rustavi. He initially joined the GTUC's staff in the International Department and also served as assistant to the president of the Public Services Workers Union of Georgia during 2004–2005. He has represented the GTUC at the National Tripartite Social Partnership Commission. In 2014 he was elected as a substitute member of the Workers Group of the International Labor Organization Governing Body.

Martha (Marty) Chen is a lecturer in public policy at the Harvard Kennedy School, an affiliated professor at the Harvard Graduate School of Design, and international coordinator of the global research-policy-action network Women in Informal Employment: Globalizing and Organizing (WIEGO). An experienced development practitioner and scholar, her areas of specialization are employment, gender, and poverty with a focus on the working poor in the informal economy. Before joining Harvard University in 1987, Chen worked with well-known NGOs in Bangladesh and India for two decades.

Sonia Maria Dias is WIEGO's waste specialist and an associate researcher at the Women's Research Studies Center (NEPEM) at the Federal University of Minas Gerais (UFMG). She has a PhD in political science from UFMG and has a certificate in solid waste management from the Kitakyushu International Techno-Cooperative Association (Japan). She is one of the coordinators of the gender and waste project. Her research interests include waste and citizenship issues, participatory governance, action-research, and popular movements.

Adrienne E. Eaton is professor of labor studies and employment relations and associate dean for academic affairs at the School of Management and Labor Relations, Rutgers, the State University of New Jersey in the United States. Her research focuses on labor-management partnerships, union organizing, and the impact of unionization on particular occupational groups including managerial workers, graduate student employees, and, most recently, informal workers. She is a coauthor, along with Tom Kochan, Paul Adler, and Robert McKersie, of *Healing Together: The Kaiser Permanente Labor-Management Partnership* and is the author of numerous articles published in journals such as *Industrial and Labor Relations Review, Industrial Relations, Labor Studies Journal,* and *Advances in Industrial and Labor Relations.* She is codirector of the Center for Work and Health at Rutgers.

Mary Evans was born in Cambodia and raised in a refugee camp. She is a lecturer at the School of Management and Labor Relations, Rutgers University, and holds a Master of Labor and Employment Relations degree. Her interests include international labor relations and economic policy.

Janice Fine holds a PhD from MIT in political science and is associate professor of labor studies and employment relations at the School of Management and Labor Relations, Rutgers University, where she teaches and writes about low wage immigrant labor in the United States, historical and contemporary debates regarding federal immigration policy, dilemmas of labor standards enforcement, and innovative union and community organizing strategies. She is the author of the groundbreaking book *Worker Centers: Organizing Communities at the Edge of the Dream* (Cornell University Press and the Economic Policy Institute, 2006). Prior to coming to Rutgers in 2005, Fine worked as a community, labor, and electoral organizer for more than twenty-five years.

Mary Goldsmith is a full professor and a member of the research unit "Mujer, identidad y poder" at the Universidad Autónoma Metropolitana-Xochimilco, México, DF. An anthropologist by profession, she is a specialist in domestic employment in Latin America, particularly in Mexico. Her publications have dealt with various facets of this topic, including the history of domestic workers' unions in Mexico, intraregional migration and care chains, and transnational organizing and have appeared as book chapters and journal articles. She also coordinated (with Martha Judith Sánchez Gómez) issue 27 of *Cahiers ALHIM Amérique Latine Histoire et Mémoire, Les migrations indigènes latino-américaines dans le contexte de la globalisation* (L'Université de Paris 8, 2014). Over the past thirty years she has worked closely with various domestic workers' organizations, including the Conlactraho; she is also regional coordinator for Latin America of the Research Network for Domestic Worker Rights.

Daniel Hawkins holds a PhD in political science from the University of Kassel, Germany. He is the author of "The Struggles over City-Space: Informal Street Vending and Public Space Governance in Medellin, Colombia," published in 2011 by NOMOS Verlagsgesellschaft. His research focuses on informal workers in the global economy, trade unions in Latin America, and state reconfigurations in the era of globalization. Hawkins works as a researcher at the National Trade Union School of Colombia (ENS). He was a postdoctoral scholar in the Center for Global Workers' Rights at Pennsylvania State University from 2012–13.

Elza Jgerenaia is currently head of the Labor and Employment Policy Department for the Ministry of Labour, Health and Social Affairs, Republic of Georgia. She holds a master's degree in management and microeconomics from Javakhishvili Tbilisi State University and is currently a PhD Fellow in business administration at Ilia State University in Tbilisi, Georgia. From 2013–2014 she was a PhD Fellow in business administration at University of Minho in Braga, Portugal. Prior to her current employment she worked for various state and nongovernmental institutions including the Ministry of Labor, Health and Social Affairs of Georgia (deputy head of Social Policy Department); Parliament of Georgia, Committee of Health Care and Social Affairs (leader specialist); responsible secretary of the Ministry of Justice of Georgia—Budget Administration Department (senior advisor on economic issues); and the American Center for International Labor Solidarity (ACILS), Georgian Trade Union Confederation (economist).

Stephen J. King an associate professor of government at Georgetown University. His research focuses on the politics of economic reform, the forms and dynamics of authoritarian rule, and regime-transition processes in the Middle East and North Africa. He is the author of *Liberalization against Democracy: The Local Politics of Economic Reform in Tunisia* (Bloomington: Indiana University Press, 2003) and *The New Authoritarianism in the Middle East and North Africa* (Bloomington: Indiana University Press, 2009).

Allison J. Petrozziello is a social researcher specializing in gender, labor migration, development, and human rights. Originally from the United States, she has been living in Santo Domingo, Dominican Republic, since 2009, where she works with UN Women and the Center for Migration Observation and Social Development (OBMICA), among others. She is the author of *Género y el riesgo de apatridia para la población de ascendencia haitiana en los bateyes de República Dominicana* (OBMICA, 2014), *Gender on the Move: Working on the Migration-Development Nexus from a Gender Perspective* (UN Women, 2013), and *Fanm nan fwontyè, Fanm toupatou: Making visible the violence against Haitian migrant, in-transit and displaced women on the Dominican-Haitian border* (OBMICA, 2011), as well as numerous journal articles, chapters, and reports. She holds a BA in women's studies from Smith College and an MA in international development and social change from Clark University.

Pewee Reed holds a bachelor's degree in international relations from the University of Liberia, West Africa, and a MBA in business administration and management from the Hamline University School of Business Minnesota, United States. In 2013 Reed served as training coordinator for Deloitte /USAID Liberia, assigned to the HR Department, Ministry of Commerce and Industry, Republic of Liberia. Reed served as director, Micro, Small, and Medium Enterprise, from November 2013 to December 2014 and was appointed assistant minister for the Bureau of Small Business Administration in the Ministry in December 2014, a position he occupies presently. He worked for the Wells Fargo Home Mortgage—Capital Markets Loan Delivery and Joint Venture Division in Minneapolis from 2004 to 2012. Reed served as research analyst at the Ministry of Foreign Affairs, Republic of Liberia, from 1998 to 2000. In 1999 he was a member of the Liberia delegation to the United Nations General Assembly. He served on the ACABQ (Advisory Committee on Administrative and Budgetary Questions) representing Liberia. Reed taught and served as dean of students of Muslim Congress High School from 1998 to 2000 and principal of St. Peters High School on Barnesville Road from 2000 to 2001. He served as assistant elections magistrate assigned to Bomi County (Suehn-Mecca District) in 1997.

Sahra Ryklief is the secretary general of the International Federation of Workers' Education Associations. She holds a master's degree in political science from the University of Liverpool and has been active in South Africa's political and labor arena for more than thirty years. She was previously the director of the Labour Research Service and contributed to and edited multiple publications produced by this institution during the past two decades.

Susan J. Schurman is distinguished professor of labor studies and employment relations in the School of Management and Labor Relations at Rutgers, the State University of New Jersey, and a former dean of the school. From 1997 to 2007 she served as the founding president of the National Labor College. She received her PhD from the University of Michigan, where she served as director of the Labor Studies Center and research investigator in the School of Public Health. She is a past president of the United Association for Labor Education, a former board member of the Labor and Employment Research Association, and is presently serving a third term as president of the International Federation of Workers' Education Associations. Her research and teaching focus on labor union effectiveness and leadership education as well as constructive labor-management relations. She is also an expert on workplace safety and health, especially on the effects of occupational stress on physical and mental health.

Vera Alice Cardoso Silva is a political science professor at the Federal University of Minas Gerais, Brazil (UFMG), now retired. She has a PhD in Latin American political and social history from the University of Illinois at Urbana-Champaign. Before retiring she helped in planning the undergraduate studies in public policies and public administration currently offered in the UFMG. Her research interests include comparative politics, Brazilian political history, social movements, and management of social policies in Brazil.

Milton Weeks is the managing director of Devin Corporation. He has worked in numerous African countries (including Liberia, Zambia, Ghana, Malawi, South Africa, and Nigeria) with financial institutions in various senior level positions over the past twenty-five years before returning to Liberia in 2007 to restart Devin Corporation. Weeks has a strong base in credit evaluation, financial assessment of corporate entities, financial structuring, and financial modeling and has served as chief executive of banks in three African countries (Liberia, Malawi, and Nigeria). His tested managerial skills have proven a major asset in his varied assignments throughout Africa, including negotiation and management in challenging financial and economic environments. He was involved in the negotiation process described in chapter 9 and is a signatory to the memorandum of understanding.

Index

CPSIA information can be obtained
at www.ICGtesting.com
Printed in the USA
FFOW03n1539180317
33484FF